Evaluating Communication for Development

Evaluating Communication for Development presents a comprehensive framework for evaluating communication for development (C4D). This framework combines the latest thinking from a number of fields in new ways. It critiques dominant instrumental, accountability-based approaches to development and evaluation and offers an alternative holistic, participatory, mixed methods approach based on systems and complexity thinking and other key concepts. It maintains a focus on power, gender and other differences and social norms. The authors have designed the framework as a way to focus on achieving sustainable social change and to continually improve and develop C4D initiatives. The benefits and rigour of this approach is supported by examples and case studies from a number of action research and evaluation capacity development projects undertaken by the authors over the past 15 years.

Building on current arguments within the fields of C4D and development, the authors reinforce the case for effective communication being a central and vital component of participatory forms of development, something that needs to be appreciated by decision-makers. They also consider ways of increasing the effectiveness of evaluation capacity development from grassroots to management level in the development context, an issue of growing importance to improving the quality, effectiveness and utilization of monitoring and evaluation studies in this field.

The book includes a critical review of the key approaches, methodologies and methods that are considered effective for planning evaluation, assessing the outcomes of C4D, and engaging in continuous learning. This rigorous book is of immense theoretical and practical value to students, scholars and professionals researching or working in development, communication and media, applied anthropology, and evaluation and programme planning.

June Lennie is a Senior Research Associate in the School of Media and Communication at RMIT University, Australia. Her work has focused on the development, application and meta-evaluation of participatory research and evaluation methodologies and ICTs for social change, sustainable community development, and rural women's empowerment. She has co-developed several participatory evaluation frameworks, toolkits and resources.

Jo Tacchi is Deputy Dean of Research and Innovation in the School of Media and Communication at RMIT University, Australia. She is a media anthropologist with a special interest in radio, digital media and communication for development. Her work in this area has been centrally concerned with issues around culture and social change, and in developing suitable methodologies for investigating this.

'This book breaks new ground by presenting a powerful and persuasive experience-based statement of the case for recognising communication and its evaluation as central to good development practice and social change. It hits many nails on the head, and draws on many sources and insights. Contriving to do this clearly and coherently is a tour de force. By skilfully drawing together and interweaving the threads and themes of complexity, participation, emergence and holism, and combining these in an approach that is critical, realistic and learning-based, the authors serve the development community well. They present a coherent and comprehensive alternative to the currently dominant approach of donors, adding impetus and credibility to the big push forward to more grounded, cost-effective and sustainable development practice.'

– Robert Chambers, Research Associate,
Institute of Development Studies, University of Sussex, UK

'We are told so often that communication for development cannot be evaluated, meaning: crops or cell phones are much easier to count. We've heard so much about the lack of indicators to measure processes of social change. By experience we know how hard it is for development managers to understand the role of communication as a participatory process and not as institutional visibility or information dissemination. Now, with this book, those who are reluctant to accept the role of communication in development and social change will lack good arguments. It presents a comprehensive framework for understanding how C4D can be evaluated and why it is indispensable for long-term sustainable development. This book is an extraordinary contribution to understanding C4D, not only from the evaluation perspective. It was so much needed.'

– Alfonso Gumucio-Dagron, Communication Specialist, Bolivia

'This work valuably weaves together insights from years of experience with emerging trends in related fields, including complexity and systems thinking, to propose a practical framework for evaluating communication for development. It is an indispensable, accessible and much-needed contribution, to guide evaluation practice in communication for development contexts and beyond.'

– Ailish Byrne, Learning & Development Specialist, UNICEF Somalia

'This is a must read for both academics and professionals in the field of communication for development. For scholars, to understand the real problems in the real world. For practitioners, to learn that muddling through has never been a viable way to sustainable social change.'

– Jan Servaes, UNESCO Chair in Communication for Sustainable Social Change, USA

'The authors provide an excellent and accessible framework for a systemic, participatory learning approach to evaluation that fully takes into account the challenges of power and positionality in development programming. This book should be essential reading for busy reflexive practitioners working to support processes of social transformation.'

– Rosalind Eyben, Convenor of the Big Push Forward (http://bigpushforward.net) and
Research Fellow, Institute of Development Studies, University of Sussex, UK

'Lennie and Tacchi have written a much-needed, readable and original book, packed with conceptual insights and practical examples. They show the maturation of participatory methodologies in the field of communication and social change, and convincingly demonstrate the implications of recent theoretical debates and conceptual developments for assessing program impact. The analysis shows the authors' breadth of practical experience, and nuanced combination of theory and methodology. The book is a trove of ideas for research and practice.'

– Silvio Waisbord, Professor of Media and Public Affairs,
The George Washington University, USA

Evaluating Communication for Development
A framework for social change

June Lennie and Jo Tacchi

First published 2013
by Routledge
2 Park Square, Milton Park, Abingdon, Oxon, OX14 4RN

Simultaneously published in the USA and Canada
by Routledge
711 Third Avenue, New York, NY 10017

Routledge is an imprint of the Taylor & Francis Group, an informa business

© 2013 June Lennie and Jo Tacchi

The right of June Lennie and Jo Tacchi to be identified as authors of this work has been asserted by them in accordance with sections 77 and 78 of the Copyright, Designs and Patents Act 1988.

All rights reserved. No part of this book may be reprinted or reproduced or utilized in any form or by any electronic, mechanical, or other means, now known or hereafter invented, including photocopying and recording, or in any information storage or retrieval system, without permission in writing from the publishers.

Trademark notice: Product or corporate names may be trademarks or registered trademarks, and are used only for identification and explanation without intent to infringe.

British Library Cataloguing in Publication Data
A catalogue record for this book is available from the British Library

Library of Congress Cataloging-in-Publication Data
Lennie, June.
Evaluating communication for development : a framework for social change / June Lennie and Jo Tacchi.
p. cm.
Includes bibliographical references and index.
1. Communication in community development—Evaluation. 2. Social change. I. Tacchi, Jo. II. Title.
HN49.C6L465 2013
306.44'9—dc23
2012027619

ISBN: 978-0-415-52207-6 (hbk)
ISBN: 978-0-415-52259-5 (pbk)
ISBN: 978-0-203-07849-5 (ebk)

Typeset in Times New Roman
by Book Now Ltd, London

To all of the people and organizations around the world who are using communication for development and alternative approaches to researching and evaluating C4D with the vision of creating a better future for all

Contents

List of illustrations   ix
About the authors   xi
Acknowledgements   xiii
Acronyms   xv

1 Introduction   1

   The need for the framework 2
   Communication for development 4
   C4D in the United Nations 6
   Evaluation 7
   Social change 8
   Participation 9
   Participation and sustainability 12
   Origins of the framework and its principles 13
   Development of the principles and framework 17
   Ensuring rigour in evaluation and sustainable development 18
   How the book is organized 19

2 Framework for evaluating communication for development   21

   Overview of the framework 21
   The framework components in more detail 24
   Comparison with other frameworks and approaches 38
   Conclusion 42

3 New thinking and trends   44

   Challenges in moving beyond dominant approaches to evaluating C4D 45
   The value of systems and complexity approaches to evaluation 46
   A systems perspective 47
   Complexity theory 56
   Distinguishing between simple, complicated and complex problems 60
   Critical approaches to understanding and evaluating social change 63
   A focus on power relations, gender and social norms 65
   Conclusion 68

4 Challenges, issues and strategies 70

Context and structure 71
Institutional and country-level challenges 73
Attitudes and policies of funders and management 74
Challenges in conceptualizing, outsourcing and managing research and evaluation 77
Challenges in assessing impacts and outcomes of C4D 79
Overcoming the challenges: key trends in C4D evaluation 83
New conceptualizations of evaluation and shifts in evaluation practice 87
Conclusion 90

5 Evaluation capacity development 92

Understanding and defining evaluation capacity development 93
The need for an alternative approach to evaluation capacity development 94
Towards a holistic approach to evaluation capacity development 96
A holistic approach to organizational capacity development 96
The value of participatory methodologies for evaluation capacity development 99
Challenges and issues in evaluation capacity development 100
Strategies for effective and sustainable evaluation capacity development 104
Conclusion 111

6 Key approaches, methodologies and methods 113

Definitions of key terms 113
Key approaches and methodologies for evaluating C4D 114
Key C4D evaluation methods 135
Indicators 137
Conclusion 140

7 Conclusion and implementation 142

Key features and benefits of the framework for evaluating C4D 142
Challenges, issues and contradictions 144
Strategies proposed to address these challenges and issues 150
Implementing the framework for evaluating C4D 152
Looking to the future 159

References 161
Index 177

Illustrations

Figures

2.1	Seven inter-related components of the framework for evaluating C4D	22
2.2	Example of a communicative ecology map	30
3.1	Communicative ecology map of Madanpokhara village, Nepal	52
3.2	Communicative ecology map of Asmita from Jhuwani village, Nepal	54
7.1	Key concepts in the framework for evaluating C4D	143

Tables

1.1	Emerging dichotomies in development M&E	3
1.2	Summary of tensions between dominant and participatory approaches to C4D	6
2.1	Similarities and differences between the framework for evaluating C4D and related research and evaluation frameworks and approaches	39
3.1	The contrasting paradigms of things and people	49
6.1	Ratings for approaches and methodologies considered 'very' or 'fairly' effective for planning C4D evaluations and/or assessing C4D impacts	114
6.2	Ratings for methods considered 'very' or 'fairly' effective for assessing C4D impacts	135
7.1	Tensions between dominant and participatory approaches to C4D	145
7.2	Tensions between dominant and alternative approaches to evaluation capacity development	146
7.3	Tensions between dominant and alternative approaches to evaluation of C4D	148
7.4	Tensions between dominant and alternative approaches to assessing the outcomes of C4D	149

Boxes

2.1	The mixed methods PM&E approach in AC4SC	32
2.2	Barriers to participation of Tamils in Finding a Voice	33
3.1	Overview of the concept 'communicative ecology'	50
3.2	The role of communication and participatory planning and evaluation in the development of Tara Shire	59
3.3	The UNAIDS communication framework	65

3.4	Self-organization in the distribution of La Boletina	66
3.5	Empowering and disempowering impacts of community-based C&IT evaluation projects	67
4.1	The benefits and challenges of incorporating ethnographic action research into C4D organizations	75
4.2	The pressure to conform to externally imposed evaluation approaches	76
4.3	Key themes in our UN consultations on challenges in evaluating C4D	78
4.4	Understanding the community context of the AC4SC project	80
4.5	Building a sense of community and understanding outcomes through visual participatory research methods	84
4.6	The value of community feedback forums in AC4SC	89
5.1	The holistic approach to evaluation capacity development in AC4SC	97
5.2	Key features of learning organizations	98
5.3	Key learnings about creative capacity development within organizations	99
5.4	Examples of effective online ECD and networking initiatives	106
5.5	Developing and embedding a research culture	109
5.6	Insights from the 'How wide are the ripples' project	110
6.1	Developing an initial theory of change for two C4D radio programmes	118
6.2	Example of a significant MSC story: 'Empowered to protest early arranged marriage'	124
6.3	New evaluation solutions to the 'problem' of gender and development	132

About the authors

Dr June Lennie is a Senior Research Associate in the School of Media and Communication, RMIT University, Melbourne, Australia. She holds a PhD in feminist evaluation methodologies, gender and ICTs. She has conducted numerous research projects and consultancies with government, non-government and international agencies, including a major UN inter-agency consulting project. From 1990 to 2012 she worked on a range of communication-related projects at Queensland University of Technology (QUT). Her work has focused on the development, application and meta-evaluation of participatory research and evaluation methodologies and ICTs for social change, sustainable community development, and rural women's empowerment. This work has included major evaluation capacity development projects in rural communities and non-governmental organizations (NGOs), including a development communication NGO in Nepal. She has co-developed several participatory evaluation frameworks and methodologies, toolkits and evaluation resources. June is a co-author of *Action Research and New Media* (Hearn *et al.*, 2009, Cresskill, NJ: Hampton Press).

Professor Jo Tacchi is Deputy Dean, Research and Innovation in the School of Media and Communication at RMIT University. She is an ARC Centre Fellow in the Centre of Excellence for Creative Industries and Innovation at QUT. She is a media anthropologist with a special interest in radio and digital media. Her research has included collaborations with a range of partners including UNESCO and other UN agencies, NGOs and corporate partners. Her research has focused both on ethnographic understanding of media and communication for development in a range of contexts, and on developing ethnographically informed participatory and mixed method approaches to understanding social change. Research in communication for development has been a focus of her research since 1999. Her work in this area has been centrally concerned with issues around culture and social change, and in developing suitable methodologies for investigating this.

Acknowledgements

This book is the product of an ongoing collaboration between the two authors, which began in 2006. Separately and together, for more than a decade, we have worked on research projects that have intensified our commitment to the approach to evaluation presented in this book, and which have greatly informed our ideas and thinking in this field. Many other people have influenced our work and our thinking.

Numerous people were crucial to the early development of ethnographic action research (EAR), including Don Slater, Peter Lewis, Greg Hearn, Lasanthi Daskon, Ian Pringle, Tanya Notley, Sunil Wijesinghe and all at KCRIP, Wijayananda Jayaweera and Savithri Subramanian. The Finding a Voice project developed EAR further and depended on support and collaborations with an international network of people, including Jerry Watkins, Andrew Skuse, Ian Pringle, Seema Nair, MS Kiran, Karma Tshering, Jocelyne Josiah, Emma Baulch, Kirsty Martin, Jo Fildes, Stuart Cunningham, Hitendra Pillay, staff, volunteers and participants in the network of community-based media and ICT initiatives, and the wonderful EAR researchers.

This book also draws on findings from the LEARNERS project which was undertaken in collaboration with Greg Hearn, Lyn Simpson, Emma da Silva, Kitty van Vuuren, Megan Kimber and Mary Hanrahan from Queensland University of Technology, staff of various project partner organizations, and community coordinators and participants in Tara and Stanthorpe Shires, Queensland (see Lennie *et al.*, 2004, for a full list of people involved).

We also draw extensively on outcomes from the Assessing Communication for Social Change (AC4SC) project which was conducted in collaboration with Andrew Skuse and Mike Wilmore from the University of Adelaide. This project simply could not have happened without the vision and commitment of Michael Bosse from Equal Access International and all at Equal Access Nepal, especially Bikash Koirala, Jiwan Sharma, Sajani Bajracharya, Sanju Joshi and Gemma Quilt. We also acknowledge the crucial role of the network of community researchers around Nepal and various community participants and stakeholders in Nepal who contributed greatly to the project. The support of Shirisha Amatya was also important to the project's success.

The consultations we conducted to develop a UN Inter-Agency Resource Pack for the research, monitoring and evaluation (R,M&E) of communication for development (C4D) gave us the opportunity to consolidate much of our thinking and have a broad range of discussions with, and input from, key thinkers, policy-makers and practitioners in the fields of C4D and participatory research and evaluation. Theresa Stuart and Paula Claycomb from UNICEF provided constant support and encouragement, useful resources and information, and valuable feedback and advice. In particular, we thank Ailish Byrne for extensive and valuable feedback on our draft reports on the project and for ongoing encouragement and support during the process of writing this book. Other participants in the consultation process who provided valuable input were: Silvia Balit, Krishna Belbase, Penelope Beynon, Gary Coldevin, Jackie Davies, Alfonso Gumucio Dagron, Will Parks, Rafael Obregon, Andrew Puddephatt, Nora Quebral, Jan Servaes, Matthew Smith, Silvio Waisbord, Kitty Warnock, Caroline Davies, Ricardo del Castello, Regina Monticone, Carla Henry, Venus Jennings, Le Le Lan, Paavani Reddy, Neil Ford, Boniface Kalanda and Masud Mozammel. Other UN participants are listed in Appendix 1 in Lennie and Tacchi (2011a). Kirsty Martin provided research assistance and compiled a large bibliography of references that we drew on extensively in writing this book.

Many ideas and inputs across these projects came from Ben Grubb, Tripta Chandola and Venu Arora.

A range of funders made the research we draw upon here possible, with the Finding a Voice, AC4SC and LEARNERS projects all supported by the Australian Research Council through their Linkage Project competitive grant scheme. This made it possible in these projects to work collaboratively, in depth, and over time with a range of partner organizations. The UN consultations were funded by UNICEF.

As well as the book *Action Research and New Media* (Hearn *et al.*), earlier work upon which we build includes the report on the UN consultations and literature review, in which we started to form early versions of some of the chapters (Lennie and Tacchi, 2011a), and the outline of a guide to designing the R,M&E process for C4D (Lennie and Tacchi, 2011b). Through the AC4SC project, and in collaboration with Equal Access, Mike Wilmore and Andrew Skuse, we developed an evaluation toolkit for C4D which has informed various parts of the book. We acknowledge Bikash Koirala's important inputs into this toolkit in particular.

We would like to thank Taylor & Francis/Routledge (Earthscan) Editorial Assistants Charlotte Russell and Helena Hurd and Associate Editor Khanam Virjee for providing support and making the process to publication smooth. We thank Maureen Allen of Book Now Publishing Services for her excellent work as copyeditor and project manager for the production process. Our diagrams were designed by Eunice Yip (with input from June Lennie), our text formatted and edited by Matthew Meng, and our reference list compiled and checked by Christine Schmidt. Our index was prepared with assistance from Frances Paterson of Olive Grove Indexing Services. Rafael Obregon, Sarah Cardey and Vandra Harris provided positive comments on our initial book proposal and three anonymous reviewers of the proposal helped us to further strengthen the book. While we received support, comments, inputs and suggestions from these people, all shortcomings in the final text are our own.

We could not have completed this book without the support of Ken Moore, Peter Barnes and other family, friends and colleagues who provided ongoing encouragement and support.

We are very grateful to all of the people who have contributed to this book in various different ways. Thank you very much.

Acronyms

AC4SC	Assessing Communication for Social Change project
ALPS	Accountability, Learning and Planning System
AR	action research
BCC	behaviour change communication
C&IT	communication and information technology
C4D	communication for development
CAS	complex adaptive system
CFSC	communication for social change
CR	community researchers
DE	developmental evaluation
EAN	Equal Access Nepal
EAR	ethnographic action research
ECD	evaluation capacity development
FAO	Food and Agriculture Organization
FAV	Finding a Voice
ICD	information and communications for development
ICT	information and communication technology
ICT4D	information and communication technology for development
ICTPR	ICT for Poverty Reduction
IDRC	International Development Research Centre
IE	impact evaluation
ILO	International Labour Organization
INGO	international non-governmental organization
IOCE	International Organization for Cooperation in Evaluation
KABP	knowledge, attitudes, behaviours and practices surveys
KCRIP	Kothmale Community Radio and Internet Project
LEARNERS	Learning, Evaluation, Action & Reflection for New technologies, Empowerment and Rural Sustainability
LFA	logical framework approach
M&E	monitoring and evaluation
MDGs	Millennium Development Goals
MSC	most significant change
NGO	non-governmental organization
OECD	Organisation for Economic Co-operation and Development
OM	outcome mapping
PAR	participatory action research

PM&E	participatory monitoring and evaluation
PRCA	participatory rural communication appraisal
R,M&E	research, monitoring and evaluation
SMART indicators	specific, measurable, attainable and action-oriented, relevant, and time-bound indicators
SPICED indicators	subjective, participatory, interpreted, communicable, empowering and disaggregated indicators
SSMK	*Saathi Sanga Manka Khura* [Chatting with my best friend] radio programme
ToC	theory of change
UN	United Nations
UNAIDS	Joint United Nations Programme on HIV/AIDS
UNDP	United Nations Development Programme
UNESCO	United Nations Educational, Scientific and Cultural Organization
UNFPA	United Nations Population Fund
UNICEF	United Nations Children's Fund
UNIFEM	United Nations Development Fund for Women
VBNK	Institute to Serve Facilitators of Development
WCCD	World Congress on Communication for Development
WHO	World Health Organisation

1 Introduction

In this book we present our comprehensive, overarching framework for evaluating communication for development (C4D). The framework is both conceptual and methodological in that it proposes ways of critically thinking about the evaluation of C4D and suggests how to go about it. It consists of seven inter-related key components – participatory, holistic, complex, critical, emergent, realistic and learning-based. Sets of principles inform each component. In the pages of this book we will describe the framework, where it has come from, what has influenced its design, and how we think it might be used.

The framework fits most comfortably within a holistic approach to development based on systems and complexity thinking. It advocates a focus on power, gender and social norms, takes a participatory, flexible, mixed methods approach to research and evaluation, and incorporates action learning and a critical, realistic, approach to social change and evaluation. The framework emphasizes people, relationships, processes, and principles such as inclusion, open communication, trust and continuous learning.

We aim to demonstrate the importance of this framework for understanding and addressing the complex social change issues that C4D contributes to. We demonstrate the value and rigour of participatory and mixed methods approaches to evaluation and the important role of evaluation in the ongoing development and improvement of C4D initiatives. We propose that the framework can help to reinforce the case for effective two-way communication and dialogue as central and vital components of participatory forms of development and evaluation that seek positive social change. This is a push back against results-based management and its negative implications for creative and innovative C4D and evaluation processes. As such it draws upon other work in this area that promotes innovative and creative approaches to evaluation, and alternative paradigms of development and organizational change.

The book outlines and critiques a number of important trends, challenges and approaches associated with evaluating, researching and assessing the outcomes of development initiatives focused on social change through C4D. This includes a detailed overview of systems and complexity theories and their value in understanding and addressing complex social problems. Such understandings are important when evaluating development initiatives that seek to address complex social and economic problems and influence social change. This requires an overview of new conceptualizations of social change that emphasize the contradictions and paradoxes in the process. The framework aims to move beyond unhelpful dichotomies and divisions, including those between different methodological paradigms and approaches, which have hindered developments in this area.

The book includes a review of the key approaches, methodologies and methods that are seen as effective for planning evaluations and assessing the outcomes of C4D activities and initiatives. We outline some practical ideas and processes for implementing the framework and strategies for overcoming the many challenges associated with the process of conceptualizing, planning and designing effective evaluations of C4D and other social change initiatives. We include examples throughout, from a number of action research and participatory evaluation projects that we have undertaken over the past 15 years, and from other C4D, participatory development and social change initiatives that have used related approaches.

The book will appeal to academics and students in a wide range of disciplines, including development, media and communications, sociology, anthropology, evaluation and capacity development. It will also be of interest to C4D practitioners, policy-makers, planners and evaluation specialists working across the whole range of development agencies.

We do not provide an extensive critique of development per se. Rather, we are focusing on evaluation and C4D, although we believe that what we have to say about this has wider implications, and our approach to development itself will become very clear. It is worth noting that this book is not an exhaustive review of all approaches to evaluation – we draw upon and discuss those that are the most relevant and appropriate to our framework, and critique dominant approaches to evaluation and ways of conceptualizing the process of social change. It is also worth noting that we use the term 'evaluation' throughout the book in a rather loose way to encompass research, monitoring, evaluation and outcome studies. This is for convenience. We explain what we mean by this term and what it encompasses below. In addition, we use the term 'C4D' through the book as shorthand for 'C4D and other social change initiatives, projects and programmes'.

The need for the framework

The project planning cycle is currently dominant in development. The linear, logical framework approach promoted by many development institutions, along with results-based management, present an upward accountability approach to development and its evaluation that is underpinned by ideas of pre-planning, and predetermining what successful outcomes will look like. In this approach, the outcomes of complex interventions are reduced to simple, cause–effect processes and the categorization of things, including people (Eyben, 2011). Contrary to this, participatory approaches, complexity theories and whole systems approaches understand social change as unpredictable, unknowable in advance, emergent, and something to learn from and adapt to. The former approaches prioritize categorization of abstract concepts, control and accountability; the latter prioritize relationships, openness, innovation and flexibility. The former are mainstream, considered rigorous, and largely based on standardized methods; the latter are alternative, considered (by proponents of the former) to lack rigour and based on a range of approaches, methodologies and methods selected according to each initiative and its context.

However, while there are some clear divisions between these two paradigms, our framework advocates taking a view that moves beyond such strict dichotomies, given its open, self-evolving, adaptive approach. For example, our approach recognizes the importance of effective planning in an evaluation but does so in participatory, realistic and flexible ways that allow for ongoing changes to an initiative and its theory of change, as those involved learn from evaluation outcomes.

These issues are important to recognize and address because participation and ideas around long-term change are being overcome by an ascendance of accountancy and linear

Table 1.1 Emerging dichotomies in development M&E

Reporting against:	Service contracts	or	Social development
	Pre-agreed plans and contracts	or	Autonomous development
	Deliverables	or	Impacts
	Technical indicators	or	Poverty reduction
Overall aims:	Serving the state	or	Serving people
	Reform	or	Transformation
	Management efficiency	or	Impact
	Short-term gains	or	Long-term change
	Formalizing institutions	or	Developmental (socio-economic–political)
Organizational impetus:	Co-optation	or	Independence
	Compliance	or	Empowerment
	Rationalizing reality	or	Enquiry
	Short-term accountability	or	Learning to do better
	Donor competition	or	Sharing learning
	Creation of a comfort zone	or	Encouraging a culture of challenge

Source: Pratt (2007: 2)

planning models (Eyben, 2011; Mebrahtu, Pratt and Lönnqvist, 2007; Quarry and Ramirez, 2009), spurred on in part by the *Paris Declaration on Aid Effectiveness*.[1] Evaluation has a key role in ensuring that we do not ignore the lessons of the past in favour of mechanistic approaches to monitoring and evaluation (M&E), that technocratic approaches do not overwhelm participatory approaches and the involvement of those on the ground, and that innovative and creative approaches designed for learning rather than accounting are promoted. In short, evaluation and our framework can help us to be searchers rather than planners (Easterly, 2006), listeners rather than tellers (Quarry and Ramirez, 2009).

There is confusion around the implications of particular concepts and words, so that the function of evaluation as downward accountability and enhanced learning is weakened (Mebrahtu *et al.*, 2007). 'Accountability' might actually mean accountancy in the way it is used, and 'participation' might refer to top-down programming (Pratt, 2007). Pratt describes the emerging dichotomies as shown in Table 1.1.

While Pratt (2007) and Mebrahtu *et al.* (2007) acknowledge that in reality many of these dichotomies might be better represented as a spectrum, they question whether we can actually choose where on the spectrum we situate our evaluation work at all. They note a de-emphasis on participatory principles, a de-prioritizing of M&E, and a fixation on greater efficiency in the disbursement of aid funding.

This book supports the call to rethink and challenge these trends, and contributes to a body of work that pushes our thinking about evaluation into an alternative, learning-centred, flexible space. To support this, the framework is designed to be both theoretically and methodologically rigorous as well as practically accessible. The idea is to enable a better understanding of the important contributions of C4D to the processes of development and change, and encourage continuous and active community and stakeholder engagement in C4D initiatives and their evaluation. This increases their long-term sustainability and effectiveness. Indeed, we argue that communication and this alternative approach to evaluation are critical for sustainable development.

The framework accommodates the complex, emergent nature of the process of social change, compared with linear, reductionist approaches. Given the complexity of social change and often rapidly changing social and communication contexts, evaluations need to take a dynamic, flexible approach that focuses on *progress* towards long-term social change and the *contribution* of C4D. This is compared with dominant 'managerialist', 'industrialized', upward accountability-based approaches to evaluation that are inappropriate in the context of C4D yet often imposed by major development institutions. In response, we will show how the framework allows for openness, flexibility and realism in planning, designing and implementing C4D and social change evaluations.

The framework supports a need to pay attention to power relations, difference (such as gender, ethnicity, educational and literacy levels, and age) and social and cultural norms in the process of researching and evaluating C4D. It can be challenging to achieve the full and equitable participation of marginalized and socially excluded people in development initiatives and their evaluation. It is particularly important to take gender issues into account in the evaluation of C4D because of the significant role that women and girls play in the development process, the fact that they are often more negatively affected by inequalities and disadvantage, and because gender can tend to slip down international development agendas (Newton, 2011). Furthermore, what is evaluated in relation to women and development is important, since positive social change in women's lives consists not simply of generating income, but a sense of self-worth and the ability to make life choices, exercise voice and influence relationships; 'it is women's capacity to exercise voice and influence in the key arenas of their lives that provides the impetus for change' (Kabeer, 2011: 1). Our approach to evaluation seeks to encompass diversity and a broad range of aspects of social change.

Communication for development

There are contested titles and definitions of communication for development, with multiple and confusing affiliations and provenances (Quarry and Ramirez, 2009). One of the most comprehensive definitions is provided by Fraser and Restrepo-Estrada:

> Communication for development is the use of communication processes, techniques and media to help people toward a full awareness of their situation and their options for change, to resolve conflicts, to work towards consensus, to help people plan actions for change and sustainable development, to help people acquire the knowledge and skills they need to improve their condition and that of society, and to improve the effectiveness of institutions.
>
> (Fraser and Restrepo-Estrada, 1998: 63)

The emphasis in this quote shifts from people who need to become aware and act to bring about change, to the need for institutions to improve their effectiveness. A focus on evaluation places the attention equally on communities and development organizations. How might development initiatives use communication to improve practices, to learn, and to help achieve sustainable development through participation with people on the ground?

C4D encompasses all forms and modes of communication, including community radio and entertainment-education programmes focused on social change and development, community-based information and communication technology (ICT) initiatives, processes such as community dialogue, participatory video, and digital storytelling activities, and the use of various combinations of new and traditional media in support of development activities. However, C4D is essentially about people rather than technologies, and is both a field of knowledge and of practice (Waisbord, 2008; Wilkins, 2000).

Surveying its multiple meanings, Waisbord (2001: 28) describes development communication as 'a sort of umbrella term to designate research and interventions concerned with improving conditions among people struggling with economic, social political problems in the non-Western world'. Servaes (2008) suggests that while the words used to define C4D might change over time, since the mid-1970s the intent is reasonably constant. Taking some of the examples Servaes (2008) cites, and adding others, there is an emerging consensus:

- Rogers (1976) described development communication as the study of social change brought about by communication research, theory and technologies, with development understood as a participatory process of social change.
- The FAO (1984) defined C4D as a social process towards common understanding and concerted action of all involved in a development initiative (in Servaes, 2008).
- For Fraser and Villet (1994) it is the planned use of communication techniques, activities and media to allow people to both guide and experience change and intensify the exchange of ideas. This is a fundamental requirement for appropriate and sustainable development.
- The UN resolution 51/172 (1997: 2), stresses 'the need to support two-way communication systems that enable dialogue and that allow communities to speak out, express their aspirations and concerns and participate in the decisions that relate to their development'.
- The World Congress on Communication for Development (WCCD) *Rome Consensus* (2006: 2) defines C4D as a 'social process based on dialogue'; it is 'about seeking change at different levels including listening, building trust, sharing knowledge and skills, building policies, debating and learning for sustained and meaningful change'.

Participatory theories and approaches are particularly highlighted in C4D because of the nature of communication itself. Yet despite the prominence of ideas around the participatory nature of communication, older modernization paradigms have not been completely displaced. In his review of trends in empirical research on C4D, Inagaki (2007) shows that the modernization paradigm and diffusion approach have a persistent influence. While we might think that ideas of communication as meanings and processes rather than the transmission of messages have concretized, this is yet to be as widely or fully practised as generally thought (Fraser and Restrepo-Estrada, 1998; Inagaki, 2007).

In our consultations for a UN project on the evaluation of C4D (described in detail below), one UN participant said *'academics are 10 years ahead of us – what they know; only about 10% of it is applied by us – we simply don't have the tools to apply it'.*[2] Our framework is intended to help bridge this gap between ideas, theories, concepts and practice that can be incorporated into the planning, managing and practice of the evaluation of C4D.

The contrasting views of dominant and participatory approaches to C4D and the resultant tensions, issues and contradictions that we have identified are summarized in Table 1.2.

There is an issue with C4D not being understood across the development arena, and a need to raise its profile. It is on the one hand marginalized; the fifth wheel on the development cart (Balit, 2010a), not even allocated the importance of the spare tyre on the development car (Gumucio Dagron, 2008). On the other hand, there is recognition that communication needs to be harnessed for development (UNESCO, 2007). The 2006 WCCD produced a set of recommendations to policy-makers based on an understanding

6 *Introduction*

Table 1.2 Summary of tensions between dominant and participatory approaches to C4D

Dominant approach	Participatory approach	Tensions and issues
Vertical, top-down, message delivery, one-way, public relations.	Horizontal, dialogue, sharing knowledge and learning.	Many C4D approaches refer to both perspectives in contradictory ways resulting in confusion and inappropriate compromises.
Communication is marginalized, lack of high-level support for and understanding of C4D.	Communication as major pillar for development, support for horizontal communication.	Institutions are often structurally unsuited for listening. C4D often located in corporate communication and external relations departments.
'Participation' is often rhetoric, not practised, or implemented in top-down ways.	Participation and ownership are seen as vital for sustainability.	Full and direct participation is incompatible with dominant organizational cultures and practices.

that communication is a 'major pillar' for development and social change. Among the 'strategic requirements' specified in the WCCD's *Rome Consensus* are: access to communication tools so that people can communicate amongst themselves and with decision-makers; recognition of the need for different approaches depending on different contexts; and, support to those most affected by development issues to enable them to have a say (WCCD, 2006). There is a stress on the need to build capacity for development communication at all levels, from community members to development specialists. It is not to be reduced to public relations or corporate communications.

C4D in the United Nations

The 11th United Nations Inter-Agency Round Table on C4D had a dual and complementary purpose – it set out both to explore ways to effectively institutionalize C4D within the international development agenda (Feek and Morry, 2009) and to find ways to demonstrate impact and thereby strengthen C4D's institutional position (Puddephatt, Horsewell and Menheneott, 2009). Feek and Morry (2009: 4) conducted a survey and interviews in late 2008 and early 2009 in preparation for the Round Table, to explore the level of 'UN agency understanding, acceptance, and implementation of C4D as a central, critical, and core element of their policy frameworks and programming strategies'. Their findings showed that C4D lacked central status in policy, strategy and planning, and lacked impact data, skilled C4D staff, and dedicated funding. Corporate communications were prioritized. Feek and Morry's survey reinforces earlier surveys from 1994 (Fraser and Fjortoft for UNICEF and WHO), 2003 (Ramirez and Quarry for IDRC), and 2006 (Fraser and Restrepo for the World Bank) (cited in Balit, 2010a: 4). Each highlights the recurring problem that few decision-makers in development organizations understand C4D or its role in development. Our 2010–2011 consultations with the UN and other C4D experts reinforce these findings. Our framework is proposed as a mechanism to promote C4D, and demonstrate the range of rigorous and insightful opportunities for evaluating and demonstrating outcomes, both positive and negative, expected and unexpected.

One way in which the UN Round Tables have tried to raise the profile of C4D is through coming up with agreed definitions. However, this task is not straightforward because different agencies have different ideas about C4D. For UNESCO, enhancing universal access to information and knowledge and fostering pluralistic, free and independent media is central; for UNICEF, C4D largely means behaviour and social change and a focus on human rights; for UNDP, C4D is intrinsic to governance and social accountability. While these are not mutually exclusive, four main 'strands' have been identified across the United Nations; behaviour change communication, communication for social change, advocacy communication, and strengthening an enabling media and communication environment (McCall, 2011).

Communication for development can mean a range of things. It can be a communication component in a broader development initiative or programme, or an initiative or programme that focuses on communication as a means to development. What is central to current understandings of C4D is that it is a social process, based on dialogue. It is 'about seeking change at different levels including listening, building trust, sharing knowledge and skills, building policies, debating and learning for sustained and meaningful change' (Gumucio Dagron, 2009: 6). Quarry and Ramirez (2009) say that rather than good communication producing good development, we should shift the emphasis to good development breeding good communication. This is development that communicates well with local communities about their development goals and solutions, rather than tells them from a policy-based, top-down approach what these ought to be. Good development by definition has good communication at its heart.

Evaluation

Moving C4D up the development agenda, giving it the recognition and attention it deserves, has been a preoccupation of UN C4D Round Tables. Achieving this depends on being able to demonstrate its impact through research, monitoring and evaluation (R,M&E). One of the recommendations of the *Rome Consensus* is that C4D programmes 'should be required to identify and include appropriate monitoring and evaluation indicators and methodologies throughout the process' (WCCD, 2006: 3). As will become clear, we prefer a focus on outcomes, rather than impacts measured through pre-defined, top-down indicators. This is because the complexity of C4D and social change makes it very difficult to assess direct cause and effect impacts, and because the outcomes and ripple effects of C4D can be difficult to adequately capture using standard approaches.

Throughout this book we use the term 'evaluation' to encompass evaluative research, monitoring and outcome studies. Here we spend a little time breaking down and defining what we mean by evaluation, its constituent parts, and how the framework approaches them.[3] We then use the term 'evaluation' in the remainder of the book as a shorthand term to encompass research, M&E undertaken to understand and critically assess C4D and its role in social change, and to continually improve and develop C4D initiatives in ways that lead to positive and sustainable social change.

We define evaluative research as the way in which we determine, through systematic, regular research, the value that primary stakeholders place on development programmes and activities, and their outcomes. Evaluation is undertaken in order to improve development's effectiveness and sustainability, to help reach objectives, to make good decisions about future activities, and, in its participatory forms, as a means of engaging and empowering people in development activities and building their capacities in evaluation.

For our framework, evaluation is seen as an ongoing, action learning, project development and improvement, and capacity development process. The aim is that this process becomes embedded into an organization's culture and its project planning and management processes, along with regular monitoring and critical reflection on the evaluation process. Evaluation enables mutual learning and understanding about the activities, opinions, values and experiences of diverse stakeholder groups (including C4D audiences and community participants). It helps us to understand and identify the expected and unexpected outcomes of development activities against a clear understanding of an initiative's vision and objectives, based on community needs and aspirations, and its theory of change.

Monitoring is a systematic and ongoing process of collecting, analysing and using information about the progress of development activities over time, and their strengths and limitations, to help guide activities and improve programmes, projects and initiatives. Monitoring performs some similar functions as evaluation but is mainly descriptive, and compares a particular programme plan with outcomes. Evaluation does the same but also looks at the various processes involved. Evaluation can move beyond monitoring, can identify and explain unexpected outcomes, and can learn from any failures to meet pre-planned activities to better develop new initiatives and innovations and improve relationships and future activities.

Participatory research and evaluation approaches are underpinned by interpretivist philosophy and a constructivist framework, in which evaluation is seen as leading to social action and positive change. In our framework, a participatory approach to evaluation is an essential principle. This means developing a partnership between stakeholders to collaboratively design and systematically implement evaluation processes, develop tools, set indicators (if they are used), and share concerns, experiences and learnings. This type of participatory monitoring and evaluation (PM&E) differs from conventional M&E in attempting to include all relevant stakeholders (staff, community participants, NGOs, donors, researchers etc.) in all aspects of the process (Holte-McKenzie, Forde and Theobald, 2006: 365). PM&E emerged from the extension of participatory action research (PAR) to evaluation (Garaway, 1995). It enables local knowledge and culturally appropriate processes to be incorporated into evaluation processes, and helps to create a clearer picture of what is happening at the grassroots level. When it is well-planned and facilitated, PM&E enables the inclusion of the diverse perspectives of women, men, young people, and various age, caste, class and ethnic groups in the data collection, interpretation and analysis process.

According to conventional approaches, impact assessment is a particular form of evaluation. It is not a separate activity but can be the focus of any monitoring or evaluation. Our framework is congruent with new evaluation and planning approaches such as outcome mapping (Earl, Carden and Smutylo, 2001), which has shifted from a focus on assessing the impacts of a programme (defined as changes in state such as reduced conflict) towards changes in behaviours, relationships, actions and activities of people, groups and organizations. The focus of this approach is on more subtle changes that nevertheless 'are clearly within a programme's sphere of influence' (Earl *et al.*, 2001: 10). We provide more information on outcome mapping in Chapter 6.

Social change

While there are many different perspectives on social change, in this book we consider social change as non-linear, dynamic, emergent and complex. Social change in complex systems such as communities occurs through multi-level, inter-connected, interdependent, non-linear and unpredictable relationships and processes (Lacayo, 2007; Ramalingam *et al.*, 2008). This means that when change happens it is often disproportionate and unpredictable, making it hard to capture in any meaningful way using evaluation approaches based on predictable and linear processes that seek measurable outcomes. Understanding the local culture and context and the relationships between people, groups and organizations in that context, is therefore vital to understanding social change.

Contemporary ideas about development emerged post World War II, incorporating modernization frameworks based on notions that countries in the 'third world' had not yet reached the stage of development of countries in the 'first world' (Crewe and Harrison 1998; Escobar 1995). Development aimed to help underdeveloped countries on the path to development, and social change meant becoming more like the West. The introduction of 'modern' technologies (Waisbord, 2001), from production technologies, medical technologies and family planning, to mass, and more recently, digital media infrastructure, were fed by notions of technology 'transfer' as a way to shape and change social and economic systems. While alternative theories and approaches to development have emerged, such deterministic and instrumentalist notions of change remain central to dominant development agendas (Gardner and Lewis, 1996). Such highly generalized discussions of development can easily become abstract goals geared to the requirements of agencies and policy discussions, and distant from practice (Eyben, 2011).

By contrast, notions of social change that encompass complexity and difference recognize that technological changes and development interventions may have complex, diverse and often contradictory effects on different communities or groups of people such as women and the very poor. The focus of C4D research and evaluation must retain a level of concrete engagement and an awareness of contradiction and complex, largely unpredictable consequences. Social change is uneven (Postill, 2011), and there is a dearth of rich ethnographic, comparative studies that explore, on the one hand, the disruptive and political potential of media and information technologies, and on the other, their social and cultural rootedness (Tenhunen, 2008).

Evaluating C4D and social change requires attention not only on the potential benefits and possibilities of communication, technologies and media in terms of development and social change, but also on the particularities of the contexts through and in which they are shaped and experienced. Social change is not linear, not predictable, and is always contextual. Effectively understanding social change requires considering broader dimensions of the process, beyond the 'social', to encompass the political, economic and cultural (Wilkins, 2009: 4). It also requires a shift in focus from the impact of particular interventions on specific groups to changes in wider social and organizational systems. This entails an open, holistic and realistic yet critical approach to development and evaluation that draws on a wide range of related theories, concepts and approaches. Such an approach allows us to raise fundamental questions about the process of development and social change and the assumptions that underpin different approaches to development and C4D.

Participation

C4D intrinsically links communication with participatory development, for example by insisting that communication relates to dialogue rather than message delivery. However, participation is a contested concept (Cornwall, 2011), with many faces (Stiefel and Wolfe,

1994). The concept of participation can be grounded in democratic theory, although what constitutes democratic participation is also contested and varied, so that democracy is at the same time the language of militarily imposed change, neo-liberal market forces and international development agendas (Appadurai, 2002; Gaventa, 2006).

Participation 'first hit the development mainstream' (Cornwall, 2008: 269) in the 1970s, and took hold in the 1980s. Even then different meanings and practices were apparent, as demonstrated in the various typologies and 'ladders' of participation developed to illustrate ranges from, in the case of the earliest ladder, citizen control (a form of citizen power), through consultation (a form of tokenism) to manipulation (a form of non-participation) (Arnstein, 2011). The practice of participation in development is considered by some as a false participation, rhetoric, incompatible with procedures and goals of aid organizations, and a threat to those in positions of power (Bailur, 2007; Cooke and Kothari, 2001; Fraser and Restrepo-Estrada, 1998; White, 1996). It has become a development buzzword (Cornwall and Brock, 2005; Leal, 2007), often assumed to be essential to development, and necessarily and intrinsically good. It holds both the potential for tyranny (Cooke and Kothari, 2001) and transformation (Hickey and Mohan, 2004), because it implicates the political and exists in relations of power.

A single definition of the concept or practice of participation in development is elusive. It is a malleable concept that can be used to signify 'almost anything that involves people' and encompasses a wide diversity of practices (Cornwall, 2008: 269). In communication and media studies, particularly in the era of Web 2.0, participation is a key concept, and yet is used to mean 'everything and nothing' (Carpentier, 2011: 14). The 'new communications environment' can be seen to offer the conditions for a shift from vertical models of communication to horizontal models; in other words, a shift from sending messages to providing an opportunity for people to engage in dialogue, share knowledge and ask questions (Deane, 2004). Yet this participatory condition is under-theorized, and its political nature largely unacknowledged (Carpentier, 2011). While dialogue, debate, the two-way flow of information, and the co-creation of knowledge are intrinsic to the idea of participatory development, some major applications of participatory strategies and processes, such as the Poverty Reduction Strategy Papers (PRSP) have been criticized for reinforcing existing structures and politics of representation (see Gould, 2005). Poverty reduction strategies are seen by some as a product of participatory sentiments obscuring central control, signalling the failure of participation as transformative and providing proof of its tyranny (Brown, 2004). The World Bank is considered by Cooke (2004) to use participatory methodologies and practitioners to enforce its neo-liberal agenda.

Ultimately, participation is about power and control and is an inherently political process (Cornwall, 2008). Carpentier (2011) grounds the concept of participation in democratic theory to highlight the importance of power, but insists that this transcends institutionalized politics to permeate all realms of society. He uses a broad definition of the political, so that all social spheres are contestable and politicized, and open to claims of increased participation. He contrasts minimalist and maximalist forms of participation, drawing on minimalist and maximalist democratic models that have more or less centralized decision-making and more or less limits on participation. He stresses the intimate connection between participation, power and decision-making processes, and indicates the wide range of ways in which they can be variously articulated (Carpentier, 2011: 16).

Participation is embedded in our political realities and struggles. Carpentier (2011: 24–28) puts forward six characteristics of maximalist participation in an effort to increase the theoretical foundation of the concept of participation:

1   The key defining element of participation is power.
2   Participation is situated in particular processes, localities and actors.
3   Participation is contingent and dependent on the ideological framework within which it is being used, or on how we 'think participation'.
4   Participation is not based on populist fantasies of the replacement or overthrow of hierarchy, but on diversity and power sharing, and equal power relations in decision-making.
5   Participation is invitational and not imposed.
6   Participation is structurally different to access and interaction.

The opening up of spaces for invitational participation or invitational social change (Greiner and Singhal, 2009) is necessary, but not enough to ensure effective participation according to Cornwall (2008). Supportive processes are needed because invited spaces for participation in development are often structured by those who provide them, rather than created by people themselves. Participation as praxis is:

> Rarely a seamless process; rather, it constitutes a terrain of contestation, in which relations of power between different actors, each with their own 'projects', shape and reshape the boundaries of action. While a frame might be set by outsiders, much then depends on *who* participates and where *their* agency and interests take things.
> (Cornwall, 2008: 276, author's italics)

Invited participation in spaces created for this purpose by those in positions of relative power, can diminish the spaces where people set their own agendas on their own terms (Cornwall, 2008; Cornwall and Coelho, 2007).

One thing we can be sure of in relation to participation is the importance of considering power, and the need to understand participation in context. We can gain 'clarity through specificity' to distinguish between different practices and understandings of participation, and spot the kind of participation that the rhetoric invokes but that has little substance, 'from forms of genuine delegated control that enable people to exercise a meaningful part in making the decisions that affect their lives' (Cornwall, 2008: 281).

In this book participation in C4D means engagement by a range of stakeholders at all points in the C4D process, including the evaluation of C4D. Indeed, because of its communicative aspects, C4D has been shown to provide a mechanism for achieving the levels of participation, voice and choice that development more broadly often struggles to achieve (Tacchi, 2009). Recognizing that participatory approaches to development, to C4D, and to evaluation inevitably bring with them issues of power, it is important to be alert to power dynamics and issues of inclusion and exclusion, empowerment and disempowerment. C4D will always, to some extent, involve challenging power relationships and structures. This is because it depends on actively engaging a range of people, encouraging voice but also encouraging active listening across difference (O'Donnell, Lloyd and Dreher, 2009).

C4D and participatory development more broadly promotes dialogue. In practice, communication as understood by development agencies is often reduced to vertical information delivery, public relations, or dissemination. Progressive proponents of C4D consider the participation of people on the ground in all processes and stages of development as a fundamental principle. Communication, understood as a two-way relationship that not only acknowledges the right of people to be heard, but includes prioritizing effective listening, and recognizing and respecting alternative forms of knowledge, is needed to achieve this (Quarry and Ramirez, 2009; Servaes, 2008; Tacchi, 2012a).

Participation and sustainability

C4D proponents insist that 'without peoples' participation, no project can be successful and last long enough to support social change' (Gumucio Dagron, 2008: 70). Community participation in planning, decision-making, evaluation and implementation of C4D and community ownership are crucial for sustainability (Baulch, 2008; Jallov, 2012; Quarry and Ramirez, 2009). Servaes *et al.* (2012: 102) suggest that 'communication and information play a strategic and fundamental role' in sustainable development. They argue that a focus on culture and participation is crucial for sustainability.

Participatory approaches that promote dialogue and engagement are often seen as costly, time-consuming, and difficult to accommodate in well-defined plans and logframes (Balit, 2010a). Our framework insists that effective two-way communication is a central and vital component. While it is true that greater time and resources are often required to use participatory evaluation approaches and methodologies effectively, our framework takes the position that a critical, long-term view of the value of participatory approaches is required. Evaluation needs to be seen as an integral part of development initiatives and a means of fostering continuous learning, evaluative thinking and a culture of evaluation within organizations and communities. At the same time it is important to be realistic, and to understand that, in practice, idealized notions of participation including and empowering everyone are not possible, and to think in terms of what Cornwall (2008: 276) calls '*optimum* participation: getting the balance between depth and inclusion right for the purpose at hand'. It is also important to recognize that participatory processes can serve to exclude people unless special efforts are made to include them (Grubb and Tacchi, 2008; Lennie, 2005a), and that some people strategically or deliberately exclude themselves (Cornwall, 2008: 279).

The framework for evaluating C4D promotes holistic, learning-based evaluation capacity development (ECD) approaches. These are needed in development and C4D organizations and initiatives from grassroots to management level in order to develop learning organizations and communities. As we discuss further in Chapter 5, learning organizations engage in constant reflection in order to continually develop and improve organizational systems and development activities in ways that meet community and stakeholder needs and goals, and their visions of the future. Indeed, this type of organizational culture is needed to effectively understand and implement the framework.

The process of engaging in well-designed and implemented participatory research and evaluation can have significant effects in terms of the empowerment and capacity development of participants and stakeholders. However, issues of gender, power and knowledge need to be taken into account to increase the effectiveness of these processes and the inclusion of disadvantaged groups. This highlights the complexity of creating sustainable C4D that facilitates the engagement of disadvantaged groups such as poor people. Baulch (2008) clearly demonstrates this in relation to the sustainability of community-based ICT centres that were involved in the Finding a Voice project, which we outline in the section below. As Jallov (2012: 29) notes: 'Sustainability is multi-faceted and complex'.

No participatory evaluation will be perfect (Newman, 2008); there are many challenges, several of which we address in this book. We take the position that participatory approaches to the evaluation of C4D will lead to improved and sustainable C4D initiatives and better long-term outcomes in terms of development and social change. We present the framework for the evaluation of C4D as a contribution towards this broad goal, and encourage critical reflection, dialogue and debate about how well this works.

Origins of the framework and its principles

The framework grows out of research we have been undertaking, together and separately for over 15 years, and our mutual interest in issues of participatory research and evaluation, and capacity development. Some of this earlier work is documented in *Action Research and New Media* (Hearn et al., 2009). Here we give an account of the work that is most significant in terms of the framework, which also serves to provide some background on the main research projects that we draw upon as examples throughout the book.

Ethnographic action research, communicative ecologies and Finding a Voice

In 2002, funded by the Department for International Development (DFID), a small team of researchers[4] set out to explore the benefits of ethnography for evaluating the use of new ICT for development (ICT4D). At this time there was much debate around the 'digital divide', which served as a driver for widespread investment in ICTs for poverty reduction. There was a sense of hype around the potential of ICTs, but little or no evidence through standard evaluation approaches. The evidence of effectiveness was through anecdotal accounts, or individual transformational stories related to connecting to market, agricultural or health information. Standard evaluation approaches were not well suited to capture the changes that ICT was felt to be achieving. The question we set out to answer was: Can ethnography – an approach designed to understand the detail of everyday lives and how social and cultural institutions within communities fit together in meaningful ways (Beattie, 1964) – help us to capture such changes?

We spent one month in Sri Lanka researching the Kothmale Community Radio and Internet Project (KCRIP), which was UNESCO's pilot community multimedia centre. We built a research team and conducted a household survey, in-depth group and individual interviews, and participant observation. This approach allowed us to develop rich understandings of the KCRIP, local communities and the use of media technologies. As an approach to the evaluation of ICT4D we found the ethnographic principles of immersion and holism especially useful. The immersion in the setting, living just down the lane from the Centre and spending our days there or travelling around and meeting local communities, provided rich data and a degree of understanding and appreciation of local populations and their issues. The holistic approach was achieved most notably through the concept of communicative ecologies, which helped us to pay attention to the actual use of, and interaction with, media and ICT in the wider context of people's lives and social and cultural structures (see Box 3.1 in Chapter 3 for an overview of this concept).

Thinking about the use of media technologies for information and communication purposes through the concept of communicative ecologies focused our attention on the complexity of local communicative environments, and on how there are many information and communication channels and flows. Different places, and different people within a place, have quite different communicative opportunities and experiences, depending on many factors, including the availability of infrastructure and technological and social networks, and particularities such as age, gender, class, education, economic situation, and so on. It cannot, therefore, be assumed, that everyone in a locality will engage with an ICT4D initiative such as a community internet project, or community radio station, in the same way.

These kinds of understandings, fleshed out through an ethnographic approach, helped us move beyond mere anecdotes, and we were able to make recommendations to help KCRIP become more effective (Slater, Tacchi and Lewis, 2002). Yet we were not satisfied with

14 *Introduction*

this. There were two intrinsic problems with this approach. First, ethnography depends on long-term engagement – longer than one month. We partly overcame this limitation by using a team of researchers and local research assistants pursuing many research threads at the same time, but we knew there were many more lines of enquiry that we were unable to follow to deepen our understanding of KCRIP and its context.

The second problem was that we wanted to develop an evaluation methodology that incorporated an ethnographic approach to help ICT projects like KCRIP to improve their work. Handing KCRIP a report and recommendations written by 'outsiders' who spent one month there did not achieve what the approach promised. This is the point at which we combined an ethnographic approach with action research, and recommended ethnographic action research (EAR) as a methodology that could be used by people on the ground working in initiatives like KCRIP, to help them understand and evaluate their own work (Slater *et al.*, 2002).

In 2003, with additional funding from UNESCO, through a project called Putting ICTs into the Hands of the Poor, or ICT for Poverty Reduction (ICTPR), we set about training a network of local researchers to be embedded EAR researchers working within and for community media and ICT centres and initiatives (Tacchi, Slater and Hearn, 2003). These EAR researchers came from nine community ICT centres in India, Nepal, Bangladesh, Sri Lanka and Bhutan (Slater and Tacchi, 2004). They collected and shared information on their initiatives, which helped us understand some of the uses and possibilities of traditional and new technologies for development, but more importantly, helped each local initiative improve their own practices. They used the research to inform their initiative's ongoing development, following and repeating an action research cycle of plan, do, reflect.

EAR provided interesting and different perspectives on how to go about researching communication and ICT for development. To develop EAR further, Finding a Voice (FAV)[5] followed on from ICTPR, starting in 2005 as a three-year research project (Tacchi, 2012a; Tacchi and Kiran, 2008; Tacchi *et al.*, 2007). We worked in 15 sites in India, Nepal, Sri Lanka and Indonesia. In each site we partnered with a local community-based ICT, media or information centre. These ranged from telecentres in Indonesia, community multimedia centres in Sri Lanka and Nepal, ICT, gender and resource centres in India, community libraries in Nepal, and community radio and TV initiatives in Nepal and India. The attention was on how new digital and traditional ICTs can be used to promote participation in content creation (especially among the most marginalized), and the consequences of such experiences of voice. This was a project with two main strands. One was a focus on establishing and researching participatory content creation activities across the 15 sites. The other was the training of and support for a network of local researchers, trained through the project in EAR. FAV informed the further development of EAR (http://ear.findingavoice.org).

Assessing Communication for Social Change

EAR was picked up by a range of other researchers and organizations, including Equal Access, an international C4D non-governmental organization (NGO). They requested a series of EAR workshops for Equal Access Nepal (EAN) because they wanted to build their internal capacity to deepen their understanding of the impact of the radio content they produced and distributed across Nepal. EAR was found to be useful, but EAN found it hard to apply it consistently or systematically. We collaboratively developed the idea of Assessing Communication for Social Change (AC4SC),[6] a four-year research project we began in 2007.[7]

The idea was to develop EAR into a methodology embedded in EAN. Previous models had relied on one or two EAR researchers working within and attempting to influence an organization (Tacchi and Kiran, 2008). Here the idea was to transform the organization by establishing evaluative systems and processes within it. Where EAR had grown in earlier research very much as a project development methodology, here we sought to transform and extend it into a strong evaluation methodology.

We worked closely with EAN staff, following a PAR approach, to develop systems and processes to assess the impacts of two popular community radio programmes: *Saathi Sanga Manka Khura* [Chatting with my best friend] and *Naya Nepal* [New Nepal]. With the collaboration and support of the Australian research team, EAN's M&E team developed research plans, built and trained a network of community researchers, collected and organized data from sites across Nepal, developed systems of analysis, and reported regularly to content teams (producers) and management. Towards the end of the four years, a transferable toolkit was produced, based on the experiences of EAN and is currently being tested by Equal Access in Niger. AC4SC provided significant learnings about evaluating C4D and evaluation capacity development in complex and challenging development contexts which we draw on extensively in this book.

The LEARNERS project

The LEARNERS project[8] was another influence on the thinking that underpins this book. This project was based on a pilot project that developed the LEARNERS process (see below), and feminist research that included the participatory evaluation and critique of a rural women and ICTs project (Lennie, 2005b, 2006a, 2009).

The LEARNERS project was conducted by a research team from Queensland University of Technology from 2001 to 2004 in collaboration with two communities in rural Queensland – the Tara and Stanthorpe Shires – and five project partners (see Lennie *et al.*, 2004).[9] Many community-based communication and information technology (C&IT) initiatives in rural Australia had failed due to factors such as small, scattered populations, limited funding and resources, and lack of training and support. The long-term sustainability of these initiatives was a significant issue and there was little effective planning and evaluation of rural C&IT initiatives.

The LEARNERS process took a whole of community systems approach to planning and analysis, used PAR and participatory evaluation, and sought to develop learning communities. The 'ideal' LEARNERS process included:

- identifying and building on existing community skills, knowledge and resources;
- engaging in continuous PAR cycles of planning, acting, observing and critically reflecting on the actions taken;
- ensuring that all participants' ideas, comments and feedback are included and taken into account;
- collaboratively planning and conducting evaluations that enable ongoing learning about and constant improvements to C&IT initiatives;
- gathering data that enable analysis of relevant differences such as gender, age, and levels of skills, knowledge and access to C&IT.

(Lennie, 2005a: 399)

Aims of the project included generating new ideas about the use of C&IT in sustainable community and economic development, and enhancing women's leadership in C&IT.

16 *Introduction*

A critical approach was taken that recognized the complex barriers to community participation and empowerment. The project included interactive workshops and other activities to collaboratively develop community capacities in planning and evaluating local C&IT initiatives such as community websites.

An important component of the project was the rigorous, continuous evaluation of project activities and impacts (see Box 3.5 in Chapter 3 for more details). This evaluation highlighted the complex and contradictory outcomes of PAR projects involving diverse participants and stakeholders, and the importance of empowering forms of leadership and rural women's empowerment to successful community capacity building and sustainable development. The project demonstrated the value of participatory research and evaluation, and the use of systems approaches, for understanding and addressing complex community development issues. It identified critical success strategies for conducting and evaluating PAR, community capacity building and community C&IT projects. These strategies, and the findings from the project, provide valuable learnings for the participatory evaluation of C4D and for evaluation capacity development in C4D.

UN consultations towards a Resource Pack for research, monitoring and evaluation of C4D

In 2010 a UN Inter-Agency Group, led by UNICEF, contracted us to develop a Resource Pack for the R,M&E of C4D for use by the United Nations and its partners. This was in response to recognition of the need to demonstrate the effectiveness of C4D in order to increase its status within the United Nations, and the need to demonstrate the rigour of approaches suitable to evaluating C4D, which mainstream evaluators within the United Nations were largely not trained in.

We undertook a wide-ranging literature review and consultations with a 15-member Expert Panel from UNICEF and various research and consulting organizations and universities in Western and non-Western countries (academics, practitioner and policy-makers in the USA, United Kingdom, Canada, Mexico, Italy, Philippines, Nepal and Africa), and 11 C4D Focal Points or M&E specialists from seven UN agencies or other bodies (FAO, ILO, UNESCO, UNDP, UNFPA, UNICEF and the World Bank). As well as providing a large bibliography of references and relevant literature that we have drawn on extensively in this book, the consultation and data gathering process involved analysis of the following data and feedback:

- qualitative and quantitative data from two detailed online surveys completed by 14 Expert Panel members and 10 UN Focal Points;
- interviews conducted with five UN Focal Points (one face-to-face and four by telephone);
- feedback received from seven Expert Panel members and two UN Focal Points on a background paper for the 11th UN Round Table on M&E for C4D by Puddephatt *et al.* (2009);
- feedback on draft principles for R,M&E of C4D, provided by nine Expert Panel members and four UN Focal Points;
- feedback on a draft of our report on the literature review and consultations, provided by six Expert Panel members, five UN Focal Points, and other specialists from UNICEF, UNIFEM and elsewhere at a series of meetings in New York in December 2010.

Outputs from this project included a comprehensive report: *Researching, Monitoring and Evaluating Communication for Development: Trends, Challenges and Approaches* (Lennie & Tacchi, 2011a) and an outline of a guide to designing the R,M&E process for C4D in the United Nations (Lennie and Tacchi, 2011b).

Development of the principles and framework

Our UN consultations included the development of a comprehensive set of principles for effective, appropriate and sustainable evaluation of C4D and an initial framework that incorporated these principles (see Lennie and Tacchi, 2011a). This work drew on evaluation principles in Chavis, Lee and Jones (2001), Hearn *et al.* (2009), Mayoux and Chambers (2005), Parks *et al.* (2005) and Regeer *et al.* (2009). The development of these principles involved seeking feedback on a set of draft principles from the UN Focal Points and Expert Panel members. Based on further literature reviews, a critical review of these principles, and our work on the framework presented in this book, we further refined and revised these principles.

General principles underpinning the framework

The framework for evaluating C4D is underpinned by some general principles. Here we divide them into four broad areas: those concerned with evaluation contexts and the social change processes; those to do with evaluation approach and design; those related to the use and selection of evaluation approaches, methodologies and methods; and finally, principles related to the outcomes of evaluations and evaluation capacity development.

Principles related to the evaluation context and the social change process

- The evaluation seeks to understand the wider systems, networks and macro and local contexts within which the initiative operates, including communication and organizational systems. In this context, social systems are seen as dynamic, adaptive and emergent.
- Social change is seen as a long-term process that is complex, non-linear, unpredictable, and often contradictory.
- The evaluation takes this complexity into account, and includes analysis of social norms and other contextual factors (including relevant social and cultural factors) that affect the process of social change.
- The evaluation focuses on *progress* towards social change and the *contribution* of C4D.

Principles related to the evaluation approach and design

- The approach to evaluation and evaluation capacity development is participatory, inclusive, flexible and creative, involves the long-term engagement of people in all evaluation stages, and draws on local and expert knowledge.
- As far as possible, the evaluation is based on action learning and participatory action research principles and processes.
- The evaluation critically addresses issues of gender, ethnicity and other relevant differences, and unequal voice, power and control.

18 *Introduction*

- Evaluation is fully integrated into organizations and the whole programme cycle.
- The evaluation design considers the strengths, limitations and cultural appropriateness of various approaches, methodologies and methods.
- The evaluation process ensures a high level of independence, integrity and honesty.
- The evaluation is open to negative findings and weaknesses, and learns from 'failures'.

Principles related to the use and selection of evaluation approaches, methodologies and methods

- The selection and use of evaluation approaches, methodologies and methods involves openness, freedom, flexibility and realism.
- Evaluation approaches, methodologies and methods are as simple, practical, responsive and rigorous as possible, grounded in local realities, and able to capture unexpected changes and ripple effects.

Principles related to the outcomes of evaluations and evaluation capacity development

- PM&E is seen as an important means of developing effective, sustainable and innovative C4D initiatives that more effectively address development goals.
- The evaluation process and ECD aims to foster the development of learning organizations. The attention here is on strengthening the whole organization and its evaluation systems, and improving coordination, cooperation and collaboration between internal and external agents and groups.

More expanded versions of these principles are provided in the descriptions of the seven framework components in Chapter 2.

Ensuring rigour in evaluation and sustainable development

There is a lack of awareness, appreciation and familiarity with participatory research and evaluation approaches in many development organizations. There is a lack of skills in these approaches and there can be issues with defining who should be involved, especially for those trained in randomized approaches to sampling and impact evaluation. Linked to this, these approaches are seen by some to lack credibility in terms of rigour and validity. Mayoux and Chambers (2005: 271) argue that participatory approaches are often seen as a 'fashionable and "politically correct" frill to the more serious task of "expert" surveys and (more rarely) qualitative research'.

In participatory approaches, the scientific ideal of objectivity is usually rejected in favour of a holistic approach that incorporates diverse perspectives, values, agendas and interpretations of participants and evaluation professionals (Lennie, 2006b). However, as we demonstrate in this book, rigour can be achieved in this approach (Dick, 1999; Lennie, 2006b; Thomas, 2000). Guba and Lincoln (1989: 233) propose that the criterion of 'trustworthiness' is more appropriate than traditional scientific criteria for assessing the quality of participatory evaluation.

The methods and underlying philosophies of participatory research and evaluation contrast markedly with traditional programme evaluation methods such as quasi-experimental impact assessments, and it is for this reason that rigour is questioned. In these traditional approaches, the evaluator is expected to adopt an impartial and objective perspective, and programme activities are usually reduced to quantitative indicators (Vanderplaat, 1995). In contrast, qualitative indicators are increasingly used in participatory impact assessments, along with multiple methods that aim to reflect 'the complexities of everyday reality' and the different perspectives of those involved (Worthen, Sanders and Fitzpatrick, 1997: 154).

There are many complex theoretical, methodological and ethical issues that have implications for the quality of an evaluation and the trustworthiness of findings and outcomes. They include the need to ensure stakeholder diversity and representativeness (Lennie, 2002; Mathie and Greene, 1997; O'Meara, Chester and Han, 2004) and the need to critique the concepts of empowerment and participation when assessing the impacts of participatory research and evaluation (Lennie, 2005b, 2006a, 2009). They also include the need to invest time, energy and resources to build evaluation capacity, to plan and conduct evaluations, and to develop relationships based on trust and open communication. Finally, these issues include the need to demystify evaluation and to encourage participants to think in an evaluative way.

How the book is organized

In this chapter we have established the background to the book and outlined and defined several key concepts that are part of the framework, including C4D, participation, social change and evaluation. There is a lack of understanding of C4D and its important role in development. We have introduced the framework, its general underlying principles, and the major action research and evaluation projects that have informed it, which we draw on throughout the book. There are important links between PM&E, C4D, social change, participation, sustainability and development. These concepts are linked through recent literature on systems and complexity theory, development and evaluation. This provides an effective way to understand development and social change processes and the importance of C4D and evaluation approaches based on dialogue, participation, emergence, continuous adaptation, learning, and capacity development.

Chapter 2 describes the framework in some detail, setting out its seven key components and linking to associated principles for effective, appropriate and sustainable research and evaluation of C4D. To highlight the value and originality of the framework, we compare it with four related frameworks or approaches to research and evaluation that have been used in the areas of international development or C4D. In Chapter 3 we review a number of significant new trends and ways of thinking about development, research and evaluation and their importance to the evaluation of C4D. We explain the value of a systems approach and complexity theory to understand and evaluate complex development and social change initiatives. We offer critiques of dominant social change communication theories, emphasizing the need to consider broader dimensions and paradoxes in the change process, and highlight the importance of paying attention to power relations, gender and social norms. Throughout Chapter 3 we critique instrumental, accountability-based approaches to evaluation that often limit the effectiveness of C4D.

Chapter 4 outlines the many complex challenges and issues surrounding the evaluation of C4D and the need for a greater appreciation of the importance of contextual, structural, institutional, and organizational issues. Key challenges in conceptualizing, managing and planning evaluations of C4D are considered, along with strategies for overcoming them. One key strategy – evaluation capacity development – is discussed in Chapter 5. Drawing on the latest thinking in this area and findings from our own research, we discuss the benefits of taking a participatory, holistic approach to ECD and some of the challenges and issues that need to be considered.

In Chapter 6 we present a detailed overview and critique of the key approaches, methodologies and methods that are considered effective for planning evaluations and assessing the outcomes of C4D. We focus on new and innovative participatory and qualitative methodologies such as EAR (Tacchi et al., 2007), outcome mapping (Earl et al., 2001) and developmental evaluation (Patton, 2011), and on the importance of feminist and gender-sensitive approaches. The strengths and limitations of the key approaches and methodologies in this field are considered. Chapter 7 presents a summary of the key challenges, tensions and issues identified in the book and suggested strategies for overcoming them. We set out a number of practical ideas and processes for implementing the framework, drawing on our work in this field and the various participatory research and evaluation toolkits and guides we have been involved in developing over the past few years. This chapter also includes key factors in selecting the most useful and appropriate approach, methodologies and methods for researching and evaluating C4D.

Notes

1 The Declaration came out of a 2005 high-level international meeting in Paris, hosted by the French Government and organized by the OECD. It set out five mutually reinforcing principles for development: ownership, alignment, harmonization, results and mutual accountability.
2 Extracts in italics indicate quotations from our consultations, as opposed to quotations from a publication.
3 In developing these definitions we have drawn on definitions and overviews of various approaches to M&E, including Estrella (2000), Gariba (1998), Gosling and Edwards (2003), Patton (2002), Wadsworth (1997), and Webb and Elliott (2002).
4 Peter Lewis and Don Slater, at that time both from the London School of Economics, and Jo Tacchi, at that time from Queensland University of Technology (QUT).
5 'Finding a Voice: Making Technological Change Socially Effective and Culturally Empowering' was funded through an Australian Research Council Linkage grant (LP0561848) with additional funding and support from UNESCO and UNDP.
6 'Assessing Communication for Social Change: A New Agenda in Impact Assessment for Communication for Development Initiatives' was funded by the Australian Research Council (LP0775252) and Equal Access.
7 The research team for this project comprised Jo Tacchi and June Lennie (both at that time with QUT) and Andrew Skuse and Michael Wilmore (University of Adelaide).
8 'Evaluating a model to improve the sustainability and success of rural community development initiatives that use new communication technologies' (the LEARNERS project) was funded by the Australian Research Council (C00107782), the Federal Department of Family and Community Services, Learning Network Queensland, The Office for Women (Queensland) and QUT.
9 The QUT research team included June Lennie, Greg Hearn, Lyn Simpson, Emma Kennedy da Silva, Kitty van Vuuren, Megan Kimber and Mary Hanrahan.

2 Framework for evaluating communication for development

Overview of the framework

This chapter presents a comprehensive framework for evaluating C4D and other social change initiatives in the development context. The framework can help to increase understanding of the important contributions of C4D and evaluation to the process of development and social change and can help develop, strengthen and improve C4D initiatives and C4D organizations.

The framework draws upon our work in this field and the latest thinking in a range of areas, including systems and complexity theory, and participatory, critical and learning-based approaches to development, social and organizational change and evaluation. It also responds to recent critiques of dominant top-down, results-driven approaches to development and evaluation. The framework presents a holistic and participatory, yet rigorous, critical and realistic approach that includes analysis of power and gender issues and local social norms. We present these concepts in this chapter and discuss them further in Chapter 3 and other parts of this book.

We present a flexible, overarching framework for evaluating C4D and other complex development initiatives that are focused on achieving positive and sustainable social change in areas such as poverty reduction, gender equality, disease prevention and discrimination. As we demonstrate through numerous examples, this framework is theoretically and methodologically rigorous, practically accessible, and highly consistent with the values and principles of C4D. An important aim of the framework is to break down unhelpful dichotomies and divisions, including those between different theoretical and methodological paradigms, which have hindered progress in this area.

The framework places a high level of emphasis on processes, principles and values (such as inclusion, open communication, trust and continuous learning), and less emphasis on achieving specific measurable results or outcomes. As Patton (2011) points out, the outcome and accountability focus underpinned by results-driven approaches downgrade or ignore these:

> But for values-driven social change activists and innovators, *how* outcomes are attained is at least as important as, if not more important than, the outcomes themselves. Process matters... given the uncertainties of complex interventions and interactions... values can become the anchor, the *only* knowable in an otherwise uncertain, unpredictable, uncontrollable, and complex world.
>
> (Patton, 2011: 246, author's italics)

The framework comprises seven inter-related components, as shown in Figure 2.1.

22 *Framework for evaluating C4D*

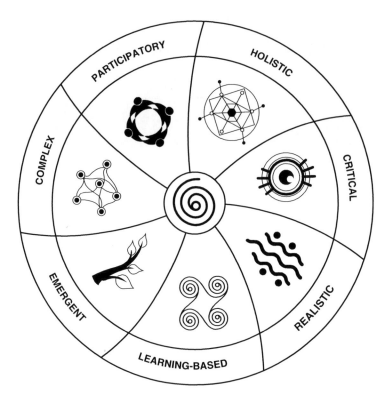

Figure 2.1 Seven inter-related components of the framework for evaluating C4D

 Participatory Evaluation is undertaken in partnership with community members, stakeholders and others, using processes that are culturally and socially appropriate, creative, and based on mutual trust, openness and transparency. This approach respects, legitimizes, contextualizes and draws on the knowledge and experience of local participants as well as relevant experts and outsiders. It is as inclusive as possible of a diversity of groups. The process aims to continuously and actively engage people in all aspects and stages of the evaluation through two-way communication, dialogue, feedback and mutual learning. It includes an action component to continuously develop and improve C4D and evaluation processes. A participatory monitoring and evaluation (PM&E) approach is seen as an important means of developing effective, innovative and sustainable C4D.

Holistic Evaluation is based on an understanding of wider social, cultural, economic, technological, organizational and institutional systems and contexts within which C4D operates. Organizations and communities are greater than the sum of their parts. This approach includes analysis and understanding of the inter-relationships, inter-connections and networks between the various organizations, groups and agents involved in an initiative (directly or indirectly) and the boundaries and local communicative ecologies (including communication flows and barriers) within which an initiative operates.

Complex The framework recognizes that social change and C4D are complex and involve processes that are often contradictory and challenging. The evaluation process is based on the recognition that C4D is often undertaken in social, economic and cultural contexts with high levels of social conflict, involving people and organizations with multiple perspectives and agendas. This means that the outcomes of C4D are often unpredictable or unknowable in advance. Evaluation approaches therefore need to be flexible, participatory, creative and well-planned and facilitated in order to adequately take the complexity of social change into account.

 Critical This approach seeks to actively and explicitly address issues of gender, caste, class, ethnicity, age and other relevant differences, and unequal power and voice among participants. Issues of gender, power and control are openly addressed in the evaluation and associated critical reflection processes. The evaluation focuses on local social norms and the challenges, contradictions and paradoxes that often characterize the process of social change. In addition, the design and implementation of the evaluation is based on an awareness of the strengths and limitations of various evaluation approaches and methods (including participatory approaches), and is open to negative findings and learning from failure.

 Emergent Social change and the outcomes of C4D are seen as processes that are non-linear, dynamic, messy and unpredictable. An emergent approach recognizes that communities and local contexts are not static, and aims to provide a better understanding of the complex process of social change. Evaluation processes therefore need to be dynamic, flexible, adaptive, alert to critical incidents and tipping points, and based on simple principles and processes such as self-organization, powerful listening and continuous feedback loops. They also need to be capable of capturing outcomes and ripple effects that go beyond or are different from underlying assumptions about the outcomes of initiatives and the process of social change.

 Realistic To be most effective, evaluation approaches and methods need to be as simple, practical, responsive and rigorous as possible. They must be grounded in local realities and based on methodological pluralism. This requires openness, freedom, flexibility and realism in planning and implementing evaluation and in the selection of approaches, methodologies and methods. This approach aims to increase the usefulness of evaluation results, which should focus on intended, unintended, expected, unexpected, negative and positive change. Long-term engagement with organizations and communities will ensure effectiveness and sustainability, and a long-term perspective on both evaluation and social change.

 Learning-based Action learning and participatory action research (PAR) principles and processes aim to achieve good communication, cooperation, collaboration and trust between those involved. This key component aims to facilitate and encourage continuous learning, mutual understanding, empowerment, creative ideas and thinking, and responsiveness to new ideas and different attitudes, values and knowledge. Evaluation is fully integrated into organizations and the whole programme cycle and involves a diversity of people taking responsibility for research and evaluation activities. This helps to develop the wide range of evaluation capacities that are required in this approach, and to create learning organizations. The process includes regular critical reflection in order to learn from experience.

The framework components in more detail

We now describe each key component of the framework for evaluating C4D and their associated principles in greater detail.

Component 1: Participatory

Guiding principles

- The evaluation approach is consistent with the values, principles and aims of C4D.
- Evaluations are undertaken in partnership with community members and other stakeholders, and, wherever possible, involve long-term engagement with these groups.
- The evaluation aims to facilitate continuous and active participation in all aspects and stages of the evaluation, through dialogue, feedback and mutual learning. Creative and engaging communication methods are used wherever possible.
- Evaluations use processes that are culturally and socially appropriate, not rushed, and based on mutual trust, open communication and transparency.
- The evaluation is as inclusive as possible of a diversity of social groups and every effort is made to include a range of voices and experiences.
- The evaluation process respects, legitimizes and draws on the knowledge and experience of community members and stakeholders, as well as relevant experts and outsiders.
- Evaluations are based on an appreciation of the long-term benefits of taking a participatory and inclusive approach.

Participation as fundamental to C4D and its evaluation

The concept of participation is a fundamental element of C4D. C4D can therefore be used as an effective means of achieving participation in development more broadly. Byrne (2009a: 3) suggests that 'contexts of multiple actors and multiple, diverse perspectives and types of knowledge call for participatory approaches'. Similarly, Chambers (2009a: 4) explains that 'participatory approaches and methods fit in a paradigm that is pluralist, evolutionary and iterative'. Chambers (2009b) argues that participatory methods open up more possibilities for impact assessment, in terms of creativity and improvisation; they resonate with complexity science, can express local diversity, and open us up to learning and being in touch with the community in ways that other methods do not allow.

The ubiquity and mainstreaming of participatory methods in development is noted by Leeuw and Vaessen (2009). Participatory forms of research and evaluation are widely acknowledged as particularly effective and appropriate in C4D, especially those initiatives that are based on the communication for social change (CFSC) approach (Byrne, 2009a, b; Parks et al., 2005). Both the UN Focal Points and the Expert Panel in our UN consultations considered participatory approaches to evaluation very important for C4D. Highlighting the value of qualitative and participatory approaches to evaluation, one Expert Panel member commented *'they are not models, they are not toolkits or toolboxes...they are open approaches that can be adapted locally, that should be adapted locally'.*

Puddephatt, Horsewell and Menheneott (2009: 10) point out that the tendency of commonly used evaluation approaches to focus on quantitative data and statistics 'often fails to provide the depth necessary for understanding more complex C4D initiatives and does not always allow for other unexpected outcomes'. They recommend that 'in the context of promoting dialogue and building capacity towards community empowerment and ownership, C4D initiatives should always aim to include a level of participatory analysis' (Puddephatt *et al.*, 2009: 10). In his detailed critique of large comprehensive, pre-set survey questionnaires with fixed categories, Chambers (2008: 19) argues that they belong to 'a paradigm of things rather than people' and represent a 'paradigmatic misfit for complexity'.

When designed and implemented effectively, participatory evaluation can contribute to developing effective, innovative and sustainable C4D initiatives, providing an approach that captures depth of understanding as well as unanticipated outcomes. However, from positivist perspectives, questions are still raised about the rigour, objectivity and validity of alternative approaches to research and evaluation (Chambers, 2008; Parks *et al.*, 2005). Participatory research is essentially a challenge to positivist research paradigms, since it is built upon the ideas of democratic practice and transformative relationships (Hall, 1993). In PAR and participatory evaluations, the emphasis is mainly on knowledge generated and constructed through the lived experience of participants, rather than through social science (Vanderplaat, 1995).

The benefits and rigour of participatory methodologies

Rigour need not be lost in participatory evaluation approaches, as Dick (1999), Guba and Lincoln (1989), Lennie (2006b) and others suggest. Participatory research and evaluation approaches and methodologies have a number of strengths and a wide range of benefits that can greatly enhance C4D and its outcomes. They include: the ongoing development and improvement of C4D initiatives and policies in ways that better meet community needs and aspirations; increased research and evaluation capacities; greater utilization of findings and learnings; and the empowerment of participants. These approaches 'open studies to the voices of those most affected by a project in ways not possible using more conventional methods and can make the realities and experiences of poor people count more' (Chambers, 2009a: 4).

Chambers also highlights the largely unrecognized ability of participatory methods to generate numbers. He explains that:

> Through judgement, estimation, and expressing values, people quantify the qualitative. The potential of these methods is overdue for recognition. As always there are ethical issues. Well facilitated, participatory methods can be win-win – empowering people as well as providing credible and reliable insights for policy-makers.
>
> (Chambers, 2009a: 6)

Mayoux and Chambers (2005: 272) argue that when used well, participatory methods 'generate not only qualitative insights but also quantitative data which are generally more accurate than those from conventional survey approaches and methods'. This is supported by Barahona (2011: 197) who outlines innovative developments in the field of participatory numbers (or 'parti-numbers') over the last 20 years, and the challenges and issues that arise when attempts are made to produce reliable statistics through participatory processes.

The approach to participation in the framework

The framework draws on PAR and PM&E methodology, which will be outlined later in this chapter. Key principles of PAR include participation, action, reflection, empowerment and the production of various forms of knowledge (Hearn et al., 2009: 13). However, it is useful to conceive of PAR as taking place along a continuum of participation, which can range from 'cooption' to 'collective action', and involves varying degrees of control by researchers (Martin, 2000: 200). This suggests the need to be aware of the challenges of achieving a high level of participation and inclusion in the evaluation of C4D, especially in situations with high levels of conflict, oppression and disadvantage.

Several decades of participatory research and evaluation have demonstrated that valuing diversity and difference and taking an inclusive approach helps to understand problems and issues, can provide new insights and perspectives, and produce new and effective solutions to problems (Hearn et al., 2009; Lennie, 2009; Morgan and Ramirez, 1983; Williams and Imam, 2006). The framework advocates processes that are culturally and socially appropriate, creative, and based on mutual trust, open communication and transparency. The process aims to continuously and actively engage people in all aspects and stages of the research and evaluation process through open dialogue, feedback and mutual learning. For example, the PAR process that we used in AC4SC included regular meetings, workshops and field-based activities that were effective in strengthening the evaluation capacities within Equal Access Nepal (EAN) and engaging community participants and other stakeholders in the evaluation process. Among other outcomes, this resulted in improved relationships between M&E and programme development staff and a greater appreciation within EAN of the benefits of continuous participatory research and evaluation. We have included some examples of the use of creative and culturally appropriate evaluation approaches and methods in Chapters 4 and 6.

However, there are a number of challenges and issues associated with participatory methodologies that need to be openly acknowledged and taken into account. They include: the greater level of time and resources required (including for capacity development), issues related to gender, power inequities and inclusion, and the potential for conflicting agendas and multiple perspectives of various stakeholder groups to hinder success (Gregory, 2000; Hearn et al., 2009; Lennie, 2005a; McKie, 2003; Tacchi, Lennie and Wilmore, 2010). We discuss these challenges and issues more in Chapters 4 and 6.

While participatory approaches to evaluation are particularly well suited to C4D, they may appear to cost more in time and resources than non-participatory approaches, and the political will to invest in these approaches is often weak or absent (Parks et al., 2005: 13). There are also issues with the dominance of quantitative approaches and the entrenched use of tools such as the logical framework approach (or logframe), which are seen by some as incompatible with alternative, participatory approaches to evaluation (Earle, 2003; Joseph, 2011). In this context, it is important to take a long-term view of the evaluation process and the benefits of adopting a participatory approach. In the long run, participatory approaches are often less costly when their many benefits are considered.

Component 2: Holistic

Guiding principles

- The evaluation recognizes that social, cultural and economic systems within which C4D is implemented are dynamic, historical and capable of continuous transformation and change.

- The evaluation aims to describe and understand how the wider systems and networks within which an initiative is implemented operate.
- Evaluations include continuous monitoring of the local communication environment.
- Evaluation capacity development (ECD) is seen as a long-term process that focuses on the whole organization and aims to improve coordination, cooperation and collaboration between internal and external agents and groups.

The importance of a holistic perspective

A holistic perspective based on systems thinking, complexity theory and action research is increasingly seen as important to better understand and address complex development problems (Burns, 2007; Byrne, 2009a; Miskelly, Hoban and Vincent, 2009; Ramalingam *et al.*, 2008; Wadsworth, 2010). From this perspective, the social systems within which C4D is implemented are seen as processes that are dynamic, historical and capable of continuous transformation and change in ways that cannot always be predicted. This emphasizes the need to understand how the wider systems, networks, inter-relationships, boundaries, and other aspects of the context in which C4D is implemented actually operate, and how they can influence the outcomes of C4D. As Hearn *et al.* (2009) point out:

> One of the implications of taking a holistic approach is the realisation that most things in any field of action (or communicative ecology) are connected. That is, it is difficult (though not impossible) to hold different variables constant or to observe the impact of one variable in isolation from others. In general we live in a very connected world.
> (Hearn *et al.*, 2009: 35)

A holistic, systems perspective strongly underpins the CFSC approach to C4D (Byrne *et al.*, 2005; Lacayo, 2006) and participatory approaches to research and evaluation (Burns, 2007; Chambers, 2008; Fetterman and Wandersman, 2005; Hearn *et al.*, 2009; Patton, 2008, 2011; Wadsworth, 2010). It is therefore highly appropriate for the evaluation of C4D.

The holistic approach in the framework

The framework considers the wider social, cultural, economic, technological, organizational and institutional systems and contexts within which C4D initiatives operate. A key aim is to understand the inter-relationships and inter-connections between the various organizations, groups and agents involved in the initiative, and the boundaries and networks that can affect the outcomes of C4D. Organizations and communities are seen as greater than the sum of their parts.

This approach seeks to understand the local *communicative ecologies* (Hearn *et al.*, 2009; Tacchi *et al.*, 2007) that can influence the outcomes of C4D. They include existing local communication networks, and information flows and barriers that are unique to each place. Hearn *et al.* (2009) suggest asking the following key questions to understand a local communicative ecology:

- What kinds of communication and information activities do local people carry out or wish to carry out?
- What communications resources are available to them – media content, technologies, and skills?

- How do they understand the way these resources can be used?
- Who do they communicate with, and why?
- How does a particular medium – like radio or the internet – fit into existing *social networks*? Does it expand those networks?

(Hearn *et al.*, 2009: 31)

An example of a communicative ecology map is shown in Figure 2.2. We provide other examples of communicative ecology maps in Chapter 3.

Using this approach, the process also includes continuous monitoring of the communication environment in order to gather timely information and feedback that will further develop and improve C4D initiatives and ensure that they meet community needs, interests and goals.

This framework also takes a holistic, participatory, learning-oriented approach to evaluation capacity development. As we discuss further in Chapter 5, this is seen as a long-term process that focuses on building the capacity of an organization as a whole, strengthening M&E systems, and improving coordination, cooperation and collaboration between internal and external agents and groups. Developing and maintaining good communication and working relationships between the various parties involved in the ECD process is critical to success (Horton *et al.*, 2003: 56; Lennie, Tacchi and Wilmore, 2012).

Component 3: Complex

Guiding principles

- The evaluation recognizes that social change is complex and that many social systems operate in ways that are non-linear, unpredictable, chaotic, disorderly and emergent.
- The evaluation takes the challenges, contradictions and paradoxes that often characterize the process of social change into account.
- The evaluation design recognizes that C4D is often undertaken in contexts with high levels of social conflict, and involves people and organizations with multiple perspectives and agendas.
- Where appropriate, the evaluation attempts to understand how and why social change happens. This includes an analysis of social and organizational norms and other contextual factors that affect the process of social change.
- The evaluation design and an initiative's theory of change are flexible and evolving and assume that the outcomes of C4D are often unpredictable or unknowable in advance.

The value of complexity-based approaches

Along with systems thinking, complexity theory and complexity-based research and evaluation approaches are increasingly seen as offering valuable alternatives to understanding how development and social change actually occurs (Jones, 2011; Lacayo, 2006; Miskelly *et al.*, 2009; Papa, Singhal and Papa, 2006; Ramalingam *et al.*, 2008; UKCDS, 2011). Complexity science represents a challenge to 'highly-planned blue-print approaches to social change, privileging self-evolving and adaptive learning approaches' (Papa *et al.*, 2006: 234). Ramalingam *et al.* (2008: 61) suggest that the value of complexity science – at its most effective – 'is to generate ideas and insights that help to see complex problems in a more realistic and holistic manner, thereby supporting more useful intuitions and actions'.

The key benefits of a complexity approach to development and social change are that it:

- takes a more realistic and holistic approach to development and change;
- can help to clarify solutions to complex problems;
- encourages greater experimentation and innovation;
- generates new insights and responsiveness to different ideas, attitudes and values;
- encourages continuous learning and utilization of evaluation results;
- focuses on multiple perspectives and inclusion/exclusion.

The approach to complexity in the framework

Social systems within which C4D initiatives are developed, implemented and evaluated are seen as operating in ways that are non-linear, unpredictable, chaotic, disorderly and emergent. The framework is based on an understanding that social change is often a highly complex process that involves people and organizations with multiple, often conflicting, perspectives, ideas and agendas. C4D is therefore often undertaken in contexts with high levels of social conflict and disagreement. This means that many outcomes of C4D initiatives can be difficult to predict. In addition, this approach to evaluation takes the challenges, contradictions and paradoxes that are inherent to the process of social change fully into account (Papa *et al.*, 2006) and attempts to understand how and why social change happens.

To be effective in adequately taking the complexity of social change and the many social and cultural factors that can hinder positive change into account, approaches, methodologies and methods for the evaluation of C4D should be flexible, participatory and creative. The evaluation design and the initiative's theory of change must be able to adapt and evolve as the initiative is implemented and changed.

Evaluations of C4D need to include an analysis of social and organizational norms and other complex contextual factors that often affect the process of social change. To be most effective they also need to use a rigorous mixed methods approach that can provide a fuller and more realistic picture of change that is able to capture the voices, concerns and values of diverse stakeholders (Bamberger, Rugh and Mabry, 2006; Greene, 2002; Hearn *et al.*, 2009; Johnson and Onwuegbuzie, 2004). Box 2.1 highlights the value of the mixed methods approach that was used in AC4SC. We discuss the value of a mixed methods approach to evaluation further in Chapter 4.

Component 4: Critical

Guiding principles

- The evaluation openly and sensitively addresses issues of gender, ethnicity and other relevant differences, and unequal power and voice among participants.
- Evaluation data is disaggregated by gender, caste, educational levels and other relevant differences.
- The evaluation design is based on an understanding of the strengths and limitations of various approaches, methodologies and methods, including participatory methodologies and methods.
- Evaluation methodologies and methods are culturally appropriate and used in culturally sensitive ways.
- The evaluation includes processes that enable those involved to critically reflect on and learn from their experiences.

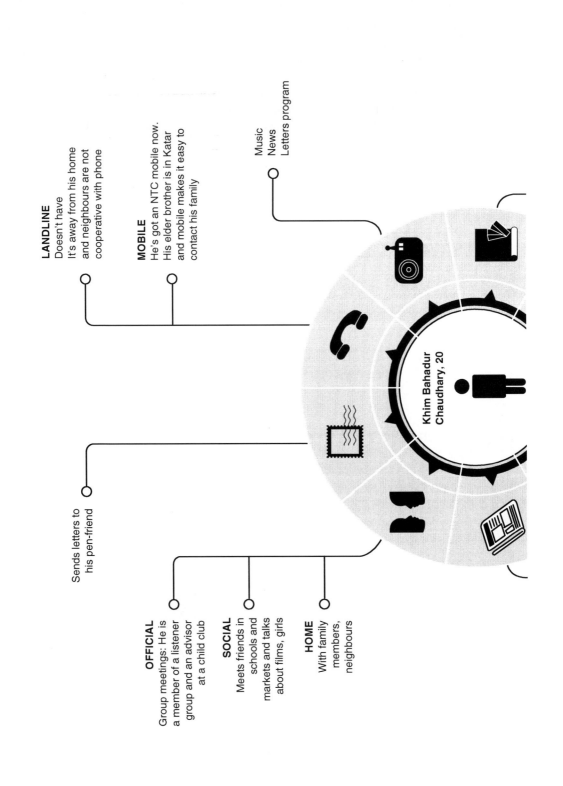

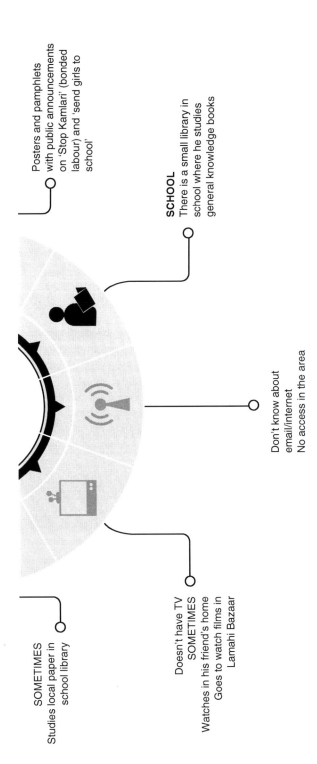

Figure 2.2 Example of a communicative ecology map

> **Box 2.1** *The mixed methods PM&E approach in AC4SC*
>
> The participatory methodology that we developed and trialled in AC4SC used a mixed methods PM&E approach. This process included community researchers using a range of participatory tools with small groups to understand local issues and to gather feedback on EAN's activities, as well as implementing the most significant change (MSC) technique to gather stories of changes that had emerged through listening to EAN's radio programmes. Other feedback and statistical information were collected from larger numbers of people through short questionnaire surveys.
>
> These data were later triangulated to increase the rigour of the results and to better understand the complex contextual factors that affect community perceptions and impacts of EAN's programmes. These factors include the uptake of communication technologies, such as mobile phones and television, and emerging changes in the social, political and economic systems within Nepal.

The importance of taking differences in gender, power and knowledge into account

Contemporary approaches to evaluation suggest that, rather than taking an idealistic view that assumes all participants in the evaluation of a C4D project are the same and equal, it is useful to openly acknowledge differences, particularly those related to gender, power and knowledge. A review of published studies on the impact of C4D initiatives found that 'the issue of power is a common cause of unsuccessful outcomes in these interventions; power imbalances in political, economic, occupational and gender domains created blockages to communication across social boundaries' (Inagaki, 2007: 40).

The effective evaluation of C4D and other development initiatives requires a high level of awareness of gender issues, given that the improvement of women's status 'is essential if we are to move the world towards a better life for all individuals' (Mongella, 1995: 121). Many of the Millennium Development Goals (MDGs) are aimed at improving the well-being and opportunities of women and girls, while the theme of the 2011 UN Inter-Agency Round Table on C4D was 'The Role and Relevance of Adolescent Girls in Transforming Society and Achieving MDGs'. However, recent research shows that gender is in danger of slipping from the agenda of international development (Newton, 2011). This suggests that new, more effective evaluation approaches that focus on gender are needed in order to maintain the important gains that have been made in this area.

The critical approach taken in the framework

The framework seeks to actively and explicitly address issues of gender, caste, class, ethnicity, age, educational level and other relevant differences, and unequal power and voice among participants, using a social construction of reality perspective (Gergen, 2009). Issues of gender, power and control are addressed in the evaluation and associated critical reflection processes. The evaluation focuses on local social norms and the challenges, contradictions and paradoxes that often characterize the process of social change. The challenges and issues in achieving inclusive participation in C4D projects are illustrated in the example from Finding a Voice in Box 2.2.

Box 2.2 *Barriers to participation of Tamils in Finding a Voice*

Finding a Voice aimed to help communication initiatives gain broader participation in their content creation activities. To do so it was necessary to understand who engaged with the initiatives, who did not, and why. The EAR researchers explored factors that prevented certain groups from participating, and helped to inform engagement strategies. This was clearly illustrated through the work with a mobile telecentre in Sri Lanka. The e-Tuktuk was developed as a mobile version of the fixed multimedia centre in a rural area of Central Province. While the centre attracted a range of people, a clear gap was identified with a particular population group that was geographically very close, but in all other ways remote from the centre. This was the extremely poor Tamil community who lived in dilapidated line houses, and worked as casual labourers, if they could get employment at all.

The factors that prevented participation were complex; to do with ethnicity, language, social positioning, economic and educational status, the history of the Sri Lankan conflict, and years of discrimination. Simply taking the centre to the community using the e-Tuktuk was not enough on its own, but gradually small gains were made by thinking creatively about how to engage with young people from the community (Grubb and Tacchi, 2008; Tacchi and Grubb, 2007). Such work can lead to small gains that need to be understood within the wider context and systems in which this community exists, in a complex situation of apparently intractable problems, which may nevertheless be considered adaptive, or evolving.

Our framework involves taking a participatory approach that aims to legitimize, contextualize and draw on the knowledge and experience of local participants, other stakeholders and those with relevant expertise and knowledge. Acknowledging the challenges involved, the aim here is to enable, as far as possible, the voices of diverse groups of participants to be heard, with the evaluator/facilitator sharing power with participants. Participants in the evaluation create shared meaning of their experiences over time.

In addition, the design and implementation of the evaluation is based on an awareness of the strengths and limitations of various evaluation approaches and methods (including participatory approaches), and is open to negative findings and learning from failure. We discuss the strengths and limitations of various approaches and methodologies that are considered effective for evaluating C4D in Chapter 6.

Component 5: Emergent

Guiding principles

- Evaluation processes, tools and methods (including theories of change) are dynamic and flexible, and can be adapted to the needs of C4D initiatives and organizations.
- The evaluation is capable of capturing unexpected, unpredictable and self-evolving changes and wider ripple effects on both intended beneficiaries and others.
- The evaluation focuses on *progress* towards social change and the *contribution* of C4D and is alert to critical incidents and tipping points.

- The evaluation aims to contribute to developing effective, innovative and sustainable C4D initiatives and continuously improving them through feedback loops.

The concept of emergence

Emergence is a key concept in complexity theory. It describes how 'the behaviour of systems emerges – often unpredictably – from the interaction of the parts, such that the whole is different to or greater than the sum of the separate parts' (Ramalingam *et al.*, 2008: 8). This highlights the importance of adopting a holistic approach when developing and evaluating initiatives, rather than just focusing on the individual elements of an initiative and their impact on participants, as standard approaches usually do.

Emergence is also about 'giving up control, letting the system govern itself as much as possible, letting it learn from the footprints' (Johnson, 2001 in Patton, 2011: 126). This emphasizes the significance of self-organization for effective social change and development (Chambers, 2008; Lacayo, 2006; Ramalingam *et al.*, 2008). Patton (2011: 150) points out that one of the implications of the concept of emergence for developmental evaluation is that it needs to be 'especially alert to [the] formation of self-organizing sub-groups who have different experiences of the programme and, correspondingly, different outcomes'. He further notes that 'the more open, participatory, individualized, and innovative the intervention, the greater the importance of such sub-groups self-organizing is for understanding programme experiences and outcomes' (Patton, 2011: 128). This highlights the need to take the experiences of different sub-groups (such as low caste girls or high caste men) into account in the evaluation of C4D and to disaggregate data in order to enable this analysis.

The approach to emergence in the framework

Social change and C4D are seen as processes that are emergent – they are non-linear, dynamic, messy and unpredictable. In order to be most effective, the process of developing appropriate evaluation approaches, methodologies and methods, and evaluating C4D therefore needs to be correspondingly dynamic, flexible and adaptive.

Evaluations of C4D also need to be alert to critical incidents and tipping points (which are often unpredictable) that can lead to significant changes in initiatives and the organizations involved. Metaphors that have been used to illustrate this concept include 'butterfly wings' and 'black swans' (Patton, 2011: 124). An example of a black swan is the global financial crisis of late 2008, a largely unpredicted and unexpected event that emerged from various critical incidents, which had a huge impact across the world.

The design of C4D evaluations therefore needs to be capable of capturing outcomes and ripple effects that go beyond or are different from the original theory of change and assumptions about the outcomes of initiatives and the process of social change. Patton (2011: 125) advises that the qualitative pattern for assessing tipping points 'involves early adopters being watched by others who, if they see or hear about positive results for those early adopters, try the innovation themselves'. An example of this process is provided in Papa *et al.* (2006: 152–153). They describe how a married couple from the village of Madhopur in Bihar in rural India heard a radio programme in which a young girl's birthday was celebrated. This led them to discuss why they had never celebrated their seven-year-old daughter's birthday. They realized that it was traditional in their village to celebrate a son's birthday with much public fanfare but not a daughter's. Inspired by the radio programme and animated by their discussions, they decided to publicly celebrate their daughter's birthday. This was the first time in Madhopur's history that this had happened. Following this event, several birthday celebrations for girls were held in Madhopur and other neighbouring villages. This example highlights the need for evaluations of C4D to be capable of capturing unexpected or unpredictable changes that can emerge from C4D-inspired discussions and subsequent community action.

The concept of emergence also suggests that evaluations need to be based on relatively simple principles and processes, such as self-organization, powerful listening and continuous feedback loops, in order to contribute to the development of effective, innovative and sustainable C4D initiatives.

Component 6: Realistic

Guiding principles

- The evaluation is based on a realistic, long-term perspective of evaluation and social change.
- Evaluation is fully integrated into organizations and the whole programme cycle from the conception, design and planning stages.
- Evaluation methodologies, methods and tools are as simple, practical, responsive and rigorous as possible, and grounded in local realities (because of a recognition of the complex nature of social change).
- Evaluation planning and the selection of methodologies, methods and indicators involves openness, freedom, flexibility and realism – it considers what is achievable.
- Wherever possible, evaluations use a mixed methods approach and triangulation.
- The evaluation process produces action-oriented knowledge, consensus about further action, and agreed visions of the future.
- The evaluation process ensures a high level of independence, integrity and honesty.

A realistic approach to development and evaluation

Among their many benefits, systems and complexity theories and PM&E can help us to conceptualize, understand, and evaluate complex development interventions in a realistic way (Miskelly *et al.*, 2009; Ramalingam *et al.*, 2008). As Lacayo (2006: 23) points out, 'instead of describing how systems *should* behave, complexity science focuses the analysis on the interdependencies and interrelationships among its elements to describe how systems *actually* behave' (author's italics). From this perspective, the focus is on the actual process of development and change and the networks of relationships and complex contextual factors that influence people's behaviour, actions, emotions and decision-making (Patton, 2011: 117–118).

Our UN consultations found that there are often unrealistic demands, targets and timeframes for the impact assessment process and donors often want to see results in an unreasonably short timeframe. We therefore identified a need to take a more realistic, long-term view of the impacts of C4D and the evaluation process and benefits of PM&E. Evaluations should be proportionate to the scale of the initiative and its timeframe in order to achieve outcomes that are realistic. For many C4D initiatives this requires longitudinal studies in order to build effective relationships with stakeholders and to assess outcomes over a much more realistic period of time. However, funding for such studies is often difficult to obtain.

The realistic approach in the framework

As the above discussion implies, to be most effective and sustainable, the evaluation of C4D needs to be based on a long-term perspective on the process of evaluation and social change. This is particularly important when a participatory approach is used. Balit (2010b: 10) highlights the importance of advocating with donors 'to foresee sufficient time and resources for research and monitoring and evaluation efforts, especially when dealing with participatory approaches for social change'. The process would involve reaching agreement with donors and stakeholders on a realistic timeframe that is needed to produce evidence of outcomes. This timeframe may need to be adjusted, given changes to local, national and global contexts and other factors.

In this approach, the evaluation of C4D is fully integrated into organizations. Evaluation is not seen solely as the responsibility of the M&E section or team, but involves all relevant staff, particularly programme development, outreach, and management staff. This includes nurturing longer-term evaluation and learning processes that are an integral part of wider organizational development and change processes. Findings are then used to inform the improvement of initiatives, and strengthen evaluation capacities. We provide examples of this process from AC4SC in Chapter 5, as well as an example of 'creative capacity development' (Pearson, 2011) in a Cambodian NGO.

Evaluation is seen as an important part of the whole programme cycle from the conception, design and planning stages. This means that evaluation becomes a responsive and integral part of the iterative process of developing, implementing, improving and adjusting C4D initiatives. This involves using an approach that is not rushed, and allowing dialogue to begin the process. In consultation with a range of participants, the process would also include developing flexible and realistic plans and timeframes for the whole evaluation process, using an organic approach that is *responsive* to unfolding developments.

In this approach, evaluation methodologies, methods and tools are as simple, practical, responsive and rigorous as possible. This implies the use of participatory research and evaluation approaches, such as ethnographic action research (EAR) and the MSC technique, that are grounded in local realities, as part of a mixed methods approach. Our research suggests that a pragmatic, mixed methods approach which draws on contrasting but complementary methodologies and methods can provide a fuller and more realistic picture of change, and increases the strength and rigour of evaluation findings (Lennie, 2006b).

Evaluation planning and the selection of approaches, methodologies, methods and indicators also involves openness, freedom, flexibility and realism. This means that if some approaches, methodologies and methods prove unsuitable, others are readily available for use in the evaluation. They should be the most appropriate for different issues and purposes, culturally appropriate for the people involved, and used in culturally sensitive ways. Constraints of the initiative and the organizational context and resources also need to be taken into account. We include various examples in this book of the use of creative, flexible and culturally appropriate evaluation approaches, methodologies and methods. They include digital storytelling, EAR, MSC, and the use of drawings and photography in participatory research and evaluation.

A key aim of the framework is to increase the utilization of evaluation results, which should focus on intended, unintended, unexpected, negative and positive change. Indicators are seen as just one component of an evaluation strategy, rather than the most important component. After all, indicators are unable to capture complex realities and relationships. They can be effective ways of measuring change but cannot capture the reasons behind such change or what this means to people's lives. As far as possible, locally derived indicators should be developed using dialogue and participatory methods, as well as externally derived indicators (Parks et al., 2005). Alternatives to indicators, such as MSC stories, and 'verifying assumptions' (Guijt, 2000) can be more useful in some C4D contexts. These alternatives may provide better ways to monitor significant and sometimes unanticipated or negative impacts associated with long-term development goals. We discuss this further in Chapter 6.

Component 7: Learning-based

Guiding principles

- As far as possible, evaluations are based on action learning and participatory action research principles and processes.
- The evaluation process aims to foster the development of learning organizations by improving organizational and M&E systems and evaluation capacities, and contributing to the development of effective policies, strategies and initiatives that address complex development goals.
- The evaluation aims to facilitate continuous learning, mutual understanding, creative ideas, and responsiveness to new ideas and different attitudes, values and knowledge.
- The evaluation is open to negative findings and weaknesses, and learns from 'failures'.

Developing a learning culture

There is a growing trend towards considering evaluation as an integral component of development initiatives and a means of fostering continuous learning, evaluative thinking and a culture of evaluation. It is also seen as an important means of strengthening evaluation capacity and improving organizational systems and performance (Gosling and Edwards, 2003; Horton et al., 2003; Lennie et al., 2012; Morariu et al., 2009; Patton, 2008, 2011; Preskill and Boyle, 2008). Critical reflection, problem solving and action learning skills are increasingly considered important to the effective, ongoing development and evaluation of development initiatives (Hearn et al., 2009; Lennie et al., 2012). This is due to the need for people and organizations to engage in ongoing learning and to adapt to rapidly changing conditions. It is now recognized that the process of participating in an evaluation can often result in positive changes to an organization, including to its capacity, processes and culture (Diaz-Puente, Yague and Afonso, 2008; Horton et al., 2003; Patton, 2008).

These wider effects of evaluation are significant, given the identified need for long-term evaluation capacity development at all levels of development organizations. As we discuss further in Chapter 5, this form of ECD focuses on organizations as a whole and the development of learning organizations in order to facilitate greater organizational sustainability and more successful outcomes of initiatives. This type of capacity development, which encourages continuous learning, adaptation and the ability to address problems and challenges, is seen as important to the sustainability and success of development initiatives (Jones, 2011; Lennie et al., 2004, 2012). In addition, it can help to improve the utilization of evaluation results, increase the relevance and value of evaluation, and enable better interpretation of findings (Imam, LaGoy and Williams, 2006; Midgley, 2006; Patton, 2008).

The learning-based approach in the framework

The approach to development and evaluation taken in the framework is based on action learning, PAR and PM&E principles and processes that aim to foster ongoing learning, effective communication, cooperation, collaboration and trust between those involved. The evaluation of C4D is seen as a continuous, active learning process that focuses on policy, programme and organizational improvement, process outcomes and capacity development at all levels, from grassroots to management.

The framework's complexity and systems approach leads to a focus on higher-level learning. It aims to facilitate and encourage mutual understanding, empowerment, creative ideas and thinking, and responsiveness of people to ideas, attitudes, values and knowledge that are 'different from their own' (Imam et al., 2006: 213). A further aim is to make stakeholders more aware of their beliefs and values and to expose their assumptions about the process of social change and 'what is valid knowledge' (Imam et al., 2006: 9). As Hummelbrunner (2006: 162) suggests, improving joint understanding across a range of stakeholders through such an approach is 'an important pre-requisite for sustainable learning effects'.

The process we advocate includes regular critical reflection and review to learn from experience and M&E findings. Unlike linear causality approaches which 'give rise to the desire to blame' (Midgley, 2006: 17), this approach encourages the open reporting of mistakes. It is open to negative findings and weaknesses, and learns from 'failures', as well as 'success stories'. This means that the evaluation seeks to ensure a high level of independence, integrity and honesty.

In this approach, evaluations assess the contributions that C4D makes to the wider impacts and outcomes of development initiatives. Drawing on contemporary learning-oriented approaches to meta-evaluation, such as those described in Hanssen, Lawrenz and Dunet (2008) and Uusikyla and Virtanen (2000), evaluators would gather lessons from across evaluations of C4D and contribute to a wider body of knowledge about how C4D is undertaken and how it works to help (or potentially hinder) social change.

As well as assessing the quality, credibility and value of evaluation practice and the utilization of evaluation results, such meta-evaluations of C4D projects would focus on important contextual issues that can have significant impacts on the outcomes of participatory evaluation projects. They include hierarchical social and organizational cultures, language and communication barriers, power–knowledge relations, and the time and resources available. In addition, they would look at wider issues such as the sustainability of evaluation systems and approaches (Lennie et al., 2012).

Comparison with other frameworks and approaches

In order to highlight the value and originality of the framework, we have compared it with four related frameworks or approaches to research and evaluation that have been used in the area of international development or C4D. Table 2.1 summarizes the similarities and differences between our framework and the following related evaluation frameworks or approaches:

1 developmental evaluation (Patton, 2011);
2 the PM&E approach to measuring CFSC initiatives outlined in Parks et al. (2005);
3 AC4SC methodology and principles (Lennie et al., 2011);
4 the conceptual and theoretical framework and methodological principles in *Action Research and New Media* (Hearn et al., 2009).

We outline the first three approaches/methodologies further in Chapter 6.

Table 2.1 Similarities and differences between the framework for evaluating C4D and related research and evaluation frameworks and approaches

	Framework for evaluating C4D	Developmental evaluation	AC4SC methodology and principles	Action Research and New Media framework and principles	PM&E for CFSC
Specific focus on sustainable social change/development	✓	✓	partly	partly	✓ (has a focus on HIV/AIDS)
Specific focus on C4D	✓	×	✓	partly – has a broader focus on new media	✓
Specific focus on evaluation	✓	✓	✓	partly – more focused on AR	✓
Includes effective principles for evaluation	✓	✓	✓ (but a limited number)	✓ (but focused more on AR)	✓
Takes a participatory approach	✓	✓ (but takes the middle ground between top-down and bottom-up)	✓	✓	✓
Draws on complexity and systems thinking	✓	✓	to some extent (not in-depth)	✓	×
Takes a critical approach	✓	to some extent – lacks an explicit focus on power, gender, etc.	✓	✓	to some extent
Takes a realistic approach	✓	✓	✓	✓	✓
Takes a learning-based approach	✓	✓	✓	✓	✓
Takes a mixed methods approach	✓	✓	✓	✓	not explicitly – focus is mainly on participatory methods
Specific focus on evaluation capacity development	✓	implied but a less specific focus	✓	to some extent – not an explicit focus	✓

Framework for evaluating C4D

Developmental evaluation

Developmental evaluation draws on systems and complexity theory, organizational development, learning theories, ethnography, action research and other methods and techniques. It was designed for use by initiatives with 'multiple stakeholders, high levels of innovation, fast paced decision-making, and areas of uncertainty [that] require more flexible approaches' (Dozois, Langlois and Blanchet-Cohen, 2010: 14). This approach supports collaborative exploration and innovation before a model for an initiative has been developed, as well as the ongoing development and adaptation of programmes or innovations in emergent and complex situations. This is an ongoing process of learning by doing that involves:

> continuous development, adaptation, and experimentation, keenly sensitive to unintended results and side effects. The evaluator's primary function... is to infuse team discussions with evaluative questions, thinking, and data, and to facilitate systematic data-based reflection and decision making in the developmental process.
>
> (Patton, 2011: 1–2)

The PM&E approach to measuring CFSC initiatives

The Parks *et al.* (2005: 1) report aims 'to support communication strategies based on CFSC principles when applied to critical social issues such as HIV/AIDS prevention and care'. In their PM&E approach to measuring CFSC initiatives, evaluation is undertaken in partnership and dialogue with community participants/audiences, project partners and staff, donors and other stakeholders. This process aims to continuously and actively engage people in all aspects and stages of the evaluation through two-way communication, dialogue, feedback and mutual learning. It includes an action component to continuously develop and improve C4D and M&E processes. PM&E tools and techniques have evolved as 'useful tools for involving local people in developing strategies for learning about their communities and for planning and evaluation' (Parks *et al.*, 2005: 11). The process is 'closely woven into the whole project cycle... It provides information that can be fed back into the project immediately to improve subsequent performance' (Vernooy, Qiu and Jianchu, 2003: 29). In this approach, the process is 'at least as important as the recommendations and results contained in PM&E reports or feedback meetings' (Parks *et al.*, 2005: 7). Another distinguishing feature of PM&E is its fundamental values of '*trust, ownership and empowerment*' (Parks *et al.*, 2005: 11, authors' italics).

The AC4SC methodology and principles

The AC4SC methodology was developed through the AC4SC project, influenced by the principles of PM&E, CFSC, and EAR (Tacchi *et al.*, 2007). The AC4SC methodology aims to help C4D organizations effectively demonstrate social change impacts, and continuously adapt and improve their initiatives and their approach to ensure their work remains relevant, useful, appropriate and sustainable. It encourages C4D organizations to become reflective, learning organizations with a strong evaluation culture that engages in ongoing evaluation capacity building. Its basic principles are participation of primary stakeholders in all aspects of the M&E process and careful planning of M&E work. This includes the use of participatory and mixed methods research and evaluation tools and techniques, and triangulation of data to increase rigour. Its basic processes are listening to audiences, learning from this knowledge, systematically processing it and feeding it back into the organization and its practices in an ongoing cycle.

The framework in 'Action Research and New Media'

This theoretical and conceptual framework includes a number of specific methodological principles for undertaking action research with new media projects, including 'adopting methodological pluralism' and 'taking an open enquiry approach' (Hearn *et al.*, 2009: 39). This framework includes:

- a *critical perspective* that questions assumptions about both action research and new media;
- consideration of the *communicative ecology* of project locations; this entails taking the wider social and cultural context and existing local communication networks into account;
- a *holistic perspective* that recognises *the connectedness of everything*;
- recognition that any explanation of a phenomenon, such as the introduction of new technologies, involves *multiple causes and effects*; our approach respects this multi-causality and seeks to *build redundancy* into the systems, interventions and inquiry processes we set up;
- respect for *diversity and differences* and *seeking inclusion* – this is seen as one of the key challenges of action research; this entails paying attention to relevant issues such as *gender and other equity and social justice issues*;
- recognising the *power–knowledge differences* inherent in action research projects;
- a *co-evolutionary perspective* on the interaction between technology and society that assumes a reciprocal relationship between the social and the technical spheres.

(Hearn *et al.*, 2009: 30–32, authors' emphasis)

Similarities and differences to the framework

All of these frameworks and approaches have a number of similarities to the framework we present in this chapter in that they can be broadly characterized as based on participatory, learning-oriented, realistic, mixed methods approaches to research and evaluation. Differences between our framework and developmental evaluation are that the framework has a specific focus on C4D, takes a strongly critical approach that includes addressing gender, power and control issues, and has a particular focus on ECD. It is also less specifically focused on the development of social innovations. Our framework naturally has a number of similarities to the AC4SC methodology and principles but is much wider in focus and is based on complexity and systems theory and key trends and issues in international development and evaluation to a greater degree.

Our framework is also similar to many elements of the conceptual framework and principles in Hearn *et al.* (2009) but has a specific focus on sustainable social change, the evaluation of C4D, and ECD. It is also in line with the PM&E approach outlined in Parks *et al.* (2005). However, our framework has a wider focus (i.e. beyond HIV/AIDS and CFSC), takes a more critical approach (including critiques of the concepts 'participation' and 'empowerment'), and is based on complexity and systems theory. In addition, our framework is more explicitly focused on the importance of a holistic approach to ECD as a means of developing learning organizations and an evaluation culture within C4D organizations.

In summary, our framework draws on the most useful and relevant elements of a number of other contemporary frameworks, methodologies and approaches to the evaluation of C4D and international development initiatives, none of which include all of the key elements of this framework that are set out in Table 2.1. It is based on new and emerging trends, concepts, ideas and practices in this field and key themes and issues that have not yet been brought together in one book. Furthermore, the framework is based on significant, rigorous research in C4D and related areas, which we have been involved in conducting over the past 15 years in Australia and South and South East Asia. We believe this combination of features makes this framework particularly original, appropriate and effective in contributing to the aim of sustainable social change through C4D.

Conclusion

In this chapter we presented a flexible, overarching framework for evaluating C4D and other complex development initiatives, as well as principles for each of its seven components: participatory, holistic, complex, critical, emergent, realistic and learning-based. This framework draws on a number of contemporary frameworks, methodologies and approaches to the evaluation of C4D and international development initiatives, and the outcomes of consultations and rigorous research in C4D and related areas, which we were involved in conducting.

Our research suggests that this framework, and its guiding principles, can be applied effectively in researching and evaluating social change in C4D and in other development initiatives. We argued that this framework is more appropriate and effective, in the long-term, than dominant upward accountability-based evaluation frameworks for providing an adequate depth of understanding, and contributing to the process of sustainable social change through C4D. It demonstrates the rigour and importance of participatory evaluation approaches to the process of social change, and the value of complexity and systems theory to development and evaluation. In this more realistic approach, evaluations focus on understanding the complexity of the local context, including gender and power issues and local social norms, and the challenges, contradictions and paradoxes that often characterize the process of social change. We discuss the various concepts and ideas behind this framework and new thinking and trends in this area in more detail in Chapters 3 and 4.

Inagaki (2007: 45) suggests that 'development communication research needs to address the gaps among different methodological paradigms in order to advance more holistic understanding of communication processes in international development settings'. He argues that: 'The existing division between methodological paradigms must be replaced by constructive dialogues between different approaches so that the empirical evidence generated in the scholarship will achieve greater legitimacy and substance' (Inagaki, 2007: 46). In addition, Ramalingam et al. (2008: 62) suggest that the concept of self-organization 'shows that actors at all levels of a given system need to be empowered to find solutions to problems, challenging the existing dichotomies of "top-down" versus "bottom-up"'. An important feature of this framework is that it suggests that a both/and approach that avoids polarizing positions is often more helpful and appropriate than an either/or approach, as Chambers (2008), Papa et al. (2006), Ramalingam et al. (2008) and Wadsworth (2010) note.

Our framework therefore aims to overcome the limitations of false divisions, such as those between qualitative and quantitative methodologies or between indigenous and expert knowledge, that have hindered progress in this area. It does this through advocating a more open, flexible, creative and pluralistic approach to evaluation which involves continuously and actively engaging people in all stages of an evaluation through open dialogue, feedback and mutual learning. The aim here is to increase the utilization of evaluation results, which focus on intended, unintended, expected, unexpected, negative and positive change.

The need for this type of approach has been clearly demonstrated through complexity and systems approaches to development and evaluation, as we discuss in more detail in Chapter 3. As one of the Expert Panel in our UN consultations noted:

The research and evaluation methodologies and processes selected should fit with the underlying aims and values of the development initiative or programme involved. Often this is not the case and people are frustrated by attempts to fit 'square pegs into round holes', without having the freedom, support and know-how to choose approaches and methods that best fit the particular context and the research or evaluation questions being considered.

Byrne and Vincent (2011) point out that in dynamic social contexts, one particular evaluation framework for evaluating social change is not feasible. The principle of methodological pluralism also suggests that there is a need to integrate and draw on all of the evaluation approaches that have been demonstrated as effective and appropriate for C4D. In this approach, evaluation becomes a vital part of an ongoing, emergent process of planning, developing, adapting and improving C4D and building learning organizations with a strong research and evaluation culture. The framework's holistic capacity development process is seen as important to the sustainability and success of development initiatives and identifying better ways of addressing development problems and challenges.

We acknowledge that there are many challenges and issues in successfully implementing this framework, given the current context which tends to work against the approach we have advocated. We discuss these challenges and issues in Chapters 4 and 7 and suggest strategies for overcoming them. As we have argued in this chapter, it is important to take a long-term view of this process and its benefits.

3 New thinking and trends

Puntos de Encuentro ('Meeting Places' or 'Common Ground') is a feminist NGO in Nicaragua, which emerged from the Sandinista revolution that transformed the social, cultural and political fabric of the nation in 1979. The creators of Puntos found that the Sandinistas' egalitarian agenda was contradicted by oppressive practices in interpersonal relationships (Rodriguez, 2005). The goal of Puntos is to transform the everyday, often invisible, inequalities that affect women and youth, to bring about changes in personal attitudes, values and behaviours by creating an autonomous and pluralistic space where women and youth can develop their own agendas (Rodriguez, 2005).

Puntos promotes youth and women's rights by challenging social norms and unequal power relationships. Its award-winning strategy combines cutting-edge media, leadership training, community education, and alliance building to create a more just society (Singhal and Lacayo, 2007). Its popular television soap opera, *Sexto Sentido* (Sixth Sense) is part of a multimedia strategy that includes a daily radio talk show, a feminist magazine, billboards, and other activities. Rather than aiming to change individual behaviour, Puntos seeks to influence the social context in which individuals act and in which discussion about different aspects of daily life, both public and private, occurs (Lacayo, 2007). Its goal is to promote alternative interpretations of reality as part of the national conversation. Rodriguez (2005: 383) has proposed the term 'activist E-E' (entertainment-education) to refer to organizations such as Puntos.

Evaluations and impact assessments are a significant challenge for Puntos. Contradictions arise when social change is approached as a non-linear, messy, *complex* problem (Lacayo, 2007). The social change approaches adopted by donors tend to imply predictable, linear processes to be measured by standard indicators of success. Donors are under pressure to invest in projects that have replicable formulas with measurable outcomes (Rodriguez, 2005). Thus, despite wide recognition of its innovative, risk-taking approach, Puntos struggled to maintain funding, and to legitimate and theoretically frame its outreach strategy. Given the Puntos approach, traditional logframes, planning models, impact indicators and standard research methods that are based on traditional behaviour change communication (BCC) theories were rejected. This is because they fail to take account of the complex, multi-level, inter-related processes through which social change actually occurs (Lacayo, 2007). Working in direct response to local needs, but with somewhat limited expertise in communication theory and in-house research and evaluation, organizations such as Puntos face challenges in articulating their work in the language used by donors or the scientific community (Singhal and Lacayo, 2007).

Puntos created complex characters in their TV dramas, to encourage people to engage with and discuss the issues amongst themselves. This presented a challenge for evaluation, since they did not use simple clear-cut messages, or characters that are simply good or bad (Lacayo, 2006). Complex changes are hard to measure, especially since the process is long-term (Panos, 2008).

Virginia Lacayo (former Executive Producer and Director of *Sexto Sentido*) came to appreciate the value of complexity theory for understanding the 'messy process of social change' (Lacayo, 2006: 10) after she was introduced to these ideas by Arvind Singhal during her Masters studies at Ohio University. She explains:

> I started to understand better the role of relationships, connection and interactions. I began to understand the concepts of emerging orders, self-organizing, nonlinearity. I began to see the importance of pattern recognition, the difference between the whole and the mere sum of the parts, the value of outliers and diversity, and how small inputs can lead to big changes and so on. Even though these concepts were familiar to me, the wholeness of them gave me eyes to see *Puntos* and its work from a different perspective.
> (Lacayo, 2007: 2)

Lacayo realized that Puntos was intrinsically working with a complexity-based approach to social change. In contrast, its operative planning followed a 'complicated' linear, step-by-step approach as required by its donors and the expectations of its collaborating partners (Lacayo, 2007: 4). Lacayo (2006: 40) asks: 'How do we reconcile the messy, unpredictable, and complex notion of social change with a short-term, cause–effect based schemata that can frame results as quantifiable and measurable?' She calls for a supportive social, political and economic environment that encourages alternative thinking, includes the construction of complexity-based indicators, and uses evaluation methodologies that 'explain rather than justify, understand rather than measure' processes of social change (Lacayo, 2006: 45).

In this chapter we review the latest critical thinking and new conceptual, theoretical and methodological advances in the field. They have significant implications for how we conceptualize the evaluation of C4D initiatives and sustainable processes of social change. We provide detailed explanations of systems thinking and complexity theory, review some critical approaches to understanding and evaluating social change, and consider the implications and value of these ideas and approaches for the evaluation of C4D. Having emphasized the importance and value of participatory approaches in previous chapters, here we highlight characteristics of complexity theory and systems thinking that have fundamental similarities to participatory and action-oriented approaches. We emphasize the need to take a critical, long-term view of the value of participatory approaches and further highlight the need to pay attention to power–knowledge relations, gender and social norms in the process of researching and evaluating C4D.

Challenges in moving beyond dominant approaches to evaluating C4D

It is difficult to capture or think about the ways in which social change occurs without accounting for the complexity of the process. Like Puntos, Equal Access, our collaborating partner in the AC4SC project, faced pressures to demonstrate their success using unrealistic indicators and unsuitable methods. They needed to do this in order to compete for funding. Equal Access recognized that the dominant linear, step-by-step approach to behaviour change and evaluation failed to capture the potentially positive impacts of having community members and collaborating partners participate directly in their C4D interventions and evaluation processes. Yet these conventional evaluation frameworks are the approaches expected by donors.

46 *New thinking and trends*

The AC4SC project was established because Equal Access was frustrated by the requirements of donors that they 'prove' impact, which was generally measured according to predetermined indicators and traditional monitoring and evaluation (M&E) approaches such as baseline studies and formative and summative evaluation. Equal Access was interested in using research and evaluation in ways that would improve their organizational systems, practices and programmes. Their discussions with donors supported their view that the ways in which they were required to prove impact could be made more relevant to them, and could be of interest to donors, even if donor requirements remained the same. This led to the development of AC4SC, which often had to compete within Equal Access Nepal (EAN) against more powerful demands for traditional evaluations, just as happened with Puntos.

Among other factors, the evaluation of the first TV series by Puntos was affected by a lack of funding. This meant that no baseline study was undertaken and the programme could only be evaluated after it had been aired. It also meant that funds were only available for a two-page questionnaire (Panos, 2008). This had an innovative quiz-like format, appropriate for 13 year olds, which enabled 'sensitive' issues to be explored that are not usually addressed in survey research (Singhal and Lacayo, 2007: 49). In addition, the process involved a team of young people randomly stopping other young people in the streets. However, the methodology and findings were criticized by evaluation and social communications experts, for lacking 'scientific rigour' (Singhal and Lacayo, 2007: 49). Development professionals began debates about what the outcomes actually meant and the 'deeper issues for assessment' (Singhal and Lacayo, 2007: 49). Despite the criticisms, the stories and understandings that emerged from this first evaluation were extremely useful to Puntos in the design of the second phase of its communication strategy.

In response to the pressure to conform, Puntos worked with those who had criticized the first evaluation to undertake a larger scale three-year mixed methods evaluation, combining qualitative and quantitative approaches (Panos, 2008). They were keen to assess impacts both at the individual and social level, and to capture some of the complexity of social change. The evaluation results showed evidence of promoting debate around taboo subjects and of the kind of interpersonal communication that the initiative encouraged. Despite this, many people were disappointed in the results because they did not clearly demonstrate large-scale direct impact (Panos, 2008). Although the donors were quite happy with the results of the evaluation, Puntos wanted to understand more about the process of change and it was mainly Puntos themselves who still had questions, along with the public health community and academics 'who were interested to see that the evaluation met their standards' (Panos, 2008).

These challenges and issues indicate a growing need to give more consideration to the 'bigger picture' issues (Byrne, 2009b) in development research and evaluation and to new thinking and trends in this field that are likely to significantly strengthen the impacts of C4D and the evaluation of C4D initiatives, making them more sustainable. This is the key aim of the framework presented in this book.

The value of systems and complexity approaches to evaluation

Lacayo's research with Puntos demonstrates the strengths of systems and complexity perspectives for researching and evaluating C4D initiatives and the importance of starting from the system/reality itself, and understanding such things as:

- The difference between *simple, complicated and complex* aspects of C4D initiatives and interventions. Lacayo (2006: 22) points out that: 'Complex problems [such as

social change] are hard to predict and control, they are not linear, adaptable and heavily influenced by context. Yet, we deal with them as if they were complicated problems'.
- The largely *unpredictable (and uncontrollable) nature of social change* processes, which means that C4D practitioners and evaluators need to be flexible enough to change the strategy or approach that is used. It also means that it is important to understand the local context and to be aware of uncertainties and feedback associated with an intervention. The flexibility of Puntos as an organization was vital to its success.
- The *importance of relationships*: It is through its relationships that Puntos was able to improve its practices and outcomes, and to constantly adapt its strategies in an environment that is dynamic and unpredictable.
- The *importance of self-organization* to social change. An example of this is the distribution network for *La Boletina,* the national feminist magazine of Puntos (see Box 3.4 later in this chapter). This magazine 'works on the principle of solidarity and is sustained by mutually supportive relationships among women's groups' (Lacayo, 2007: 3).

A systems perspective

A holistic perspective based on systems thinking is increasingly seen as important to better understand and address complex or 'wicked' problems such as poverty, gender inequality, HIV/AIDS and domestic violence (Burns, 2007; Byrne, 2009a, b; Eyben, 2011; Hearn *et al.*, 2009; Rihani, 2002). There is a growing appreciation of the value of systems thinking to researching and evaluating initiatives that seek to address such problems (Hearn *et al.*, 2009; Imam, LaGoy and Williams, 2006; Patton, 2008, 2011; Wadsworth, 2010). This type of approach is also becoming more widely used as a strategy to facilitate sustainable community and economic development (Hearn *et al.*, 2009) and has significant implications for the ways in which we conceptualize, plan and implement C4D initiatives and their evaluations.

Systems concepts have been applied in a wide range of fields, including health, management and organizational studies, natural resource management and international and community development. Examples of the application of systems thinking include the 'whole systems' approaches to involving the community in sustainable planning and development as advocated by Oleari (2000), the 'sustainable livelihood' approach to rural development in South Asia outlined by Rajbhandari (2006) and Rice and Foote's (2001) systems approach to communication campaigns for improving health conditions of young children in developing countries.

Overview of a systems framework

Systems thinking is a very broad field which includes complex adaptive systems, soft systems methodology and systems dynamics (Imam *et al.*, 2006; Patton, 2011; Rihani, 2002). In contrast to linear, reductionist approaches to research and evaluation based on Newtonian thinking which tries to isolate variables and focuses more on 'things' (Chambers, 2008: 172), a systemic perspective aims to understand the relationships between the different elements in a system and what happens when they interact and combine (Burns, 2007: 29). Patton (2008) summarizes the fundamental premises of a systems framework as follows:

- The whole is greater than the sum of the parts.
- Parts are interdependent such that a change in one part has implications for all parts and their inter-relationships.

- Systems are made up of subsystems and function within larger systems.
- The focus is on inter-connected relationships among parts, and between parts and the whole.
- System boundaries are necessary and inevitably arbitrary.

(Patton, 2008: 367)

Systems thinking assumes that social dynamics are not always visible through scrutinizing individual interactions because any explanation of a phenomenon cannot point to a single cause and effect (Hearn et al., 2009). Positive and negative outcomes have more to do with complex patterning of inter-relationships (Burns, 2007). Eyben (2011) provides further insights into the differences between dominant reductionist approaches to international aid based on a 'substantialist' mode of thinking, and a systems/relational perspective. The substantialist mode considers pre-formed entities rather than relationships between entities, and 'categorizes things, including people and abstract concepts', ascribing essential properties to them (Eyben, 2011: 28–29).

The logical framework (or 'logframe') approach, a key planning tool in international development, is based on a substantialist perspective in which the impacts of complex interventions are reduced to simple, linear, cause–effect processes. In contrast, the relational perspective is based on a systems/complexity framework. From this perspective, individuals are embedded in relational contexts. While some development interventions, such as building bridges or schools, might lend themselves to a substantialist approach and a focus on bounded problems, where there is broad agreement on the nature of the problem and some mutual understanding of the solution, many do not. Here, complexities of history, power and culture must be brought into the frame (Eyben, 2011). Robert Chambers (2008), a long-term champion of participatory and alternative approaches to development research and evaluation, clearly demonstrates the differences between these two perspectives, as shown in Table 3.1.

While setting out these dichotomies is useful for emphasizing differences in ways of thinking, we need to be alert to polarization, distortion and caricature (Chambers, 2008: 172). This emphasizes the need to avoid an either/or perspective, and the value of adopting a both/and view. This is what the communicative ecologies approach that is part of ethnographic action research (EAR) (Tacchi et al., 2007) is trying to do.

The holistic, systems perspective is a key component of our framework for evaluating C4D and has significant implications for the way in which development initiatives are conceptualized and evaluated. It raises important questions about the appropriateness of dominant top-down, centralized approaches to the evaluation of social change that do not adequately take the complex inter-relationships and interactions between people into account, or the actual process of social change. They value measurements and outputs such as reports over outcomes such as increased capacities and improved relationships and trust between people.

The communicative ecology approach (see Box 3.1) is based on a holistic, systems perspective. EAR and communicative ecology were developed to avoid a reductionist approach that insists on 'indicators' and measures. Rather, they were designed to align with the people and processes column of Table 3.1.

In both Finding a Voice and AC4SC, the concept of communicative ecology was used to emphasize the importance of understanding any communication activity within a wider understanding of the diversity, even within single locations, of people's lives, their access and use of communication technologies, and the availability of communication channels to them. Simple exercises in exploring how information and communication flows – who discusses what with whom, how news and local knowledge circulates – led to an appreciation

Table 3.1 The contrasting paradigms of things and people

Generative basis	Things and procedures	People and processes
Orientation, planning and access	Top-down Centralized Controlling	Bottom-up Decentralized Empowering
Key words	Planning Design Blueprint	Participation Emergence Process
Methods	Standardized Reductionist Universal Fixed	Performative Inclusive Contextual Flexible
Embodying	Rules	Principles
Expressing	Conventions	Values
Implicit assumptions about causality and change	Linear Controllable Predictable	Non-linear Uncontrollable Unpredictable
Valuing and relying for rigour and quality on	Regulation Precision Measurement Statistical analysis	Responsibility Fitness Judgement Triangulation
Roles and behaviours	Supervising Enforcing	Facilitating Enabling
Typical procedures and processes	Questionnaires Randomized control trials Logframes	Participatory methodologies
Mode and ethos	Hierarchical	Democratic

Source: Chambers (2008: 173)

of the persistent dominance of face-to-face and very local flows of information and modes of communication.

EAR researchers in Finding a Voice mapped their own communicative ecologies and compared them in our first EAR training workshop. This highlighted how, while each researcher was part of a digital world with access to mobile phones and the internet, their different geographic, social and economic positioning led to quite different communicative ecologies, and to discussions of why and how these differences exist. Availability of infrastructure and affordability of services came out strongly, with implications for national regulation and legislation of communications. Later, undertaking communicative ecology work in their various communities, another complicating and complex layer of differences emerged in often striking ways. Among other factors, this exposed the impacts of ethnicity, gender and caste on difference and diversity, illustrating blockages and flows, inclusions and exclusions, in the larger system.

Sensitivity to contextual factors, organizational norms and societal values is critical in systems-oriented evaluations (Patton, 2011: 120). The critical reflection, problem solving and action learning skills that are required in systems approaches are increasingly seen as important to the effective, ongoing evaluation of development initiatives. However, at the

> **Box 3.1** *Overview of the concept 'communicative ecology'*
>
> In order to understand the potential and real impacts of individual media technologies in any given situation, you need to place this experience within a broader understanding of the whole structure of communication and information in people's everyday lives.
>
> Each instance of communication or information takes place within an already existing 'communicative ecology', and each place has its own unique communicative ecology that we need to understand.
>
> It is important to look at *everything* that could count as a medium of communication. That is, not just press, broadcasting or telecoms but also roads, buses and trains, visits to neighbours, gossip, and public and private places where people meet to communicate. It is also important to look at how people *combine* different media.
>
> Communicative ecologies focus our attention on the communication-related aspects of the contexts in which the people we are studying operate. It places media technologies in the context of all the ways of communicating that are significant locally, including face-to-face interaction.
>
> It is recognized that any 'new' connections and networks (social and technical) that develop as a result of the introduction of individual technologies will be far more effective if they are somehow interconnected with existing, locally appropriate systems and structures.
>
> Through this approach we can ask how new media technologies articulate with more traditional ones: how do different media serve different purposes, and how do they combine in people's everyday lives?
>
> (Hearn *et al.*, 2009: 31)

same time, organizations that rely on funding from major donors have to contend with managerial and operational systems and processes based on the substantialist mode of thinking, as the experiences of Puntos and Equal Access illustrate.

Some of the characteristics of complexity theory and systems thinking have fundamental similarities to participatory monitoring and evaluation (PM&E):

1. a shift in focus to inter-relationships and processes rather than snapshots, seriously challenging dominant linear explanations of systemic phenomena;
2. an understanding of development as complex, emergent and transformative;
3. a shift to the bigger picture and inter-connections, with much focus on boundaries and the values they reflect.

(Byrne, 2008: 9, based on Williams and Imam, 2006)

Participatory forms of research and evaluation that take the wider context and inter-relationships into account such as empowerment evaluation, utilization-focused evaluation, EAR, feminist participatory communication research and developmental evaluation have been influenced by, or can be seen as fitting well with, systems perspectives (Hearn *et al.*, 2009; Imam *et al.*, 2006; Patton, 2011; Rattine-Flaherty and Singhal, 2009). There are close synergies between action research and systems thinking, with both relying on a holistic and inter-connected view of the world (Burns, 2007; Greenwood and Levin, 2007; Hearn *et al.*, 2009; Imam *et al.*, 2006; Wadsworth, 2010).

The usefulness of a systems perspective

A systems perspective provides a valuable lens through which to understand the complex process of development and social change, helping us conceptualize development interventions such as C4D realistically, to clarify messy solutions to complex social problems, and improve mutual understanding and relationships among a diversity of stakeholders (Imam *et al.*, 2006; Miskelly, Hoban and Vincent, 2009; Ramalingam *et al.*, 2008; Rihani, 2002). Systems thinking 'takes on and provides new insights into the enduring issues of human experience, interaction and efforts at development' that include complexities of power, control, actors differing motivations and rapid change (Patton, 2011: 122). Such a holistic approach is crucial because issues cannot be isolated from the wider systems of which they are a part (Burns, 2007). The communicative ecology assumes that the role of a radio intervention or a facility such as a computer centre, for example, cannot be understood without understanding the wider communicative ecology of which it is a part, and the diverse positioning and communicative opportunities and experiences of people in any locality.

For example, Sita Adhikari, a Finding a Voice EAR researcher working across two library and computer initiatives in rural Nepal, found that within the same village, women's ability to access media and information, and to take part in communication activities were radically different, depending on a range of factors. Sita used her detailed understanding of how women communicate to inform the design of library activities, directly responding to women's local situations. Communicative ecology mapping can demonstrate:

- differences between men and women, young and old, rich and poor, and so on;
- who are included in and excluded from which flows of information and communication channels; and
- how geography, distance and cost can influence communication.

Figure 3.1 illustrates the communicative ecology of Madanpokhara village in the Palpa district of Nepal. It shows the main communicative channels available in this village, including the local village FM radio station, or community station. Jiwan Sharma, the researcher from EAN who investigated the communicative ecology of Madanpokhara was of course interested in which radio stations could be received here, so that he could work out which EAN programmes, which are broadcast through a range of radio services, were able to be received. In addition, he found that the community library had closed, but a local youth group was planning to reopen it. He discovered that while some families here use email and the internet, only one household has a computer, others have to travel 10 kilometres to use this service in the market place of the nearest town, Tansen. There are many active youth groups, and these are considered by the researcher to be an important component in the communicative ecology of the village. He found that most households owned a mobile phone – not most individuals, but most households had access through a family member. There were very few landline telephones. A local newspaper was available daily, while national papers were brought into the village by NGOs and through the school.

While Figure 3.1 helps us to start to appreciate the availability of communicative channels and flows, looking at individual communicative ecologies helps us to understand how different people experience them.

Figure 3.2 depicts the communicative ecology of 20-year-old Asmita, who lives in Jhuwani village, in Chitwan, Nepal. Asmita is a college student. She visits the community library daily where she uses the computers to email and chat for around an hour. She also

LIBRARY

There was a community library in this place but it is now closed. The library on the school premises is not accessible to the general public except students of that school. But the youth clubs have planned to resume the community library. The Forest Consumers Club has also shown their interest in this regard.

TV

People are using televisions to watch news-related programs and some entertainment programs, and also

EMAIL/INTERNET

Though some of the households use computers, email/internet have not been used by all of them except one family for their private use. For other people, they have to walk approximately 10 kilometers to reach Tansen Bazaar to use this service.

Madanpokhara VDC, 7 Sangam Tole

YOUTH GROUP

Many youth groups are formed at Sangam Tole in Mandanpokhara village. Many such clubs ranging from Madam Club (deriving its name from the Tole itself) to children's clubs, women's clubs, farmers' clubs and Forest Consumers Club are run. These are initiated to conduct some community welfare programs. They have recently started a discussion after listening to the programs SSMK/NN.

POST OFFICE

People are found using this service to deliver letters to their relatives and to send feedback to the radio programs

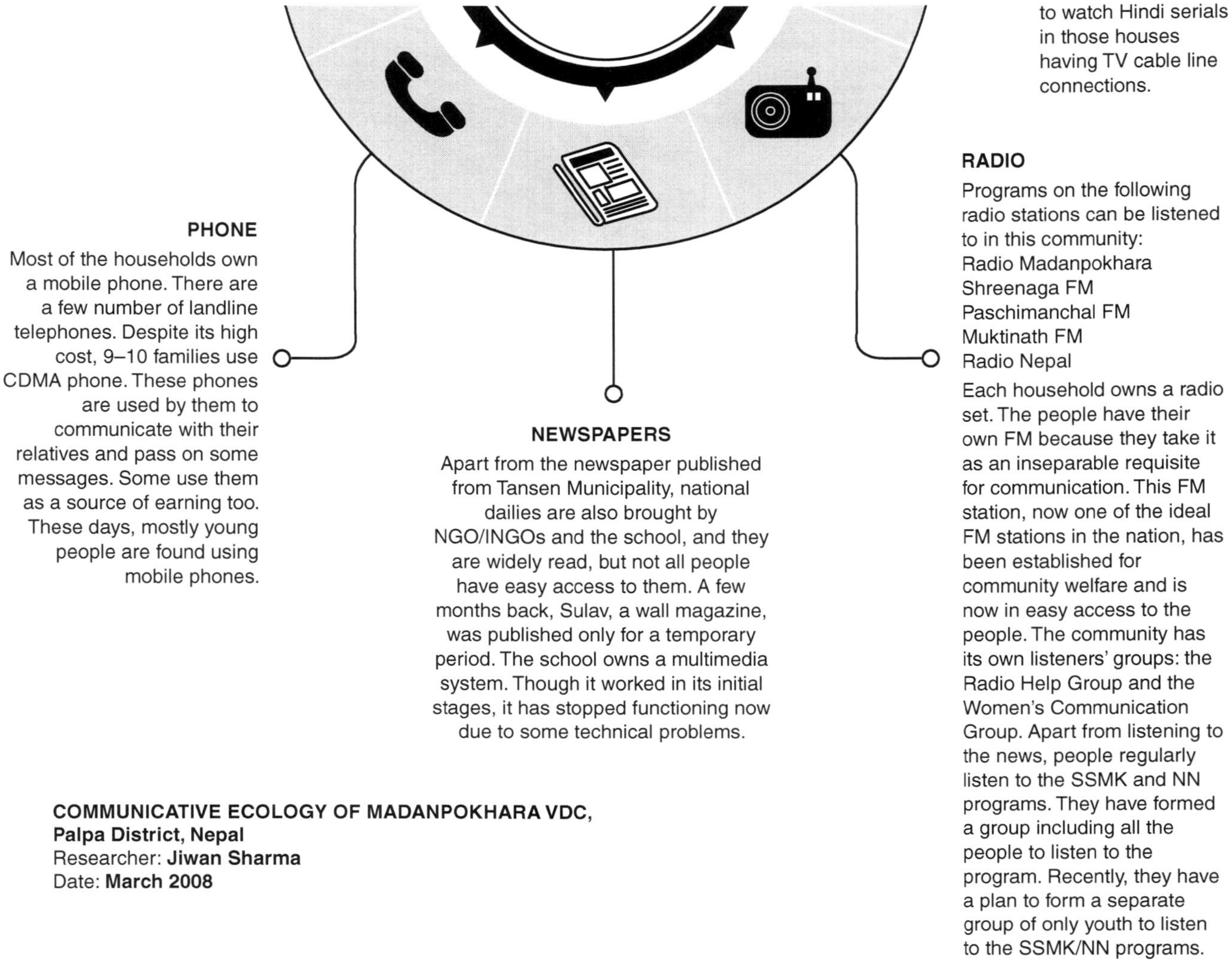

PHONE

Most of the households own a mobile phone. There are a few number of landline telephones. Despite its high cost, 9–10 families use CDMA phone. These phones are used by them to communicate with their relatives and pass on some messages. Some use them as a source of earning too. These days, mostly young people are found using mobile phones.

NEWSPAPERS

Apart from the newspaper published from Tansen Municipality, national dailies are also brought by NGO/INGOs and the school, and they are widely read, but not all people have easy access to them. A few months back, Sulav, a wall magazine, was published only for a temporary period. The school owns a multimedia system. Though it worked in its initial stages, it has stopped functioning now due to some technical problems.

RADIO

Programs on the following radio stations can be listened to in this community:
Radio Madanpokhara
Shreenaga FM
Paschimanchal FM
Muktinath FM
Radio Nepal

Each household owns a radio set. The people have their own FM because they take it as an inseparable requisite for communication. This FM station, now one of the ideal FM stations in the nation, has been established for community welfare and is now in easy access to the people. The community has its own listeners' groups: the Radio Help Group and the Women's Communication Group. Apart from listening to the news, people regularly listen to the SSMK and NN programs. They have formed a group including all the people to listen to the program. Recently, they have a plan to form a separate group of only youth to listen to the SSMK/NN programs.

to watch Hindi serials in those houses having TV cable line connections.

COMMUNICATIVE ECOLOGY OF MADANPOKHARA VDC,
Palpa District, Nepal
Researcher: **Jiwan Sharma**
Date: **March 2008**

Figure 3.1 Communicative ecology map of Madanpokhara village, Nepal

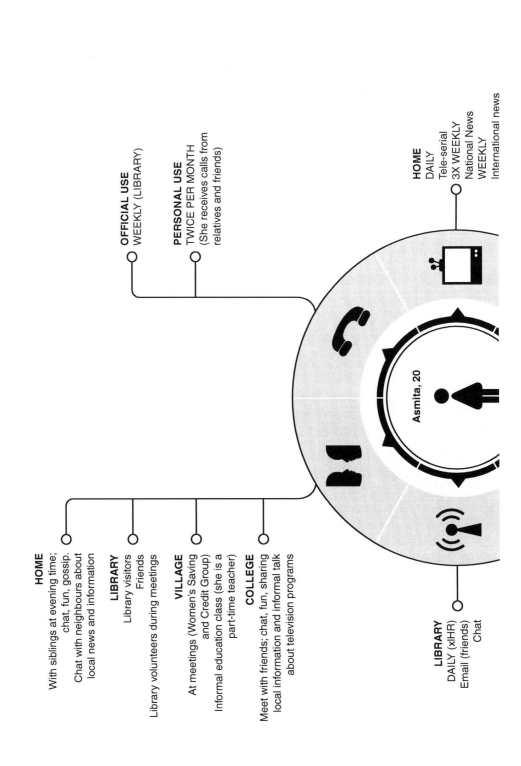

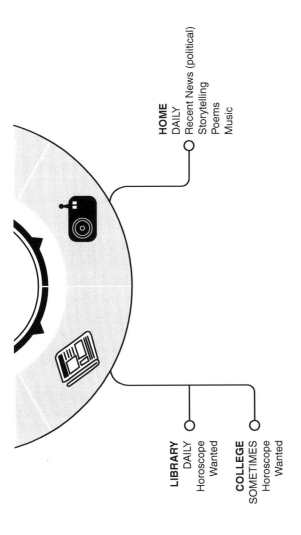

Figure 3.2 Communicative ecology map of Asmita from Jhuwani village, Nepal

reads the newspapers at the library, and she likes to look up her horoscope. She listens to the radio every day in the evenings, for the news, and to listen to stories, poems and music. She watches soaps on TV every day, the news less regularly. She volunteers at the library, and so uses the landline telephone occasionally for official business. She also uses a landline a couple of times a month to receive calls from relatives. Face-to-face communication takes place at home, at the library, in the village and at college with a range of people, for a range of purposes, including fun and gossip, news and information.

Not everyone in Jhuwani village will have the same communicative access and patterns of use. Diagrams illustrating the communicative ecologies of illiterate villagers, for example, would look quite different. Moreover, over time, these communicative ecologies will shift and change. Focusing on the whole helps us to further focus on the deep underlying process of social change (Byrne, 2009a). Yet it is important to note that there are no single isolated systems, only a complex of interwoven, interlocking and overlapping systems and networks of social relations, all implicated with dynamics of power, politics and culture (Burns, 2007).

The conceptual framework of the communicative ecology takes a holistic approach, but understands that different perspectives within the same social groupings can produce different understandings because of differential social status, levels of access and engagement, and power. This framework encourages a focus on, and respect for, the complex inter-relationships within the local social and cultural context in which people live and the way 'each media initiative, event, and relationships will change and shift the power relations at both an individual and community level' (Hearn et al., 2009: 33).

Complexity theory

Complexity theory is seen by many to offer a valuable alternative to understanding how development and social change occurs. It provides a sophisticated, realistic, effective and sustainable way of conceptualizing, implementing and evaluating development projects and initiatives (Chambers, 2008; Jones, 2011; Miskelly et al., 2009; Papa, Singhal and Papa, 2006; Ramalingam et al., 2008; Rihani, 2002; UKCDS, 2011).

Interest in complexity theory has grown rapidly in recent times. Indeed, Guijt et al. (2011: 13) suggest that it has become the latest 'buzzword' in the international development field. Development practitioners are increasingly questioning the dominance of top-down evaluation approaches based on simplistic, cause–effect models of development and change and associated managerial, results-based approaches which are increasingly imposed on development initiatives, often in inappropriate ways (see http://bigpushforward.net; Chambers, 2008; Jones, 2011; UKCDS, 2011).

Leach emphasizes the benefits and challenges of complexity science to international development:

> ...it seeks to comprehensively reflect the full range and diversity of a social system and its environment. It helps to recognize that there are multiple ways of understanding and representing a system; and that all analyses of a system involve framing... The fundamental implication of complexity and dynamics is that there are limits to what is known and what can be controlled and planned. This means dealing with incomplete knowledge in situations where uncertainty and surprise are inevitable, and tailoring actions and strategies where dynamics of change and their drivers are not always tractable to control.
>
> (Leach quoted in UKCDS, 2011: 8)

The paradigm of complexity presents a major challenge to dominant approaches to development planning and evaluation that are based on linear, highly predictable systems, a sense of order and control over long-term events, top-down management, and assumptions of replicability (Rihani, 2002).

Complexity theory or 'complexity science' is highly interdisciplinary and seeks answers to fundamental questions about living, adaptable, dynamic systems. It brings together insights from a wide range of disciplines such as biology, anthropology, economics, sociology and management (Lacayo, 2007). Systems are seen as complex when they 'have large numbers of internal elements that interact locally to produce stable, but evolving, global patterns' (Rihani, 2002: 6).

Complexity theory has been described as 'a loosely bound collection of ideas, principles and influences from diverse bodies of knowledge. It is a discovery of similar patterns, processes and relationships in a wide variety of phenomena' (Guijt *et al.*, 2011: 14). It considers that many human and non-human systems operate in ways that are non-linear, unpredictable, chaotic, disorderly and emergent. Lacayo (2006) points out that:

> Contrary to the cause–effect Newtonian paradigm, complexity provides us with the opportunity to look at problems with multiple perspectives, studying the micro and macro issues, and understanding how they are interdependent. So, instead of describing how systems *should* behave, complexity science focuses the analysis on the interdependencies and interrelationships among its elements to describe how systems *actually* behave.
> (Lacayo, 2006: 23)

This highlights the value of complexity theory to the evaluation of complex social change initiatives. It is not a single theory but the study of complex adaptive social systems, patterns of relationships, and how they change or remain the same. It debunks substantialist approaches to evaluation and, instead, privileges self-evolving and adaptive approaches (Papa *et al.*, 2006).

The emergence of complexity approaches

The recent application of complexity theory to development and social change can be linked to the global interest in a range of alternative holistic, critical, feminist and postmodern perspectives, and participative and creative ways of fostering development and social and organizational change (Stevenson and Lennie, 1995). It can also be connected to the alternative co-evolutionary perspective on technological change and society that 'offers ways around the bi-polar positions that bog us down' (Hearn *et al.*, 2009: 27).

This philosophical position can be seen as part of an alternative view of the world emerging through systems thinking, ecological awareness and feminism, and in the philosophy of human inquiry (Reason, 1988: 3). Complexity theory can be considered as a kind of bridge between 'the naturalism of rationalism and the anti-naturalism of postmodernism', and demands a broad and open-minded approach (Geyer, 2003: 15–16). It implies methodological pluralism, important for flexible and adaptive or responsive evaluation practice (Midgley, 2006: 26), and is essential in the evaluation of complex C4D interventions, as we discuss further in Chapter 4.

Key complexity concepts

The following key complexity theory concepts have been identified by Lacayo (2007), Ramalingam *et al.* (2008), Patton (2011) and Rihani (2002). They have significant implications for understanding and evaluating C4D and other development and social change processes.

- Complex systems are made up of inter-connected and interdependent elements. They are fluid and dynamic, and characterized by change and continuous interaction between elements. The whole is different to or greater than the sum of the separate parts of a system.
- Interacting agents within systems respond and adapt to the system, to each other and to their environment. From these interactions, they make sense together, change and evolve over time. A system changes when it chooses to be disturbed by the information it receives and it understands the world differently.
- Complex systems are made up of non-linear and unpredictable relationships and processes. As a result, when change happens, it is often disproportionate and unpredictable. Strategies therefore need to be flexible enough to adapt. Small differences in the initial state of a system can lead to major differences later on.
- The free flow of diverse information is essential for a system to evolve. This means that both diversity and participation are important. Feedback loops and processes affect how change happens; this process is unpredictable and non-linear.
- Under conditions of complexity, processes and outcomes are uncertain and unknowable in advance. This is due to turbulence in the environment and limits to our knowledge. The concept of emergence implies that a system must be given the freedom to govern itself as much as possible, and to learn from history and experience.
- The concepts 'chaos' and 'edge of chaos' suggest that, paradoxically, in complex adaptive systems, the more freedom there is in self-organization, the more order. In this process, order is emergent and self-organizing.

When complex systems are capable of evolution they are also known as complex adaptive systems (CAS). However, in order to evolve successfully, a CAS 'must change in response to shifting conditions, but it must survive long enough for the next cycle of adaptation to begin' (Rihani, 2002: 8). Complex adaptive systems such as communities and organizations share the following traits:

1 They have 'active internal elements that furnish sufficient local variety to enable the system to survive as it adapts to unforeseen circumstances' (Rihani, 2002: 80). This is similar to the idea of the need for 'requisite variety' in systems in order for a system to deal with variety and change in its external environment (Morgan and Ramirez, 1983: 4).
2 The systems' elements are 'lightly but not sparsely connected' (Rihani, 2002: 80).
3 The elements 'interact locally according to simple rules to provide the energy needed to maintain stable global patterns, as opposed to rigid order or chaos' (Rihani, 2002: 80–81). This can be related to the principle of 'minimum critical specification' which encourages system designers to 'specify no more than is absolutely necessary for a system to begin operation, so that a system can find its own design' (Morgan and Ramirez, 1983: 7). This is a key principle in action learning.
4 'Variations in prevailing conditions result in many minor changes and a few large mutations, but it is not possible to predict the outcome in advance' (Rihani, 2002: 81).

Rihani (2002) argues that development and its underlying political, social and economic processes behave as a CAS. This is illustrated in a case study from the LEARNERS project, shown in Box 3.2, which indicates the complex character of the Tara Shire's systems and inter-connections. This example highlights the importance of proactive community

Box 3.2 *The role of communication and participatory planning and evaluation in the development of Tara Shire*

Tara Shire is in rural Queensland, Australia. At the time of the LEARNERS project the Shire was experiencing significant communication problems, including poor telephone services, and had no local newspaper or radio station. Most roads were unsealed, and public transport services were minimal. Many people were living in impoverished circumstances with few services and facilities.

The Shire's extensive geographic area, small, scattered population and changing demographic profile had created a divided community. People were not working well together, many townships operated in isolation and there was little proactive leadership. Consequently, the area lagged behind in its development, including in the uptake of new communication and information technologies (C&IT).

A year before the project started, a new mayor and new shire councillors began providing positive leadership, instigated new community development initiatives, and actively began building a more cooperative and pro-active community. Community leaders, particularly women, began generating motivation through community workshops and successful events such as a multicultural festival. A committee of community representatives was formed to address key problems in the Shire. A number of C&IT initiatives were implemented, including a community website, public internet access, and computer and internet training and support services. Given this positive new energy and outlook, the Council expressed interest in using the LEARNERS process to help the community work more effectively together to reach its goals and to engage in more effective planning and evaluation. They hoped that the holistic and participatory LEARNERS process could help improve communication across the Shire and training and access to new C&IT.

The Council's community and economic development officer was enthusiastic about the project and used her good relationships with community organisations to generate interest and support. Following a community leaders meeting, women and men working in diverse areas, including education, youth development and agriculture, participated in the project's first community workshop. A local project steering committee nominated the community website and IT training and access across the Shire as projects that would be evaluated using the LEARNERS process.

Local participants collaboratively planned the evaluation of these projects, analysed results of a survey of residents, and planned key actions. While some participants such as school principals understood it immediately, others found the LEARNERS process difficult to understand. Although there were some unintended and disempowering outcomes, the project helped to improve the networking, communication, and information sharing between community groups through email and the Shire website. More people began using C&IT, and new ways of using C&IT to overcome communication problems were identified. While the loss of the Council's IT Officer had a major impact on some project activities, participants expected to continue using and learning from the knowledge and capacities they had developed from engaging in the project.

(Lennie *et al.*, 2004)

leadership, participatory planning and evaluation with diverse groups of community members, and the effective use of new communication technologies in the process of community development, adaptation and change.

Distinguishing between simple, complicated and complex problems

A recent conceptual advance in the area of systems and complexity-based evaluation that is highly relevant and useful in planning, designing and evaluating C4D is the typology 'simple, complicated and complex' (Patton, 2011: 85). This is a useful means of understanding differences between the diverse types of problems that need to be addressed, and matching an intervention or evaluation approach to the nature of the situation. Making these distinctions can strengthen programme theory (Funnell and Rogers, 2010). However, Patton (2011: 84) makes the important point that: 'What may be appropriately understood as simple at one level can be understood as complex at another level and from a different perspective'. These distinctions are relative, rather than absolute, and matters of 'perception and judgment' (Patton, 2011: 95).

Patton (2011) explains that the simple, complicated and complex typology is based on the degree of uncertainty/degree of conflict matrix developed by Zimmerman. This matrix maps the situation along two dimensions: (1) the degree of certainty about what should be done to solve a problem, and (2) the degree of agreement among stakeholders about the desirability of an intervention or their degree of conflict about this. For instance, the relationship between vaccination and preventing disease is highly predictable, while there is considerable uncertainty how to best design and implement anti-poverty initiatives. There is widespread agreement that preventing polio is a good thing and that children should be vaccinated to eradicate polio, but there is 'substantial political conflict about almost all aspects of global warming' (Patton, 2011: 86).

The use of this typology in assessing the impacts of C4D requires considering the multiple paths to achieving impacts and the role of the intervention in achieving them, in relation to the context – that is, whether the context was favourable or otherwise (Rogers, 2009). This has significant implications for how interventions operate, the ways in which we understand them, and how we can use these understandings (Rogers, 2009: 25).

Simple situations

A simple situation is characterized by high degrees of certainty and agreement. They are situations 'in which knowledge and experience tell you what to do and there is widespread agreement about what to do' (Patton, 2011: 86). Cause and effect are well understood in simple interventions (Rogers, 2011). Patton (2011) explains that in a simple situation,

> ...it is both possible and appropriate to intervene from the top down, as in the worldwide campaign to eradicate polio. A high degree of predictability and agreement permits detailed planning, controlled execution, and precise measurements of the degree to which predetermined targets are achieved. A best practice model can be generated and subjected to a summative test.
>
> (Patton, 2011: 86)

Simple aspects of interventions 'can be tightly specified and are standardized – for example, a specific product, technique or process' (Rogers, 2009: 25). In simple situations, 'best practice' can be seen as being like recipes in that they provide clear, tested directions that are likely to work again in the future (Patton, 2011: 87). An example of a simple element of an agricultural extension development programme provided by Patton (2011) is extension agent technical training. This has a high degree of certainty since 'there is scientifically valid knowledge about specific production techniques and training approaches' and 'high agreement that extension agents should be competent and knowledgeable about production and education techniques' (Patton, 2011: 104–105).

Complicated situations

These are situations that are less predictable, with less certainty of producing desired outcomes. They occur when the degree of uncertainty and agreement are such that 'what needs to be done is challenging and difficult, but knowable. That is, how all the parts will fit together is initially unknown but can be figured out, and is therefore knowable' (Patton, 2011: 87). Complicated aspects of interventions also have multiple parts, are part of a 'larger multi-component intervention, or work differently as part of a larger causal package' (Rogers, 2009: 25). In complicated interventions, success requires a high level of expertise in many specialized fields, along with coordination of this knowledge (Rogers, 2011).

However, in the context of C4D we need to distinguish technical complications from social complications. For example, sending a rocket to the moon is *technically complicated* but 'if all of the many technical calculations are done well, coordinated, and executed precisely, it is likely that the desired outcome...will be accomplished' (Patton, 2011: 87, author's italics). In contrast, *socially complicated situations* 'involve situations with many different stakeholders offering different perspectives, articulating competing values, and posing conflicting solutions' (Patton, 2011: 87–88). A human rights campaign is an example of a socially complicated intervention.

Socially complicated situations, such as those that C4D deals with, are particularly challenging when those involved 'have fundamentally different perspectives and values, or operate from different paradigms about how the world works and what's important to do' (Patton, 2011: 89). An example of this is the interaction and collaboration between diverse stakeholders in an agricultural extension development programme who have diverse views about 'the nature and degree of collaboration that is possible and desirable', a 'history of operating in silos' and 'much resistance' to change (Patton, 2011: 104–105).

Complex situations

Complex situations are characterized by high uncertainty and high social conflict and refer to interventions in which the outcomes are unpredictable and unknowable in advance (Patton, 2011: 90). This concept also refers to 'dynamic and emergent aspects of interventions, which are adaptive and responsive to emerging needs and opportunities' (Rogers, 2009: 25). This means that patterns are only evident in retrospect. In complex situations, 'cause and effect is unknown and unknowable until after the effect has emerged, at which point some retrospective tracing and patterning may be possible' (Patton, 2011: 92). Rogers (2011) also suggests that in complex interventions, expertise can help but is not sufficient, and that relationships are the key to successful interventions.

Anti-poverty programmes and peace-building C4D initiatives are examples of complex development interventions. Research and evaluations have clearly shown that what works in one culture does not necessarily work in another, as the vastly different outcomes of HIV/AIDS prevention programmes in different countries demonstrate (Singhal and Rogers, 2003). Complex aspects of the agricultural extension development programme example include 'Networking and emergent initiatives among leaders and actors brought under the auspices of the programme: spin-offs and ripple effects [and] self-organized subgroups exchanging information and taking action together' (Patton, 2011: 104–105).

The value of complexity theory to development and social change initiatives

As the diverse examples we have drawn on indicate, systems and complexity theories have been used to understand complex interactions between people and organizations in a wide diversity of systems including agricultural extension, preventative health organizations and international development (Lacayo, 2006; Ramalingam *et al.*, 2008; Rihani, 2002). The example of Puntos de Encuentro, which highlighted Lacayo's use of complexity theory to understand the 'messy process of social change', is one of the few instances we have identified of the application of complexity theory to researching and evaluating a C4D initiative. It demonstrates the need for greater acceptance among donors of the type of holistic, relational framework of evaluation that we are advocating in this book. Our work on the UN consultations suggests that at least some major international agencies are open to such a significant shift in attitude and approach.

The application of complexity theory to international development provides a realistic view of our world that can help us develop appropriate strategies for change. It improves our understanding of complex problems and gives us concepts and ideas that bring together old and new insights to develop new theories of change and greater appreciation of underlying processes (Jones, 2011: viii). Its value is in providing a way of thinking about human relations that can help us form realistic and holistic understandings which in turn can lead to effective action – it makes us think about the way we are thinking (Burns, 2007; Ramalingam *et al.*, 2008).

We can identify the following benefits. Applying complexity theory and systems approaches to the evaluation of C4D:

- can help us to conceptualize complex development interventions and their evaluation in a *more realistic way*, and to focus on the *actual* process of development and change and the networks of relationships and contextual factors that influence people's behaviour, actions, emotions and decision making (Patton, 2011: 117–118);
- can help to *clarify messy solutions to complex problems* 'in a clear manner that facilitates comprehension, understanding and proactive action' (Forrest, 2006 in Imam *et al.*, 2006: 7);
- highlights the *need for an intervention or evaluation approach to be matched to the nature of the situation*: this requires identifying the simple, complicated and complex elements of interventions and considering the implications of these elements of an initiative for the evaluation questions and design;
- *verifies the importance of participatory approaches* and a focus on social issues: this provides a rationale for focusing on the local context and the need for context-relevant indicators (Miskelly *et al.*, 2009: 10);
- suggests that international development strategies should *encourage experimentation and innovation* in research methodologies and policies, consider multiple perspectives, support the development of innovations, and use 'methodological flexibility, eclecticism, and adaptability [and] ... creative and critical thinking' (Patton, 2011: 26);
- can be a powerful means of *generating new insights and responsiveness to other ideas and attitudes*, which can help us to see the world in different ways, make stakeholders more aware of their beliefs and values, and expose their assumptions about 'what is valid knowledge' (Imam *et al.*, 2006: 9);
- encourages *continuous learning and utilization of evaluation results* and leads to a focus on higher-level learning and participatory, bottom-up processes (Jones, 2011; UKCDS, 2011) and 'the trajectories of societies over long time frames' (Miskelly

et al., 2009: 5): this encourages the *open reporting of mistakes*, and suggests that capacity development which encourages continuous learning, adaptation and the ability to better address problems and challenges is important to the success of development initiatives (Jones, 2011); this can also help to increase the relevance and value of evaluation, and enable better interpretation of findings (Imam *et al.*, 2006; Midgley, 2006; Patton, 2008);

- *increases our focus on boundaries* that are put around the system that we are trying to understand or evaluate (Imam *et al.*, 2006): Patton (2011: 34) notes that dealing with boundaries is 'a common and constant issue ... for all kinds of social innovations that start out with a narrow focus and find that changing what they've targeted morphs into changing other systems that affect what they've targeted';
- *encourages us to seek and include multiple perspectives* on an issue: this forces us to ask 'Whose reality is being considered? Who is defining what the situation is? Where do the limits of that situation lie?' (Imam *et al.*, 2006: 9); systems concepts help us to answer these questions;
- helps us to focus on the *inclusion or exclusion of different voices* in the development and evaluation process and to consider the potentially negative effects of interventions on certain groups of people.

Critical approaches to understanding and evaluating social change

Social change is a contested and complex concept, with many different definitions and perspectives. We have argued that systems concepts and complexity theory provide valuable new lenses, through which to understand the process of social change, that have significant implications for how we conceptualize and undertake the evaluation of complex social change initiatives. We have also suggested that we need to take a more critical approach to understanding development and social change, which questions the fundamental theories and premises on which development and C4D are based.

Deconstructions and critiques of traditional development theories have highlighted the paradoxes and contradictions that are inherent in current development practice and the persistence of the 'hegemony of behaviour change theories and steps to change models' (Lacayo, 2006: 21). They have also highlighted the need to consider issues of gender, power and control, oppression and empowerment, participation and dialogue, given that these are all important to the process of social and community change (Burns, 2007; Lacayo, 2006; Lennie, 2005b, 2006a; Papa *et al.*, 2006).

Critique of dominant social change communication theories

As the experience of Puntos highlights, there is a contradiction between the way in which development organizations conceptualize social change and how most organizations frame their strategies. Lacayo suggests that traditional methods are steeped in BCC theories, which rarely question how social change occurs. These models come from health organizations that tend to take a linear cause–effect approach to health and population problems (Lacayo, 2006: 20). Large-scale BCC interventions such as HIV/AIDS prevention programmes have primarily focused on knowledge provision and the promotion of health services and have seldom resulted in massive changes in HIV infection, 'unless they have been accompanied by strengthened local level mobilization' (Parker, 2004: 3).

Singhal and Rogers (2003: 211–212) note that BCC strategies for HIV prevention that focus on individual-level changes mistakenly assume that people can necessarily control their context, or work outside of social, cultural, economic and political factors. They assume that people operate on an 'even playing field' without reference to gendered power inequalities, and that people make decisions rationally, of their own free will. In addition, Singhal and Rogers (2003: 213) point out that due to their focus on biomedical concerns, HIV/AIDS prevention programmes fail to take into account how sexuality is socially and culturally constructed. Thus, they 'are culturally rudderless and flying blind'. The earlier BCC and social change models can also be critiqued for downplaying the contradictions, paradoxes, struggles and power relations inherent in social change processes, which as Papa *et al.* (2006) demonstrate, represent the basic drivers of social change.

Another problem with traditional approaches is that social change is conceived *for* rather than *by* communities. Complexity theory suggests that sustainable development requires active and meaningful participation of those affected, since development (as well as empowerment) cannot be effectively achieved by outside experts (Lennie, Hatcher and Morgan, 2003; Papa *et al.*, 2006; Rihani, 2002).

Beyond a focus on individual change

Puntos believes that social change results from individual and collective change. BCC has started to incorporate wider social change as its intention (McCall, 2011). Singhal and Rogers (2003: 214) note that many communication scholars agree that we need to move away from older individual-level theories of preventative health behaviour towards 'more multi-level, cultural, and contextual interventions'. Box 3.3 provides an overview of the UNAIDS communication framework which illustrates this new approach.

A new report for UNAIDS by Byrne and Vincent (2011) draws on systems thinking and complexity theory and a range of new evaluation methodologies such as outcome mapping to develop a new framework for evaluating social change communication for HIV/AIDS. They argue that approaches that better address the complexity of social change are urgently needed.

The importance of self-organization

In complex adaptive systems the more freedom there is for self-organization, the more order. The process of self-organization is important because it suggests that social change interventions and their evaluations will be more effective if they are based on relatively simple, flexible frameworks, principles and processes which allow the process to 'find its own design' (Morgan and Ramirez, 1983: 7). In this way, self-organizing capacities are developed with only as much structure as needed (Morgan and Ramirez, 1983: 7). For example, birds flying in formation follow simple rules that result in beautiful order and energy conservation, thus enabling them to fly long distances.

The concept of self-organization demonstrates the benefits of people finding their own solutions, and of distributed rather than centralized control. This results in outcomes emerging from self-organization rather than external inputs and control. 'Order emerges from the interactions among the individuals... as the environment changes, the system changes to adapt itself to the new conditions' (Lacayo, 2006: 24). This phenomenon is illustrated well in Box 3.4, which highlights the challenges that complexity-based approaches face in demonstrating the impact of such self-organized activities.

Chambers (2008: 176) argues that participatory methodologies can be seen through the lens of 'self-organising systems on the edge of chaos' since 'they generate self-organising

> **Box 3.3** *The UNAIDS communication framework*
>
> Influenced by social scientists, the UNAIDS communication framework (UNAIDS/Penn State, 1999) represents a move away from focusing on individuals as the main target of preventative interventions. Instead, the UNAIDS model provides a multi-level cultural, and contextual guide to designing HIV/AIDS communication interventions. The UNAIDS framework urges program managers and communication specialists to ascertain the role of communication in influencing the social and cultural environment for HIV/AIDS prevention, care and support, including the communication action needed to create access to health services. Communication is ascribed an important role in grassroots advocacy, mobilizing political action, and in creating the context for more gender-sensitive and culturally appropriate HIV/AIDS intervention programs.
>
> The UNAIDS framework calls for refocusing communication interventions on five key contextual domains: (a) government policy; (b) socioeconomic status; (c) culture; (d) gender relations; and (e) spirituality... The five contextual domains of the UNAIDS communication framework signify that the forest is more important than the trees... By focusing on the five contextual domains, communication experts can create a flexible, culture-based, holistic strategy in which the interventions are located in the social patterns of relationships among individuals, as may be determined by their age, seniority, gender, socioeconomic class, and cultural and spiritual beliefs.
>
> (Singhal and Rogers, 2003: 216–217)

systems with emergent properties, the detail of which cannot be foreseen'. Patton (2011: 150) suggests that one of the implications of the concept of emergence for developmental evaluation is that it needs to be alert to the formation of self-organizing sub-groups who might have different experiences and who might contribute to different outcomes. Being alert to this requires mapping networks, relationships and sub-groups and tracking information and communication flows and their relationships to emergent issues. This process can be captured through mapping communicative ecologies. This enables researchers to track the flow of information and to identify communication channels, as well as blockages and challenges, and how these change over time.

A focus on power relations, gender and social norms

Many contemporary and participatory approaches to evaluation openly acknowledge and take into account the gender and power relations that are an inherent part of social interactions and organizations, as well as the political nature of research and evaluation practices (Burns, 2007; Gosling and Edwards, 2003; Hearn *et al.*, 2009; Lennie, 2005b; Martin, 1996; Tacchi, Lennie and Wilmore, 2010). Burns (2007: 39) makes the important point that 'change emerges from the spaces in between, in the interrelationships and in the discussion, and it is mediated by complex power relations'.

While the participation of women is a fundamental principle for development, it is often difficult to carry through because of gender inequalities in many societies (Gosling and Edwards, 2003: 33). Clearly, the evaluation of social change initiatives requires a high level of awareness of gender issues. Cornwall (2000: 1) believes that rethinking the concept

Box 3.4 *Self-organization in the distribution of La Boletina*

The distribution network of *La Boletina*, the national feminist magazine of Puntos de Encuentro, is a good example of self-organization. *La Boletina*'s circulation gradually increased from 500 copies in 1991 to 26,000 copies in 2007, making it the largest circulation magazine in Nicaragua. The reasons for this increase include that *La Boletina* is free of charge, and is distributed by hundreds of volunteers who travel long distances. They hand-carry the magazine to towns and villages all over the country, distributing the magazine to local groups. These groups may then distribute the magazine further in their communities.

This distribution network is a unique phenomenon of self-organization. It works on the principle of solidarity and is sustained by mutually supportive relationships among women's groups. Puntos did not plan this distribution strategy, and has no direct control over it. The system emerged on its own.

The absence of centralized control provides freedom for emergence, which in turn has, ironically, jeopardized its own existence. The lack of control by Puntos over the delivery and use of *La Boletina* makes it hard to demonstrate its impact, using the indicators established by donors. Donors have pressured Puntos to increase its level of control over the magazine, for instance by charging a cover price. It has been difficult for Puntos to justify to its donors how charging might actually 'kill' the most important distinctiveness of *La Boletina*: its volunteer, self-organized distribution network and the collective ownership of the magazine by women's groups. Complexity science, on the other hand, values this lack of centralized control as an essential quality of healthy systems. The most illuminating paradox of all is that in complex adaptive systems, order is emergent and self-organizing.

(Lacayo, 2006: 24–25)

of gender might more directly address 'issues of power and powerlessness that lie at the heart of both Gender and Development'. Wilkins (2005: 262) makes similar arguments and notes the paradox that 'despite more and better programmes and research efforts, women's conditions are not improving'.

We need to recognize power differentials between those involved in evaluations and ask whose version of reality is privileged (Mertens and Chilisa, 2009). This would include asking questions such as: Who do I need to involve? How do I involve them? Whose values do I represent? These issues clearly have significant implications for the way in which we conduct the evaluation of C4D and the extent to which the processes used are inclusive and empowering.

Instead of assuming, idealistically, that all participants in a C4D evaluation are the same and equal, it is more useful to openly acknowledge the differences between those involved, particularly those related to gender, power and knowledge (Hearn *et al.*, 2009; Lennie, 2006a, 2009). We also need to take the type of critical approach advocated by our framework, which recognizes that participation in community-based evaluations can have disempowering, as well as empowering, effects on participants. This point is illustrated well in the example in Box 3.5 from a critical evaluation of the LEARNERS project.

Lennie's (2005a) critical analysis of the LEARNERS project highlights the need for an open, realistic, critical and emergent approach to evaluating claims for the empowering

Box 3.5 *Empowering and disempowering impacts of community-based C&IT evaluation projects*

June Lennie's research indicates that both empowering and disempowering impacts and outcomes can be anticipated in PAR projects that involve people from diverse backgrounds with different levels of status, power and knowledge, unequal access to communication and information technology (C&IT), and different goals and agendas. While empowerment and disempowerment were seen as separate and distinct for the purpose of this analysis, Lennie's research demonstrated the inter-relationship between these two processes.

Her critical, feminist theory-influenced evaluation of the LEARNERS project employed a framework comprising four interrelated forms of power: social, technological, political and psychological. Corresponding forms of disempowerment were also analysed, and gender and other differences between participants taken into account. Outcomes of this research provided critical insights into the complexity of building community capacities in evaluating rural C&IT projects. They indicate that participatory evaluations and PAR are political processes that can have contradictory and unintended impacts and effects.

The ideal LEARNERS framework and the reality of implementing the process were somewhat different. The framework provided a flexible and inclusive whole of community process for participation in the evaluation of rural C&IT projects. It built on existing community strengths and capacities, resources and goals, generated mutual trust and understanding between the diverse groups involved, and produced various forms of empowerment. The project's PAR and participatory evaluation processes were effective in identifying strategies to increase the sustainability of C&IT projects in the two communities. Outcomes of the project were particularly positive in Tara Shire, a disadvantaged community with significant need for improved communication systems and better community networking and cohesion.

However, due to inequalities in power and knowledge, the different values and agendas of the community participants and the academic researchers, pre-existing relationships and networks within the communities, and other complex issues, the project also had a number of unintended and disempowering impacts. They included a perceived lack of ownership and control of some project activities, and some confusion and misunderstandings about the project and the LEARNERS process. Other barriers to community participation, empowerment and capacity building were identified, such as a lack of time and/or capacity to participate, loss of key champions in the communities, and lack of access to or limited experience with C&IT.

As a result of the ongoing evaluation of the project, a much more simple, practical and easy to understand process for the evaluation of community-based IT projects was developed in the form of an online resource kit called EvaluateIT (see Hearn *et al.*, 2009 and www.evaluateit.org).

(Lennie, 2005a)

impacts of participatory evaluation and C4D projects and the development of evaluation capacity building processes. This requires rigorous analysis of both the intended and unintended impacts of such projects. Gender and power issues need to be taken into account, particularly issues related to leadership, communication and control. The framework of empowerment and disempowerment that was used to analyse the impacts of the LEARNERS project provided a useful means of undertaking such an analysis.

Power–knowledge, culture and social norms

As Burns (2007: 36) notes, Foucault's conceptualization of power has underpinned a considerable amount of contemporary systems thinking. This framework of power has also been drawn on by many social science and feminist researchers (Lennie, 2009). In this conceptualization, power is seen as 'constantly in motion, multi-directional and systemic in patterning' (Burns, 2007: 36). From this perspective, power is something that exists in action, in a network of inter-connected relations. It is enacted in everyday social practices, rather than wielded by powerful groups such as corporations or large institutions. Foucault's work shows 'how objects of knowledge are not natural, but are ordered or constructed by discourses which determine what is "seeable and sayable"' (Jennings and Graham, 1996: 171).

This power–knowledge nexus highlights the power relations that are enacted in all interactions, whether or not those involved have an emancipatory intent (Lennie, 2009). In this framework, power is intimately connected to knowledge, including the technical knowledge of specialists and the tacit knowledge of community members or workers (Hearn *et al.*, 2009). It is embodied in the social hegemonies that constitute social norms – 'the attitudes and behaviours that people regard as normal for their peer group' (Burns, 2007: 35). Burns (2007) highlights the urgent need to pay attention to social norms in order to win community support, without which development interventions will not be sustainable. This has major implications for C4D initiatives that aim to challenge harmful practices such as child marriage and female genital mutilation.

A holistic, complexity-based perspective emphasizes the importance of local context and cultures. As Servaes and Malikhao (2005) and Waisbord (2005) note, a cultural perspective has become central to debates about development and communication. However, Waisbord (2005) identifies key tensions in C4D related to cultural diversity and change. He asks: 'Who [has] the right to determine which cultural practices are desirable and need to be preserved?' (Waisbord, 2005: 89). This is especially salient in the field of development where culture is often mistakenly considered to be associated with tradition and the past, while the imperative of development is progress and the future (Appadurai, 2004).

Conclusion

This chapter has reviewed a number of new conceptual, theoretical and methodological advances and trends that have significant implications for how we approach the evaluation of complex social change initiatives, how we understand the process of social change, and how sustainable C4D and social change might be achieved. Systems and complexity theories are seen as particularly important to better understanding, evaluating and addressing the 'messiness' that C4D and much of international development practice involves working with. Among their many benefits, these approaches can help us to conceptualize development interventions in a more realistic way, to clarify messy solutions to complex social problems, and improve mutual understanding and relationships among diverse stakeholders.

We have highlighted some of the many paradoxes and contradictions that C4D and other development organizations have to contend with. They include using complexity-based and relational frameworks in their work but having to use operational systems and processes based on the substantialist mode of thinking, exemplified by linear logic models and pre-defined indicators. We argue that this raises important questions about the appropriateness of dominant substantialist and upward accountability-based approaches to the evaluation of C4D. Irela Solorzano, an M&E team member with Puntos, noted the following issues with current impact evaluation designs and indicators:

> We need to gain external legitimization of our work, but we also want to have an opinion and to participate in the design [of the evaluation] to guarantee that it will be coherent with our vision and mission. The problem is we still haven't developed enough theoretical and methodological frameworks that allow us to offer effective alternatives. We need new indicators, but they can only be validated during implementation, and that affects the evaluation because it cannot be planned in detail at the beginning of the project.
>
> (Lacayo, 2006: 44–45)

As this quote suggests, there is a need to take more effective and critical approaches to understanding and evaluating development and social change. Such an approach would question the fundamental theories and premises on which development and C4D are based and the dominant evaluation approaches and methodologies that are typically promoted. This requires acknowledging paradoxes and contradictions inherent in development practice, and moving beyond simplified dichotomies such as dominant and participatory approaches to development and evaluation. It also requires integrating complementary evaluation approaches to develop a new paradigm that moves beyond the dichotomies that have bogged down progress in this field. Broader dimensions of the change process, beyond the 'social' also need to be considered. Self-organization is seen as important because it suggests that social change interventions and their evaluations will be more effective if they are based on relatively simple, flexible frameworks, principles and processes that allow order and effective designs to emerge.

A critical approach also involves paying more attention to gender, power–knowledge relations, culture and social norms in the evaluation of social change. This approach takes gender discrimination and inequalities in the development context into account and recognizes that participation in community-based evaluations can have disempowering, as well as empowering, effects. We have suggested that the evaluation of C4D needs to consider the gender and power–knowledge relations that are inherent in all social interactions and that organizations need to attend to local social norms in order to make interventions more successful and sustainable.

Having firmly located our framework as one that incorporates holism and systems and complexity thinking, in the next chapter we consider some of the challenges and issues that emerge in the evaluation of C4D and suggest strategies for overcoming them, drawing on our UN consultations and new conceptualizations of evaluation and shifts in evaluation practice.

4 Challenges, issues and strategies

In the introductory chapter of his book *Developmental Evaluation: Applying Complexity Concepts to Enhance Innovation and Use*, Michael Quinn Patton (2011: 2–4) tells the story of how he was contracted to conduct an evaluation of a community leadership programme in Minnesota. It was a five-year contract consisting of two and a half years of formative evaluation for programme improvement, followed by two and a half years of summative evaluation to assess effectiveness. This is a standard approach to evaluation.

The evaluation started well. Feedback from participants in the formative evaluation stage led to many major programme improvements, including recruitment processes, new curriculum elements and support initiatives. The programme team welcomed the feedback enthusiastically, since formative evaluation focuses on improving programmes and models. They were very happy with the improvements being made as a result.

When the two and a half years of formative evaluation ended, and the summative evaluation was due to begin, Patton met with the programme team to explain this new phase. He explained that for the summative phase no further programme improvements and changes should be made, because it was now time to make an overall judgment about the value of the model, whether it worked, and if the programme should be continued and expanded. To do this, the model they had developed needed to remain the same over a period of time in order to adequately measure and attribute outcomes in a credible way.

Programme staff were disturbed by the idea of a fixed model that could not be improved, since a major learning over the formative phase had been about the benefit of continuously adapting and adjusting according to the particular needs of different groups. They had learned that communities are different, and broader economic, political and technological environments keep changing – they are not static. They could see how fixing the model would stop them from making the kinds of improvements they knew would be required – for example, to get more young people involved, and to engage with emerging immigrant communities. They saw what Patton was suggesting as a recipe for standing still and becoming less relevant, which they felt they could not afford to do. They insisted that they needed to continue to improve the programme, to never use a static model, to keep developing and changing.

In response, Patton developed the idea of developmental evaluation (DE), a learn-by-doing process. At this point the evaluators stopped acting like external consultants and became part of the programme design team, bringing evaluative thinking and data into the conceptualization and development of the programme. This relationship continued for six years. Each year the programme changed and the evaluation evolved, new questions emerged, different evaluation designs were developed, and the programme continued to adapt. While formal summative evaluation never took place, and no final evaluation report was written, periodic summative decisions were made and supported by documented results.

Programme development was facilitated through DE. The ongoing development of the leadership programme was informed by an understanding of changing conditions, ongoing learning, and identification of the emergent needs of a range of participants (Patton, 2011).

Developmental evaluation, just like ethnographic action research (EAR), was developed in response to an identified need to move beyond more conventional approaches to research and evaluation, and develop approaches and methodologies that help initiatives and programmes to become more effective. Both DE and EAR are essentially developmental. They can be used to demonstrate effectiveness to external agencies, but their main purpose and audience is the development programme, initiative or activity, along with its participants and the communities they are trying to reach.

A key question for both DE and EAR is: How can an initiative improve its effectiveness while staying appropriate to shifting and complex conditions and environments? Both are participatory, they appreciate the complex nature of the environments in which development initiatives operate, and they consider whole systems and emergence. DE and EAR fit well within our framework in that they include all seven key components, to varying degrees. They are participatory in their approach; they are holistic, taking the whole system and the communication flows and relationships and barriers to change into account. They appreciate the complex nature of the contexts in which activities take place and need to be understood; and, particularly in EAR, they are critical, reflecting upon and critiquing difference and issues of power and control. These approaches are also emergent in that they appreciate that many changes are unknowable in advance, and they prefer an approach based on self-organization. They are both realistic and seek to support appropriate long-term processes of change and to capture intended and unintended outcomes; and they are learning-based in their action research approach, continuously adapting based on new understandings, ideas and knowledge. Yet such approaches face many challenges, as they do not conform easily to standard approaches.

Some of the challenges involved in using these kinds of new approaches and methodologies are faced in evaluation for development more broadly, while others pertain to their application in C4D in particular. In this chapter we explore the challenges and issues that we consider to be the most important in the evaluation of C4D. We begin this chapter by introducing some of the contextual, structural, institutional and organizational challenges and then explore some implementation issues, from planning and managing the evaluation of C4D, to assessing the impact of C4D. Our understanding of the main challenges and issues comes from our experiences researching in this field for a number of years, from our reviews of literature, and, most recently, our consultations for the UN Resource Pack. Our framework grew out of our growing appreciation of the shortcomings of mainstream evaluation practices, the particular requirements of C4D, and the challenges and possible solutions that face more adaptive, participatory approaches.

We go on to discuss new conceptualizations of evaluation and shifts in evaluation practice that have significant implications for understanding and evaluating C4D. They offer strategies that are likely to be effective in overcoming the challenges and issues we have identified, which is of course also the purpose of the framework. Later chapters will elaborate on some of the strategies that we introduce here.

Context and structure

The evaluation, sustainability and success of C4D and other development initiatives are affected by contextual and structural factors. Complex social, economic, political, cultural, environmental and technological factors are at play, including issues of gender and power. Neither development nor communication can be extracted from the contexts and structures within which they take place, thus they require political will on the part of governments, local authorities and other power brokers, 'After all, enabling poor communities to participate directly challenges existing power structures' (Balit, 2010a: 6).

For C4D, context includes communities, organizations and institutions as well as geography, history, culture, political systems, media and funding rules. 'Listening to the context is about appraising, learning, recognizing and appreciating all those dimensions so that we can make well-informed decisions' (Quarry and Ramirez, 2009: 113). The impacts and implications of the wider environment need to be better understood in evaluations of C4D (Byrne, 2009a). Inagaki (2007) calls for academic research in C4D to bridge the divide between critical theory and empirical research, currently experiencing a disjuncture and threatening the legitimacy of scholarship. Ignoring or paying scant attention to structural issues that have major implications for C4D makes academic research instrumental, which implies that it 'will lose its authenticity as a voice questioning fundamental development problems' (Inagaki, 2007: 44).

Our framework attempts to counter such a disjuncture, by taking adequate account of contextual and structural factors in a number of ways, including through the key components of holism and complexity and through engaging a critical lens. The emergent, realistic, and learning-based components help to allow the framework to take account of often rapidly changing information and communication technologies (ICTs), media, political, social and economic contexts. Paying attention to, and adapting in light of changing environments, is crucial for C4D and evaluation, especially in a communications environment that is changing at an unprecedented rate, with the case of mobile phone penetration and use in developing countries a case in point. Souter (2008: 179) points out that technology can become obsolete within the lifetime of a development initiative, or at least no longer appropriate. The changed communication environment might suggest a completely different approach to the use of ICTs or media than was envisaged at the start. Such observations informed the concept of communicative ecologies that are continually evolving.

Participation is also a crucial component of our framework, not least since issues of access to ICTs clearly affect the outcomes of C4D initiatives and their evaluation. This would be most evident when evaluation methods are used that employ ICTs such as online surveys or multimedia, but equally if those who take part in evaluation form only a part of the community an initiative seeks to include. Some people are harder to reach, and here special effort must be made (Grubb and Tacchi, 2008). Who gets to have a voice in C4D initiatives and their evaluation, as well as who listens, and with what consequences, all need to be considered (Quarry and Ramirez, 2009; Tacchi, 2012a).

In many developing countries, such as Nepal where the AC4SC project took place, there are particular barriers associated with the geography, the political situation, as well as gender, caste, communication infrastructure, language, and social norms. Such an environment can significantly affect communication among stakeholders and evaluators, and can make travel to research and evaluation sites and data collection time-consuming and difficult. AC4SC experienced major communication and travel challenges over the four years of the project, due in part to the wide cultural and linguistic diversity in the country, the limits of internet access and reliable telephone infrastructure outside the Kathmandu Valley, and the country's mountainous terrain and poor roads which are subject to landslides. Added to this, ongoing political instability and major political reform, discontent and regular strikes, including disruption to transport systems, greatly affected field research and capacity development activities. The very factors that made the work of Equal Access Nepal (EAN) important – including its focus on raising awareness of the political change happening in the country and associated rights and responsibilities – made their work, and their evaluation of that work, difficult. C4D and wider development initiatives by definition take place in locations where there are many challenges to be addressed, and therefore evaluation of C4D must take those challenges fully into account.

Institutional and country-level challenges

Quantitative approaches dominate evaluation in the field of development, with a stress on measurable outcomes and results-based planning, so that evaluation units are largely made up of mainstream evaluators with traditional evaluation training. This raises significant problems for C4D because there is a lack of capacity within agencies like the United Nations to evaluate an approach to development, which is itself a social process based on dialogue. As Balit (2010a: 4) explains, it is a 'soft and social science that has to do with listening, building trust and respecting local cultures – not easy concepts to understand for policy makers and programme managers with a background in hard sciences'. To understand social change, and appreciate the role of C4D in it, the wider environment and social structures and the complex nature of everyday life and cultural norms must be considered, and since we are interested in change, this must be done over time. Our consultations with UN Focal Points reinforced that there is a clear emphasis on quantitative approaches across UN agencies, with a very clear separation of evaluation and evaluation expertise from programme planning and implementation. As a member of our Expert Panel noted:

> *A key issue underlying the challenges and difficulties is that the M&E of C4D (like much other development) is typically approached in a vertical, non-integrated manner, rather than being an integral part of programmes. It is an add on, for 'M&E experts'. This reinforces the tendency towards top-down, 'expert driven' approaches and actively works against participatory approaches (skills which the former do not typically have).*

A further obstacle is that many C4D units are still located in corporate communication and external relations departments. Communication here is largely instrumental, not part of the actual process of development. While the role of communication is considered highly important to many development agencies, it tends to be understood as message delivery, disseminating information and telling people what to do, rather than listening and giving people a voice (Balit, 2010a; Tacchi, 2012a). As successive UN Round Tables for C4D, UN Resolutions and the *Rome Consensus* (WCCD, 2006) have declared, C4D goes beyond information dissemination, 'C4D is about seeking change at different levels including listening, establishing trust, sharing knowledge and skills, building policies, debating and learning for sustained and meaningful change. It is not public relations or corporate communication' (Gumucio Dagron, 2009: 6). The effective use of participatory evaluation approaches and methodologies, which are more congruent than standard quantitative approaches with the underlying ethos of C4D, is made difficult by misapprehensions of C4D as message delivery within organizations or institutions that operate through control and authority rather than inclusion and dialogue.

One challenge then is that C4D might be viewed narrowly as instrumental message delivery or dissemination of information. A second is that the environment may not be conducive to media diversity or a range of voices, and a third compacting challenge might be that evaluation fails to either critique the C4D approach itself, or contextualize activities within a realistic appreciation of the environment.

The first of three considerations for designing media development programmes, as proposed by Waisbord (2011), is nuanced assessments of the availability and suitability of an environment that might allow for media diversity and promote a range of voices. Such nuanced assessments can lead to understanding institutional weaknesses for media diversity, assessing the obstacles at system, organization and community levels, and prioritizing areas of intervention according to past experience, available knowledge and resources. This can all help to provide an evidence-based approach that tackles obstacles and challenges at all levels.

Waisbord's (2011) second consideration is that media change needs to be approached as an endogenous, long-term process, locally driven and tapping into ongoing trends such as technological and political change. Not all media environments are the same or similarly disposed to change. This idea of endogenous, self-reliant development echoes work from the mid-1970s calling for 'another development' (Dag Hammarskjöld Foundation, 1975). Yet while today the rhetoric of participation and locally grown development is strong, if not pervasive, analysing a sample of policy texts published between 1998 and 2009 by UN agencies and the World Bank regarding the role of information, communication and technologies for development, Mansell (2011) reveals the predominance of a Western-centric, exogenous model of development. Waisbord's (2011) third consideration relates to this challenge of exogenous models of development; it is to align international aid for media development to the support of ongoing efforts based on local experiences, and through partnerships of international and local actors. The concerns of donors should not determine what constitutes appropriate actions.

One of the challenges of planning and implementing research and evaluation of C4D identified by one of the Expert Panel members in our UN consultations was '*the lack of coordination between central HQ policy staff who want evaluations, and field staff for whom evaluation is an irritation*'. Our consultations, and most of the other research projects we report on in this book, emphasize the need for a long-term, sustained focus on capacity development in evaluation for staff at all levels of development agencies and organizations (see Chapter 5). Our UN consultations suggested that without the understanding, funding, support and commitment of senior UN managers and donors, improvements to capacity and moves towards greater use of more innovative and participatory approaches and methods are unlikely to be successful. Box 4.1 illustrates some of the challenges and benefits of incorporating EAR into C4D organizations.

Attitudes and policies of funders and management

A key challenge identified through our UN consultations was that senior managers and funders were seen as lacking an appreciation of the value and importance of C4D, and research and evaluation, so they rarely support innovative or participatory approaches. One Expert Panel member listed the following as key challenges in planning and conducting research and evaluation of C4D:

> *The assumptions and biases of funders/those commissioning research and evaluation, combined with a lack of openness to less mainstream, more innovative, less prescriptive and predictable approaches. Both conceptually and in terms of resourcing these*

Box 4.1 *The benefits and challenges of incorporating ethnographic action research into C4D organizations*

Finding a Voice operated in 15 locations in South and South East Asia, in a range of contexts and different institutional structures. Each location presented different challenges, and each organization was driven by different imperatives. By becoming a part of FAV, organizations were signing up to a commitment to achieving greater participation in content creation (in whatever ways were appropriate to their contexts and goals), and to work to understand and inform this process through research. The usefulness of EAR and the embedded local researchers depended on an openness on the part of the organization, first of all to reviewing its goals and activities in relation to content creation; and, secondly, to learning from and changing and adapting according to research findings.

To be really effective, EAR needs to be an embedded component of an organization, adequately resourced and ongoing. It can help to build flexibility into initiatives so that they can adapt to local needs and changing situations. It can help organizations recognize and document successes *and* failures, opportunities *and* challenges, recognizing that in order to overcome obstacles they need to be fully understood. To achieve all of this, the idea is that the organization develops a *research culture* through which knowledge and reflection are made integral to ongoing development. The research aims, methods and analysis arise from, and then feed back into, a rich understanding of the particular place. It provides a way of listening carefully to what people know from their own experiences and then brings this local knowledge into the ongoing processes of planning and acting.

In some cases, especially where there was a large and hierarchical organizational structure, it was difficult or impossible for the EAR researcher to develop a research culture within the organization, or penetrate the barriers to those in decision-making positions who needed to know about the research if it was to have any impact on the initiative. Typically, these kinds of organizations prioritized survey type research over the largely qualitative and participatory approaches undertaken in EAR. In other more flexible and responsive organizations, EAR was seen to be a driver for the ongoing development of the initiative, and we saw EAR itself being adapted to suit the needs of the initiative.

It was clear to see a number of factors at play at different times, including the ability of an organization to adapt, along with internal and local issues of power, gender, class and caste.

(Tacchi and Kiran, 2008)

processes, an unquestioning 'more of the same' is all too commonplace, regardless of the suitability and fit with the aims of and values underlying the particular programme involved.

Byrne (2008: 4) highlights difficulties with funding innovative evaluation practices in C4D and the frustrations of many at the field level with having to fit their achievements into externally imposed 'SMART' indicators and objectives, along with tabular cause and

> **Box 4.2** *The pressure to conform to externally imposed evaluation approaches*
>
> In AC4SC we often assumed consensus concerning some aspect of the development of the project, only to discover that there were in fact major misunderstandings or lack of clarity, and a degree of concern about innovative approaches. A good example of this is the work we did with EAN staff towards developing theories of change for two of their radio programmes, which involved working with teams that included programme producers, management and M&E staff. This happened in year three of the project, after earlier work on developing theories of change had stumbled or become too complex for EAN staff to feel they were useful.
>
> At this time, we followed the Keystone Accountability (2008) approach to developing a theory of change (ToC), which involves creating visions of change and including multiple stakeholders. It was seen as a useful approach by members of the M&E team who had come across it, as well as by us, since it seemed to provide a clear process for gaining a high level of participation and agreement in terms not just of the social change goals of the radio programmes, but also a grounded way to develop indicators of that change, and the actions required by various stakeholders to achieve the vision of success.
>
> Initially this worked extremely well, and staff from across the organization invested time and energy. However, at some stage, this was followed by the realization of the amount of time and work that would be required to complete the ToC with a range of stakeholders external to EAN. This was the thing that had most attracted us to the approach, and ended up being the factor that made the EAN M&E team the most uneasy about it, making it difficult to pursue.
>
> Already stretched in terms of the demands of the organization on their time, the M&E team felt overwhelmed by the seemingly 'extra' work this task required, and were unable to weigh this positively against perceived benefits. While initially the ToC seemed to offer an ideal mechanism for joining up M&E work with agreed social change objectives, it shifted to an additional task with ill-defined benefits. That is, it was seen as a task that was extra to the standard, and more conventional cause and effect work that they accepted as part of how funders expected them to work.
>
> Indeed, within the academic team itself there emerged different opinions of how we should progress, with conflicting views between following a standard logframe approach or the more flexible ToC approach. This can be understood as a manifestation of a pragmatic (work within the system) versus transformational (change the system) approach. In reality, for a C4D organization on the ground, we found it was necessary to accommodate both approaches, and hoped for a good balance between working successfully within the conventional development landscape, whilst trying to innovate and change it for the better.
>
> (adapted from Tacchi, Lennie and Wilmore, 2010)

effect approaches such as the logframe approach, which we discuss in Chapter 6. We came across these frustrations in AC4SC, as Box 4.2 illustrates.

Certainly, it is challenging for individual development organizations to challenge approaches such as the logframe, and argue for more flexible and innovative approaches. Changes need to come from larger movements and networks of practitioners, such as the Big Push Forward (http://bigpushforward.net) who recognize the need to work together to positively influence the evaluation and impact assessment agendas and approaches of development funders and implementers, as discussed in Chapters 5 and 7.

Souter (2008: 181, author's italics) argues that impact assessment of information and communications for development (ICD) requires 'sustained commitment on the part of implementing agencies, from project design through to project completion *and beyond*'. He suggests that donors also need to understand and be willing to recognize the need to identify and understand unexpected or negative impacts, that 'impact assessment is not about validation of past decisions but about the improvement of those that will be made in the future' (Souter, 2008: 181). Identifying failure empirically is an excellent way to feed into effective planning, to avoid similar failures in the future, and learn from and build on experience. However, it is highly risky for implementation organizations to talk about failures when they are funded by donors who take a standard approach to evaluation, and where evaluation is used to decide whether an initiative is extended, expanded, replicated or closed.

For the leadership programme in Minnesota out of which DE grew, and for EAN and AC4SC, it was a desire to improve practice, rather than prove impact for the sake of ticking donor-required boxes, that inspired them. How an initiative responds to things that do not work can provide useful insights into a programme's effectiveness. Nevertheless, across the board, it is the success stories that proliferate in reports to donors, rarely are we able to learn from detailed stories of failures or negative outcomes. The ways in which donors operate make this a highly risky enterprise for donor-dependent development organizations.

Challenges in conceptualizing, outsourcing and managing research and evaluation

In our UN consultations, we asked UN Focal Points to name up to four challenges they face in conceptualizing, outsourcing and managing research and evaluation in their C4D programmes. We also asked the Expert Panel members about the challenges they face in planning and conducting research and evaluation for C4D. Weak expertise or capacity in conceptualizing, managing and planning research and evaluation of C4D was identified. One respondent pointed out that '*C4D is often an organic process that follows opportunities which means the evaluation needs to be flexible enough to move with a programme as it develops without missing opportunities for baselines*'. Yet the ability to plan for such an approach to evaluation is missing. Compounding the situation is a lack of understanding of C4D itself. There is, according to one of our Expert Panel respondents, '*Poor understanding of C4D concepts, its role and adequate use in programmes*', while another commented on a '*Lack of understanding of C4D by agencies commissioning research, monitoring and evaluation*'. Box 4.3 provides examples of the responses to our questions about challenges, grouped under key themes.

The responses in Box 4.3 indicate a lack of appreciation and understanding of the value and importance of research and evaluation of C4D, and of C4D itself. Given that participatory approaches to evaluation for C4D, considered by respondents to be most appropriate, are time-consuming and resource intensive, the issue of lack of resources is particularly important. As Leeuw and Vaessen (2009: 32) comment, 'in general, the higher degree of participation, the more costly and difficult it is to set up the impact evaluation'. However, if issues of capacity development, local ownership, empowerment and sustainability are valued as important outcomes, and could be factored into a cost–benefit analysis, participatory approaches would be seen to offer value for money.

78 *Challenges, issues and strategies*

Box 4.3 *Key themes in our UN consultations on challenges in evaluating C4D*

Funding and other resources such as time for research and evaluation of C4D is a low priority, or inadequate

Resources needed for research, if available (which they are usually not) would be disproportionate to the scale of the project/programme.

Under-resourcing the effort, expecting impact results from what is really just 'a drop in the ocean' case study.

The second most important challenge is to convince the contractor that it also takes money to do it well. A fixed percentage of budgets should be allocated to research, monitoring and evaluation from the design phase, instead of adding the activity at the end and looking for funding when the project or programme funds are already exhausted.

Finding the time to design evaluations for diverse programmes, where each requires specialised analysis.

Low levels of skills, capacity, understanding or awareness of research and evaluation and social change

Uneven understanding of behaviour and social change.

Few skilled practitioners in many countries to conduct research, monitoring and evaluation of C4D.

Weak or non-existent expertise of personnel within the national agency(ies) with whom the UN agency is working.

Weak capacity for research and evaluation, especially at organizational levels, and inadequate resources to strengthen capacity at all levels, over a realistic timeframe.

Lack of capacity to design and implement research and evaluation, and lack of useful indicators or baseline data

Weak design of indicators, baseline information, and conceptual approach to assessing impact at start of implementation.

Evaluation is not really conceptualized at the beginning of programmes.

Lack of clarity about objectives for the commissioned research, monitoring and evaluation.

Diffuse, long-term and hard-to-measure results expected from our projects and programmes.

Indicators for some aspects of C4D programming are not well defined or understood.

Lack of importance and value given to research and evaluation for C4D

Convincing decision-makers and project managers that R,M&E of C4D is important.

Low level of realization among partners of importance and value of R,M&E for C4D.

Lack of interest among programme staff, governments, other stakeholders in activities and use of evaluation results.

The most important challenge is convincing the contractor that research, monitoring and evaluation are processes that take time, and they are not just quick mechanical operations.

Attitudes to evaluation approaches, methods and processes

To convince the contractor that quantitative methodologies will not provide the necessary information on how peoples' lives changed. Only qualitative methodologies which allow people to participate and speak can provide quality information about social change.

The apparent obsession with methods and tools, to the neglect of deeper, fundamental questions like: Who is the evaluation for? What is it for? Who are the intended users of the evaluation? What are the intended uses? How will the process itself empower those involved and strengthen wider communication for development processes?

Too much jargon and mystification of the process, lack of simplicity and lack of clarity about what is being evaluated.

In the ICT for Poverty Reduction (ICTPR) project, we trained nine local researchers in India, Nepal, Bhutan, Bangladesh and Sri Lanka. They worked for 12 months as local researchers, providing research and feedback to their community-based interventions, and as a coordinated network of embedded researchers provided important learning about ICT and development for UNESCO (Slater and Tacchi, 2004). This research component of ICTPR, which included training the local researchers, cost US$80,000. Compared to the cost of an external evaluator, evaluating nine initiatives across five countries, and the level of insights and usefulness of the data produced to help those initiatives become more effective, we felt this was extremely good value. Furthermore, in terms of capacity development, local researchers trained through ICTPR went on to become trainers, coordinators and lead researchers in the larger Finding a Voice (FAV) project.

What appropriate evaluation looks like for C4D was raised in our UN consultations as a key concern. Baseline studies are useful, but in fact quite rare, and often look at factors that turn out to be less important as an initiative develops (Gosling and Edwards, 2003). What standard baseline and endline studies consist of therefore needs careful consideration. In AC4SC, rather than standard baselines, members of the M&E team conducted 'scoping studies'. Box 4.4 is an example of the type of participatory scoping research in communities that can provide an understanding of the complex contextual factors that affect the process of social change and can successfully begin the process of engaging local stakeholders in the ongoing research and evaluation process.

Without some kind of baseline, it is not possible to assess impact (Souter, 2008), although how we understand baseline and what it consists of can be broad, locally informed and periodically reviewed, and, in some situations, retrospective baselines can be effectively created. Similarly, as discussed already, the idea of impact is problematic with its cause and effect logic. Timings of impact-focused evaluations and programme cycles tend to work against evaluative learning. Social change needs to be recognized as non-linear, complex, uncertain, unpredictable and long-term. A moving baseline would fit this conceptualization of social change better than standard ideas, since change requires 'an in-depth understanding of both context and the baseline against which change is being measured' (Souter, 2008: 161).

Challenges in assessing impacts and outcomes of C4D

Impact studies have in the past been quite rare in development (Cracknell, 2000), but are now high on the development agenda, as evidenced by the growing number of resources in

80 *Challenges, issues and strategies*

> **Box 4.4** *Understanding the community context of the AC4SC project*
>
> As an initial step in the AC4SC project, Bikash Koirala and Jiwan Sharma, M&E Officers with EAN, undertook scoping studies in four districts of Nepal in which regular participatory research was later conducted by embedded community researchers. The main purposes of the initial scoping studies included:
>
> - to identify and engage key stakeholders who could provide relevant information about the community and help to identify potential community researchers;
> - to explain the AC4SC project to key stakeholders and the benefits of the project to the community;
> - to collect demographic data and relevant contextual information about the area;
> - to undertake communicative ecology research and mapping.
>
> Methods used in the scoping studies included interviews, observation, focus group discussions, social mapping, well-being ranking and gender charts. The researchers also gathered government statistics and other data about population numbers, age distribution, gender, ethnicity/caste, religion, educational/literacy levels, economic activity and migration to and from the area. Communicative ecology mapping was used here to understand the communications and media landscape, what communication channels were available and to start to get some insights into how they were used and by whom.
>
> One of the first scoping studies, in the Dang District, was undertaken by Bikash Koirala. He prepared a report, which included contextual information and a range of communicative ecology diagrams. The report gave details about the location and populations broken down by ethnicity and caste, language groups and gender. Details were provided about levels of poverty, education, literacy levels, livelihoods, industries and migration patterns.
>
> Radio was reported as the only reliable source of information in many villages. There were five FM radio stations in the district. Internet access was very limited or non-existent. The report described the presence of listener groups for EAN's radio programmes in the area and the range of different awareness-raising activities these groups conducted in the community. EAN had provided the groups with satellite radios in an effort to build listening and promote dialogue and activities within the community. The scoping reports were able to identify and report on these, providing a starting point for understanding and designing the local research to follow, through local researchers that EAN would train as part of the AC4SC project.

this area, including the very comprehensive guide *Impact Evaluations and Development*, recently published by the Network of Networks for Impact Evaluation (Leeuw and Vaessen, 2009). However, perspectives on the 'definition, scope and appropriate methods of impact evaluation differ widely among practitioners and stakeholders' (Leeuw and Vaessen, 2009: ix).

Impact evaluations are resource and time intensive. There is a distinct lack of published reports on high quality impact assessments of C4D (Inagaki, 2007: 43). Some of the difficulties in demonstrating the impacts of C4D were aptly summarized by one of the Expert Panel members in our UN consultations:

Impact is a holy grail, it requires considerable funding and effort to gain credible results because communication impact is challenging. It is not counting latrines that have been built, it is about assessing changes in how people think and respond to issues and contexts and this can be impacted by many variables.

The attribution problem

Attribution is considered to be 'the central problem in impact evaluation' (Leeuw and Vaessen, 2009: 21). It is a key problem in assessing impacts of C4D compared to other development initiatives such as polio eradication programmes where it can be easier to isolate changes in rates of the disease in a particular population. Souter (2008: 175) suggests an open-minded approach to analysis and interpretation of findings 'particularly to issues of attribution, aimed at learning from experience'. The processes and effects of communication can be difficult to measure. Balit (2010b: 1) suggests that in some cases we can think about measuring changes in 'knowledge, behaviour, attitudes and access and use of services', yet the sticky question of attribution remains, given the difficulty of attributing causality.

Causality is complex, and change is likely to be due to a whole range of factors, which in turn act on each other. Different factors may become relevant over time. It is often quite difficult to track and isolate those related to C4D. This is, in part, due to C4D often being a component of a larger development initiative that is usually conducted in collaboration with a number of partner organizations and involves a range of media and community-based activities. This presents a particularly difficult challenge, because of the politics of aid, which means that implementing agencies are 'often tempted to claim credit for impacts because that is what those they are accountable to want to hear' (Souter, 2008: 162). The complexity of assessing the impacts of C4D is effectively highlighted by Inagaki (2007):

... general categories such as mass media and interpersonal communication can potentially conceal varying effects among specific channels within each mode, such as one-to-one interpersonal contacts versus group discussion, broadcast media versus printed materials... different communication channels interact with one another, and this interaction can form a complex network of communication effects encompassing multiple, direct and indirect paths of influence. When measured alone a mass media message may have negligible direct impacts, but the same message can have significantly greater impacts when mediated through other channels of communication, such as interpersonal communication and group communication.

(Inagaki, 2007: 34–35)

An apparently intractable problem with the desire to attribute impact is the one highlighted by Patton (2011) and DE – a programme needs to remain static and subject itself to conventional formative and summative evaluation to provide such evidence in any convincing form. The value of this can be weighed against the benefits of an initiative that adapts and responds to changing environments. The idea of cause and effect and causal relationships is not terribly helpful here. We might consider its usefulness in relation to whether any particular problem, question or activity can be thought of as simple, complicated or complex, with cause and effect becoming decreasingly useful as the complexity increases.

As Inagaki (2007) suggests, it is unlikely that the impact of a communication initiative could be considered in isolation from wider contextual factors and underlying social change. Contribution analysis (Mayne, 1999) is one response to the challenge of attribution, which attempts to move beyond standard approaches to impact assessment. Rather than attempting to prove direct impact, it focuses on the contributions of a programme to observable outcomes. It may not be considered directly responsible for the outcome, but it can be plausibly demonstrated that it contributed to it. Contribution analysis takes into account that impacts can take a long time to occur or become evident. However, while this is a useful advance on the standard approach, our critical review of this approach suggests that it is not highly suitable for the evaluation of complex C4D initiatives. Contribution analysis is underpinned by linear cause–effect programme logic models that we consider inappropriate for the assessment of C4D outcomes since they do not provide the type of 'flexible thinking-action logic' (Retolaza, 2011: 4) that is required for initiatives focused on transformative change. We discuss this further in Chapter 6 in our overview of the theory of change approach.

Timeframe issues

There are often unrealistic demands, targets and timeframes for the impact assessment process, with donors expecting to see measurable results in an unreasonably short timeframe, most likely determined through measurable pre-set indicators. This can lead to the creation of 'results' that may have little connection with work on the ground. Members of our Expert Panel for the UN consultations noted:

> *If donors demand 'results', it is hard to link improvements in public knowledge and discourse with actual changes on the ground... imprecise results from unrealistic targets and dubious indicators (for which data can't be collected) planned at the beginning.*
>
> *Inadequate time and resources to do justice to effort expended, to achievement and to the learning potential and interest. This typically accounts for limited follow-up opportunities, including those for collective critical reflection and learning, which should lie at the heart of evaluation processes.*

If social change is understood as an ongoing and complex process, it will be very difficult to understand and demonstrate the impact of a C4D initiative through measurable pre-set indicators within a short timeframe. Yet impact assessment is usually undertaken immediately after the end of a project's implementation. Social change is ongoing; outcomes of interventions often lie in the future, beyond the immediate project (Souter, 2008). The main issues here are the timeframe of development funding, and the reporting requirements based on dominant evaluation approaches. These two factors negatively impact the likelihood for success, as well as concepts of what constitutes success, and how therefore it might be demonstrated.

In Inagaki's (2007: 41) review of 37 studies on the impact of C4D programmes, only four gave any indication of long-term impacts, 'and even among these studies impacts going beyond the immediate timeframe of the project are discussed through anecdotal accounts rather than systematic analyses'. Project implementation timeframes are too short to be able to assess long-term impacts. The average length of funding for projects reviewed by Inagaki (2007) was two years, and over half of the 37 studied had active project periods of one year or less.

Parks *et al.* (2005) suggest that assessing the impact of communication for social change (CFSC) programmes should look at short-term, intermediate and long-term impact. While Skuse (2006: 25) points out that understanding the behavioural impact of radio programmes is 'notoriously difficult and can only occur over the long-term', he nevertheless argues that 'there is scope to set interim behaviour change indicators within ICD programmes that can and should be evaluated'. Souter (2008: 164) suggests that the best way of assessing 'lasting and sustainable change' is to use longitudinal studies 'undertaken some time (six months, two years, five years) after project closure'. However, he notes that the reluctance of donors to fund such studies is a particular problem in areas like ICD 'where there is no strongly established evidence base of past experience on which to build' (Souter, 2008: 164).

The value of alternative approaches

The challenges of inadequate resources for evaluation make formal evaluation hugely costly to practitioners, so that one of the challenges to donors is to make evaluation less complex and costly, and provide easy to use tools 'that will allow broadcasters to quickly and easily assess the impact of their outputs' (Skuse, 2006: 26). Such approaches, however, pragmatically serve donor requirements and timelines without actually helping to improve the evaluation experiences of implementation organizations and making the evaluation useful to them, unless it takes an alternative approach to evaluation that allows for ongoing adaptation. Instrumental and donor-responsive approaches to impact assessment do not sit comfortably with alternative approaches such as DE, as they aim to prove rather than develop or improve. Yet alternative approaches are in fact more likely to be able to demonstrate incremental impacts or outcomes. As Patton (2011) found, working on the Minnesota leadership programme, DE was able to provide useful periodic inputs into summative decisions not after the project ended, but during its application. Therefore it is less important that donors make evaluation less complex or provide simple tools, than that they fundamentally examine the purpose of and approach to evaluation, and who its users and participants are or should be.

It is helpful to have evaluation and impact assessment embedded in all stages of 'the programme spiral' (Gosling and Edwards, 2003: 126). Cracknell (2000: 340) suggests 'the key issue is to ensure full participation of all the stakeholders right from the start of the project's life ... unless the primary stakeholders are fully involved, progress could be slow and success problematic'. Based on this and other research that clearly demonstrates the value of participatory forms of evaluation, our framework includes a holistic, participatory approach to the assessment of outcomes and highlights the importance of taking the social economic, cultural and political context into account, not just in the C4D activity itself, but also in its evaluation.

Overcoming the challenges: key trends in C4D evaluation

In this section we discuss a range of strategies to address the challenges set out above. These include using innovative and creative research and evaluation approaches and a mixed methods evaluation approach. In the next section of this chapter we present what we consider to be four particularly important new conceptualizations of evaluation and shifts in evaluation practice. All of these strategies and responses to the challenges have contributed to the development of our framework. Evaluation capacity development is another essential and highly effective response to most of the challenges highlighted in this chapter. Capacity development links closely in particular to the learning, holistic, emergent and realistic components of our framework. We discuss the importance of a learning-based approach to evaluation capacity development in C4D in Chapter 5.

Innovative and creative approaches to evaluation of C4D

A key finding from our UN consultations was that more openness, freedom and flexibility is needed in the selection and use of various evaluation approaches, methodologies and methods to ensure that they are appropriate and fit the aims of the C4D initiative. Innovative and creative participatory approaches, such as DE and EAR, can foster new understandings of local issues, and facilitate community engagement and dialogue, and personal and community change. They are highly appropriate and effective in the evaluation of C4D. Creative processes such as storytelling, drawing pictures, and taking photographs and video are increasingly used in different stages of development research and evaluation as key elements of ethnographic and participatory action research methodologies (see Liamputtong, 2007).

As we illustrate in Box 4.5, images can be important to sense-making in participatory learning processes since they can 'capture the essence of the issue' and can act as 'catalysts for change in a hundred unknown areas' (Burns, 2007: 129–130). They provide access to

---

Box 4.5 *Building a sense of community and understanding outcomes through visual participatory research methods*

Elizabeth Rattine-Flaherty and Arvind Singhal have analyzed the social change practices of Minga Peru, an NGO in the Peruvian Amazon that promotes gender equality and reproductive health. Minga Peru's outreach activities include a radio programme and community-based interventions facilitated by community health workers or *promotoras*, local women leaders who act as catalysts for change. Their research highlights the feminist orientation of participatory research approaches. Feminist perspectives are seen as encouraging forms of self-expression such as drawing and storytelling that are rejected in traditional Western research approaches that privilege linear logic. They suggest that participatory methods directly support the notion that emotion clarifies rather than clouds understanding and judgment.

Participatory research with Minga Peru *promotoras* included participatory exercises in which groups of *promotoras* created drawings and took photographs that aimed to capture the reality of Amazonian life and Minga Peru's influence on the communities. Participants discussed sketches of themselves before and after their involvement in the activities of Minga Peru. The dialogue generated through these exercises was found to help connect participants, creating a sense of community and enabling participants to view their experiences from multiple perspectives. This process highlighted both self-development and collective development; it enabled critical reflection and gave voice to the women involved. In addition, participants developed skills such as group facilitation and public speaking, along with technical skills such as how to use a camera. However, these methods are not free of risks. They can lead to greater anger, shame and resentment, they require extensive time and energy, and time must be taken to develop relationships and trust.

(Rattine-Flaherty and Singhal, 2009)

different forms of knowing, can act as triggers to open up areas of inquiry and interpretation that may not have been anticipated, and can help us to conceptualize a system and to articulate complex relationships (Burns, 2007: 117–118). Pink (2007) suggests that visual research methods should be rooted in a critical understanding of local and academic visual cultures, visual media and technologies, and the ethical issues they raise. Not all visual cultures are the same, and in some cultures, oral rather than visual methods are more appropriate.

Processes such as communicative ecology mapping can help participants and evaluators to understand and explore communication systems, patterns and issues in a community and identify barriers to information and communication access among different groups. 'Rich pictures' have been used in soft systems methodology as a way to collectively learn not only about the obvious facts of a situation, but also about abstract or emotional ways of knowing such as the social atmosphere among different actors or stakeholders (McKegg and Wehipeihana, 2011). Rich pictures can be used in DE to capture the real situation through a no-holds-barred, cartoon-like representation of all the ideas, connections, relationships, influences and relationships that are part of the context (McKegg and Wehipeihana, 2011).

Chambers (2008: 99) points out that 'Symbols, objects and diagrams can represent realities that are cumbersome or impossible to express verbally'. He suggests that visual and tangible approaches and methods can reverse power relations by 'generating a positive sum synergy through which all can contribute and learn'. Through the process of collective analysis and learning and facilitator assessment, the rigour and credibility of outputs are also increased (Chambers, 2008: 99). These methods are considered to empower through enabling local people to represent complex realities and relationships:

> The visual diaries of ILS [Internal Learning System] in South India empower low caste women, arming them with visual representations of their realities and experiences, enabling them to track and discuss changes in their lives over time, and to take action when patterns of marginalization (such as caste or gender discrimination) persist.
> (Chambers, 2008: 100)

Digital storytelling has become a regular feature in many of the community-based media centres that took part in Finding a Voice. The process can stress individual or group voices and stories (Hartley and McWilliam, 2009). In FAV, digital storytelling and other forms of mediated storytelling were found to open up dialogue between groups and communities about social issues such as domestic violence that had previously been difficult to discuss (Watkins and Tacchi, 2008).

In our UN consultations, some respondents suggested that there is a need for greater focus on innovative, 'non-dominant' approaches and experimentation. Byrne (2009a: 5) suggests that we urgently need 'more honest and reflective stories of innovation in practice, in social change, communication for social change and their evaluation, from across the world and across the development sector'. The Nicaraguan C4D initiative Puntos de Encuentro, discussed in Chapter 3, is a good example of innovation, as is DE, and the approaches used in FAV and AC4SC. All of these examples used an innovative mixed methods approach to research and evaluation.

The value of a mixed methods approach

The systems and complexity theories that underpin our framework for evaluating C4D highlight the need for methodological pluralism. Midgley (2006) notes that this is important in developing a flexible and responsive evaluation approach, which is essential in the evaluation of complex C4D interventions. A pragmatic, mixed methods approach can also provide a fuller and more realistic picture of social change, shed light on different issues, and increase the strength and rigour of evaluation findings (Bamberger, Rao and Woolcock, 2010; Hearn et al., 2009; White, 2009). The importance of a mixed methods approach in the evaluation of C4D is demonstrated in our UN consultations, which found that 80 per cent of the UN respondents and 79 per cent of the Expert Panel consider a mixed methods approach as 'very important' in their work.

Johnson and Onwuegbuzie (2004: 17) suggest that a mixed methods research approach is the 'third research movement', moving past paradigm wars between qualitative and quantitative proponents. They define mixed methods research as 'the class of research where the researcher mixes or combines quantitative and qualitative research techniques, methods, approaches, concepts or language into a single study' (Johnson and Onwuegbuzie, 2004: 17). The features of this approach are an expansive and creative form of research, inclusive, pluralistic, and complementary, suggesting an eclectic approach to method selection and critical thinking about planning and conducting research.

The use of mixed methods is promoted in EAR training materials. For example, the EAR training website (http://ear.findingavoice.org) encourages researchers to think about the value of using more than one method. Methods are referred to as tools, and the analogy of building a house is used to explain the need to draw on a range of tools:

> None of the tools should be used on their own to fully understand an issue – just as you would use a range of tools to build a house; you need to use a range of tools to build your research and understandings. For example, you might use a participatory technique, in-depth interviews and participant observation to explore what poverty means in a particular place. You would never attempt to understand this fully through just using participatory techniques, just using in-depth interviews, or just using participant observation. Through combining these tools you get to a deeper and more rounded understanding of any issue, topic or group.
> (http://ear.findingavoice.org/toolbox/index.html)

In the frequently asked questions section of the website, the question 'why do I need to use different tools' is answered by local researcher Govinda Prasad Acharya, who was the EAR researcher working with a local television initiative in Palpa, Nepal:

> We need different kinds of data to become clear about a particular issue. An EAR researcher should look at the same issue from different angles. To collect different kinds of data from different angles, we need different research tools.
> (http://ear.findingavoice.org/started/5-0.html)

The selection of approaches, methodologies and methods, as we outline further in Chapter 7, must be related to the purpose and goal of evaluation. There are a broad range of approaches, each suitable for specific applications, and often able to be used to complement each other or provide triangulation.

A mixed methods approach can capture and enable respect for different perspectives as part of a 'democratically-engaged' evaluation approach (Greene, 2002: 24). It is suitable for exploring complex situations and problems, can help provide detail on local contexts, collect sensitive information, include hard to reach groups, and significantly strengthen rigour (Bamberger *et al.*, 2010: 3–16). It allows us to select from a broad range of methods, providing exactly the kind of flexibility that is required in the evaluation of C4D.

However, Bamberger *et al.* (2010) highlight a number of challenges in using a mixed methods approach to evaluate international development projects. While mixed methods have been used by many development agencies for several years, many of these evaluations have taken a somewhat ad hoc approach, and the professional, financial and other resources have usually not been available to increase their conceptual and methodological rigour (Bamberger *et al.*, 2010: 23). This highlights the need to improve the capacities of evaluators to undertake mixed methods evaluations. A participatory, mixed methods approach requires a wider range of skills and knowledge to be used effectively than do standard approaches to evaluation.

New conceptualizations of evaluation and shifts in evaluation practice

We now present four new conceptualizations of evaluation and shifts in evaluation practice that have significant implications for understanding and evaluating C4D. These shifts fit well with our framework, respond in significant ways to the challenges and issues set out above, and help to provide an environment for C4D evaluation practices that is ultimately supportive of better development planning and practice at all levels.

- evaluation as an ongoing learning and organizational improvement process;
- a shift from proving impacts to developing and improving initiatives;
- the use of evaluative processes to support the development of innovations;
- a shift from external to internal and community accountability.

Evaluation as an ongoing learning and organizational improvement process

There is a growing trend towards seeing evaluation and meta-evaluation as an integral part of development initiatives and a process that effectively enables continuous learning and the development of learning organizations as a means of strengthening capacities and improving organizational systems and performance (Horton *et al.*, 2003; Lennie, Tacchi and Wilmore, 2012; Morariu *et al.*, 2009). This type of 'pedagogical' approach to evaluation entails a teaching and learning process, one that is:

> ...more about learning than judging; more about participants becoming critically aware of their own positions on issues and developing an understanding and appreciation of new and different perspectives... This learning process is made possible by dialogues of several kinds.
>
> (Schwandt, 2001, in Byrne, 2008: 14–15)

Such an approach highlights participation, self-evaluation and the importance of trust (Souter, 2008: 181). Ideally development practitioners and funders are learning organizations, open to feedback and responsive to new ideas (Gosling and Edwards, 2003; Raeside, 2011). There are some evident basic incompatibilities between this kind of approach and the aims of accountability and measuring impact (Cracknell, 2000; Earle, 2003). The development of a learning culture requires the active support, leadership and involvement of senior management within organizations, empowerment of local staff, an openness to collaboration, critical reflection and learning from the things that did and that did not work, and a commitment to putting these learnings into practice (Forss *et al.*, 2006; Lennie *et al.*,

2012; Raeside, 2011; Taut, 2007). However, the imperative of proving immediate impact makes this longer-term view of how to achieve lasting social change highly risky, as illustrated by both Puntos and AC4SC, as discussed earlier. Moving to this kind of learning culture in the current context of results-based management is problematic primarily due to the contradictory aims of these approaches (Chambers and Pettit, 2004; Earle, 2003), and yet is essential to improving development effectiveness.

A shift from proving impacts to developing and improving initiatives

The approach to evaluation that we advocate in this book is focused on developing and improving C4D initiatives rather than on attempting to prove impacts, which is often extremely difficult given the complexity of the social change process. Sankar and Williams (2007: 1) make the important point that the increasing emphasis on 'proving' the impact of programmes 'can undermine and sometimes even distract from program delivery efforts, where a focus on "improving" could be more meaningful. It is not easy to design evaluations that both "prove" and "improve"'. They consider the overemphasis on impact as limiting options for innovation and the longer-term achievement of sustainable results.

When evaluations of development initiatives are underpinned by a holistic, learning-based framework, there is a shift away from '*measuring* and *proving*' towards '*understanding* and *improving*' (Byrne, 2008: 9, author's italics). Here, progress towards long-term social change and appreciation of the contribution being made, rather than attempts to measure and attribute impact, is increasingly considered a more realistic measure of effectiveness (Byrne, 2008). This shift from proving to developing and improving is exemplified by the emergence of relatively new planning and M&E methodologies such as outcome mapping (described in Chapter 6), which focuses on constant improvement, understanding and the creation of knowledge (Earl, Carden and Smutylo, 2001). It is further illustrated by DE, and is the key driver behind EAR.

Increasingly there is an understanding that simple baseline and endline measurements, considered rigorous by mainstream evaluation standards, and using random samples, are not the best way to improve practice (Mayoux and Chambers, 2005). The new impact assessment agenda of pro-poor development has moved from a focus on 'proving impact' to 'improving practice', which requires a new paradigm of impact assessment with credible and practical recommendations and approaches to challenge and shift 'the policy and practical impact of impact assessment itself' (Mayoux and Chambers, 2005: 273). The development of the AC4SC methodology (see Chapter 6) was in direct response to this imperative.

The use of evaluative processes to support the development of innovations

The work of Patton (2011), Wehipeihana and McKegg (2009), Wadsworth (2010), Burns (2007) and others has recently highlighted the value of using evaluative processes to support the development of innovative social change and community development initiatives. A key aim of DE is to support innovation development 'to guide adaptation to emergent and dynamic realities in complex environments' (Patton, 2011: 1). It can be seen as a form of strategic thinking and acting, as an intervention unfolds. The five purposes and uses of DE, outlined in Patton (2011: 21–22), are:

1 ongoing development;
2 adapting effective principles to a new context;

3   developing a rapid response in the face of a sudden, major change or crisis;
4   pre-formative development of potentially scalable innovation;
5   adapting effective principles to a new context.

A shift from external to internal and community accountability

Another related key trend is the shift from evaluations being mainly focused on upwards, external accountability to donors, to a greater focus on internal, personal and downwards, community-level accountability. David and Mancini (2011: 245) note that over the last decade there has been an increased focus on accountability to primary stakeholders, accompanied by experimentation with 'participatory approaches that address issues of power, justice and rights and open up new frontiers of enquiry, learning and understanding of change'. Likewise, Jones (2011: ix) observes the emergence of innovative systems for feedback and increasing emphasis on transparency and accountability in development interventions.

A growing number of initiatives have emerged that aim to develop better accountability to communities and stakeholders. Jones (2011: 27) cites Action Aid's Accountability, Learning and Planning System (ALPS), which stimulates ongoing change in Action Aid's 'planning, strategy, appraisals, annual reports and strategic reviews, bringing them more in line with principles of downward accountability'. Another example provided by David and Mancini (2011: 246) are the processes and mechanisms developed by Oxfam Australia and

---

Box 4.6 *The value of community feedback forums in AC4SC*

In January 2009, Bikash Koirala, an M&E Officer from EAN, and four community researchers (CRs) held five community forums in the Dadeldhura and Dang districts of Nepal to provide feedback on the research undertaken by the CRs and to discuss key findings from this research. These meetings consisted of three main parts:

1   asking the community what they knew about what the CRs are doing in the community;
2   presentation of a report based on data collected by the CRs;
3   finding out what social change means to the community.

A key aim of the forums was to learn more about how much the CRs were able to involve community members in the research. The meetings were also seen as helping the CRs to be more accountable to the community in their research work. The meetings went well overall and had a number of useful and positive outcomes.

At one meeting, participants said they liked the most significant change stories, which the CR presented in his report, because they helped them to learn about the experiences of other people in the community. They asked him to present these stories to them regularly. Another meeting enabled parents and their children to meet together and discuss for the first time issues such as changes in discrimination between sons and daughters. Various useful ideas about the process of social change in the community and the role of communication in social change were also identified.

Oxfam New Zealand, which include complaints mechanisms, annual reflection processes, stakeholder surveys and processes for transparent sharing of analysis and feedback with stakeholders.

An example of the use of community feedback forums in the AC4SC project to enable community researchers to be more accountable to their local communities is provided in Box 4.6.

There are key challenges here to do with knowledge, power relations and structural barriers to participation. In their account of the development and implementation of ALPS by Action Aid, David and Mancini (2011: 245) suggest that a workshop on power and power relations was pivotal since it challenged participants to grapple with and acknowledge their own personal experiences of power and power relations within their organization.

The inclusion or exclusion of the type of information that EAR researchers in FAV could bring to the table was often related to conceptions of the relative importance of, and what is thought to constitute, 'knowledge'. This calls our attention to the way that development's preference for one knowledge system fails to appreciate the political nature of knowledge, and the importance of multiple knowledges (Mansell, 2011). Local knowledges are complex cultural constructions, often with different modes of operation and relations to social and cultural fields (Escobar, 1995). Development attempts to recodify local knowledge to make it useable for development activities, with a goal of enhancing expert knowledge and increasing the chances of success for development brokers, rather that tapping into, engaging with and learning from local knowledge. We need to find better ways to engage with, incorporate, account for and respond to 'worlds and knowledges otherwise' (Escobar, 2007; Tacchi, 2012b).

Conclusion

This chapter has explored some key challenges and issues that face alternative and innovative approaches to the evaluation of C4D, and suggested some strategies for overcoming them. Key challenges are contextual, structural, institutional and organizational. While neither development nor communication can be extracted from its contexts and the structures within which they operate, conventional approaches to evaluation are not best placed to fully engage with or critique them. The attitudes and policies of funders and of development managers further challenge the use of innovative and participatory approaches. A lack of flexibility of approach towards evaluation for C4D, and a privileging of mainstream results-based approaches, compounds the situation. Impact assessment and requirements to define attribution, further challenges an approach to development that builds upon notions of relationships, values, dialogue and debate.

Approaches like DE and EAR are attempting to practise research and evaluation that serves a fundamentally different purpose than mainstream impact assessment. We recommend innovative and creative approaches to evaluating C4D, and the use of mixed methods, to help ensure trustworthiness and rigour and the inclusion of multiple perspectives. We have presented new conceptualizations of evaluation and shifts in evaluation practice that are highly significant in understanding and evaluating C4D and development, as the examples we have drawn on demonstrate.

In practice, the challenges and solutions tend to exist in a form of tension, as many of our examples in this book illustrate well. The increasing emphasis on short-term accountability competes with the desire to prioritize user interests and needs and to take a long-term perspective (Mebrahtu, Pratt and Lönnqvist, 2007). All of this means that we have to approach our evaluation practice with a highly critical lens, because all that seems to be participatory is not necessarily what it appears, due to issues of power and control. As Mebrahtu *et al.* (2007) demonstrate, different development actors may use the same terminology to mean very different things. They challenge us to put people back at the centre of development, and use evaluation to help to achieve real outcomes and positive change in people's lives rather than perform development accountancy. This is, indeed, the bigger challenge that sits behind the challenges and issues we describe in this chapter.

5 Evaluation capacity development

The Institute to Serve Facilitators of Development, whose English acronym is VBNK, is a not-for-profit NGO in Cambodia. VBNK is a support organization that offers a range of services for capacity development to Cambodian and international development organizations. In her 2011 book *Creative Capacity Development: Learning to Adapt in Development Practice*, Jenny Pearson tells the story of the development of the organization over more than a decade, of how creative capacity development evolved, and the various challenges and learnings that emerged along the way.

Pearson (2011) found that culture and history, especially the recent traumatic violent history in the country, required creative approaches to capacity development, because people were resistant to change and fearful of exploring or stirring emotional depths. Pearson defines creativity in very broad terms, to encompass artistic notions of the creative, such as performance and drawings, but also creative or innovative approaches to encouraging different ways of thinking. These approaches were useful to penetrate beyond understandings of what constitutes learning.

A major challenge and consideration, evident perhaps most starkly in post-conflict countries with traumatized populations, is the importance of considering culture, context and an inherent resistance to change. The idea of challenging control, or of trainers facilitating learning rather than bestowing knowledge on others in a rote fashion, along with a difficulty in accepting the notion of 'shades of grey' over right or wrong, correct or incorrect, presented a raft of challenges to VBNK. Only an understanding of local culture and the recent history of the people could help to explain these points of apparent resistance to new ways of thinking and learning.

Over the years, and working through many challenges, Pearson grew to understand that the complex systems within which we work demand that we take creative risks and learn from them, to bring about new ways of being, doing and thinking. At the same time, contexts can actively work against this, meaning progress in capacity development needs to be considered over the long-term, approached creatively, and will often be incremental.

Capacity development presents opportunities to have positive outcomes at the local level, to offer creative responses to the needs of development organizations, and to proactively introduce new ideas when old approaches are failing. But capacity development faces a series of challenges. Not least, there is a lack of capacity in developing country contexts, and therefore any effort at supporting capacity across the local development sector first needs to develop the capacity of local support organization staff. Only then can they in turn facilitate the capacity development of other organizations. This kind of 'training the trainer' approach was used by VBNK to good effect, but the real imperative for capacity development lay in shifting thinking away from the concept of training, to one of 'learning'.

Pearson (2011) made a major breakthrough in her thinking about capacity development in Cambodia when she learned about a perspective called the Action Learning Cycle. This takes into account the complexity of development and is based on a typical action research cycle of planning, action, reflection and learning. She applied this approach to VBNK over a few years, and gradually saw the organization become more of a learning organization, but it was not straightforward, and was always, and continues to be, faced with challenges. Over the years Pearson learned that development itself, as an activity, a goal and a process, needs to be carefully scrutinized, and organizations and individuals need to regularly reflect on their motives and aims. Likewise, with capacity development, its very purpose, and the ways in which we think about it need to be reviewed and revised as circumstances change and our learning increases.

While the example of VBNK refers to capacity development broadly, in this chapter we focus on evaluation capacity development (ECD) and argue that there are many benefits to be gained from strengthening capacity in evaluating C4D. A holistic approach to ECD increases the sustainability of C4D organizations and initiatives. To do this requires a long-term approach and a shift in how both evaluation and capacity development are approached and understood. Institutionalizing evaluation, developing an evaluation culture within organizations at all levels, and building the evaluation capacities of staff and stakeholders improves the quality of evaluation, understanding of evaluation and its role in the learning process, and improves C4D design and outcomes. Yet as Pearson (2011) found in Cambodia, there are many challenges and points of resistance that need to be identified and overcome.

We begin this chapter by reviewing various understandings and definitions of the concept 'evaluation capacity development'. We outline the need for an alternative approach to ECD and then set out the holistic, participatory, learning-oriented approach to ECD that is an important part of our framework. We explain the principles of this approach, emphasizing its relationship to participatory research, evaluation and learning processes, and the importance of the organizational culture for developing learning organizations. Following this we highlight the many challenges and issues in building evaluation capacities in development contexts, and in C4D in particular. Finally, we suggest strategies and processes for effective and sustainable ECD at the global, national, organizational and community levels, along with strategies for the design and evaluation of ECD.

Understanding and defining evaluation capacity development

Capacity development is essentially about learning – about building skills, knowledge and adaptability (Pearson, 2011), at whatever scale, level or stage in the development process. Yet as Pearson (2011) illustrates very well, we are not all similarly disposed to learning. Learning is not a set of skills that can be taught, but a process and way of thinking and perceiving. Learning and capacity development are approaches, or processes, that can lead to improved and sustainable development outcomes. They challenge approaches that prioritize upward accountability, control, predetermined outcomes, and one-off training activities. Johnson and Wilson (2009) stress the importance of social engagement in learning, and opportunities for learning through joint action. Evaluation capacity development is particularly important for C4D as it struggles to demonstrate its importance to development more broadly, and both capture and demonstrate outcomes.

The process of ECD is about developing the ability of people and organizations to themselves define and achieve their evaluation objectives. This involves three interdependent levels: 'individual, organizational and the enabling environment' (Lundgren and Kennedy, 2009: 81). Preskill and Boyle (2008) highlight the need for capacity building to lead to sustainable evaluation practices within organizations, which means taking a learning-oriented approach, gaining support from management, providing adequate resources, and developing strong systems and processes for evaluation. Ba Tall (2009: 123) notes that capacity 'includes different realities from individual to institutional level' and is usually defined as 'the power of something to perform or to produce'. Like Lundgren and Kennedy (2009) and Preskill and Boyle (2008), she suggests that it is 'a continuing process of learning and change management' (Ba Tall, 2009: 123) and that, like development, it is a long-term process.

Developing evaluation capacity can be seen as part of the process of institutionalizing evaluation and creating an evaluation culture within development agencies and their government and NGO implementing partners. These processes are vital components of any strategy to widen appreciation of the value and significance of C4D in reaching development goals. Bamberger (2009: 14) advises that the institutionalization of impact evaluation (IE) at the sector or national level will only take place if it is locally led, there is strong buy-in from key stakeholders, processes and methodologies are well-defined, it is adequately funded, and there is a focus on evaluation capacity development. Bamberger (2009: 30) advises that an ECD strategy for IE must target at least five main stakeholder groups: 'agencies that commission, fund, and disseminate IEs; evaluation practitioners who design, implement, and analyse IEs; evaluation users; groups affected by the programmes being evaluated; and public opinion'. He explains that users include 'government ministries and agencies that use evaluation results to help formulate policies, allocate resources, and design and implement programmes and projects' (Bamberger, 2009: 30).

However, there is a significant need to provide adequate resources and time for effective ECD and associated learning and reflection processes. A key lesson from the international ECD experience is that 'building an effective capacity for monitoring and evaluation is neither quick nor easy' and there is a need for 'steady and sustained support by international donors' (Schiavo-Campo, 2005: 13). The UN and Expert Panel members we consulted also emphasized the importance of a long-term, sustained focus on capacity development in evaluation for people at all levels. They indicated that this process needs to include staff who are conceptualizing, planning and managing the evaluation of C4D initiatives, as well as staff and stakeholders of NGOs and government partners who are working with development agencies to implement and evaluate C4D. One of the recommendations made by Byrne (2008) in her paper on evaluating communication for social change is the need to redress imbalances at all levels by providing adequate resources and support in order to strengthen evaluation capacity.

The need for an alternative approach to evaluation capacity development

The rationale for more holistic, learning-oriented approaches to ECD includes:

- the need to focus on the long-term, 'big picture' issues of development, sustainability and institutional and organizational change;
- the need to move away from instrumentalist approaches to capacity development towards more holistic, learning-based approaches that include a focus on organizational culture, development and change;

- the need to move beyond technical transfer approaches to training towards action learning methods and the incorporation of indigenous innovation and ideas in the capacity development process.

(Djamankulova, Temirova and Sobirdjonova, 2010; Hay, 2010; Horton *et al.*, 2003)

These needs are exemplified by Hay (2010) in relation to evaluation field building in South Asia:

> In the context of capacity building, evaluation field building entails moving away from an instrumentalist approach that sees the overall goal as improving evaluation for donors, to supporting researchers and evaluation practitioners to build evaluation communities, culture, theory, and practice in support of local, national, and regional development strategies and programs.
>
> (Hay, 2010: 228–229)

Hay also tells us that we need to move beyond an approach to training that is about technical transfer. As Horton *et al.* (2003) suggest, local initiative is required for positive local capacity development. While external agencies can provide training, information and other services, 'each organization must ultimately take responsibility for developing its own capacities to meet its own needs' (Horton *et al.*, 2003: 54). Horton *et al.* (2003: 52) argue that the traditional linear approach to capacity development is flawed since it makes the assumption that developing individual and project-level capacities 'will lead to improved organizational capacity and performance'. From their extensive evaluation studies of capacity development in research and development organizations around the world, they conclude that 'organizational capacities are not developed through training individuals, delivering information, or participating in collaborative projects alone. These can be important components of a capacity development strategy, but only when they address organizational priorities' (Horton *et al.*, 2003: 50). Their research identifies the following weaknesses of traditional approaches to capacity development:

- Individual staff or project-focused support seldom addresses the organization's priority needs.
- A focus on individuals or projects misses the 'big-picture' issues facing the organization.
- Trained individuals may not find an environment conducive to the use of their new knowledge, skills, and attitudes.
- A focus on individuals and projects may even undermine the organization's capacity.

(Horton *et al.*, 2003: 52–54)

Other research has identified a need to move from the instrumental, single-loop organizational learning associated with technical forms of evaluation towards a more 'political type of learning' known as double-loop learning that encourages people to 'question in depth the role of the framing and learning systems underlying the organization's goals, strategies and assumptions' (Suárez-Herrera, Springett and Kagan, 2009: 323). This latter type of learning is particularly important to developing learning organizations that are able to look critically at their systems, processes, and internal and external relationships, and to identify ways they can be improved.

Towards a holistic approach to evaluation capacity development

The 'learning-based' and 'holistic' components of our framework are related in two particular ways to ECD. First, on a broad scale, ECD is seen as a long-term process that focuses on building the capacity of whole organizations along with their partners and stakeholders. It needs to take place at all levels of development organizations to encompass the conceptualization, design, planning, management, implementation as well as the evaluation of C4D. It needs to be approached holistically. This requires evaluation that is embedded into every part of the development process. ECD needs to lead to awareness of the important role of evaluation, and development of required skills, attitudes and knowledge that are appropriate to each evaluation. This must be approached critically and not with automatically applied standard models and methods. It also requires strengthening communication, feedback and evaluation systems in C4D organizations. This will lead to an increase in the usefulness and effectiveness of evaluation and improved relationships, communication, coordination and collaboration between internal and external stakeholders. The whole development cycle and approach to C4D needs to use ECD to become learning- and improvement-oriented.

Second, and following the framework's participatory underpinnings, ECD must be embedded into C4D practice, on the ground, at the practitioner/implementation level. This incorporates the emergent and realistic components of the framework, involves local stakeholders, and taps into local knowledge and social change aspirations and needs. As Box 5.1 indicates, this is the type of holistic, participatory, learning-based approach to ECD that we sought to use in the AC4SC project.

A holistic approach to organizational capacity development

Horton *et al.* (2003: 46–48) highlight the value of adopting participatory, learning-oriented, self-assessment processes for managing and improving organizational capacity development. Based on learnings from their extensive global research, Horton *et al.* (2003) advocate a holistic approach to organizational capacity development. Its principles include:

- take ownership of your organization's capacity development initiative;
- focus on the needs and priorities of the organization as a whole;
- management of capacity development processes is crucial for success;
- prepare for monitoring and evaluation at the outset of a capacity development initiative;
- capacity development is more than a one-off event;
- engage stakeholders in the capacity development process;
- establish an environment conducive to learning and change.

(Horton *et al.*, 2003: 55)

Horton *et al.* (2003) suggest that rather than focusing on building the capacities of individuals and parts of an organization, as in traditional approaches, it is more effective to focus on building the capacity of the organization as a whole and to encourage the active participation of a broad range of staff and stakeholders in the process. This is the approach that we used in AC4SC. Organizational capacity building is a process that 'evolves over a number of years' and development and maintenance of good working relationships between those involved is 'crucial to its overall success' (Horton *et al.* 2003: 56). This approach is highly congruent with the participatory, holistic, learning-based approach to evaluation that our framework advocates.

Box 5.1 *The holistic approach to evaluation capacity development in AC4SC*

The AC4SC project included a significant capacity development component that built on a participatory action research (PAR) approach. Its key aim was to develop the capacity of Equal Access Nepal (EAN), through evaluation, to learn from and improve its activities, as well as influence the evaluation practices of development donors. The research team encouraged EAN staff to see participatory evaluation as an ongoing action learning and programme improvement process that could foster the development of a learning organization and an evaluation culture within EAN. A partnership approach to capacity building was used by, for example, encouraging EAN staff to take some responsibility for facilitation of workshops and meetings, and organizing meetings that engaged various stakeholders (including EAN's competitors) in the project.

Management, radio programme development, outreach and M&E staff took part in key capacity development and critical reflection activities. These activities were collaboratively designed and implemented and based on an initial needs assessment and a critical review of EAN's M&E systems and the effectiveness of the ethnographic action research (EAR) methodology that had been introduced to EAN a couple of years before.

Interactive capacity development activities included practice in the use of various participatory techniques and facilitation of group discussions with community groups, and exercises that encouraged active listening. During capacity development workshops participants took turns to present feedback at the end of each day, reflecting on what they had done and learned, and suggesting what might be given more attention. The M&E team later used the new knowledge, skills, experience and confidence they had gained to train a network of community researchers to regularly collect research data, using a range of participatory methods in the EAR toolkit, which was adapted for the impact assessment process.

As well as face-to-face critical review meetings in Nepal, regular Skype chat meetings held in years 3 and 4 of the project and frequent email communication was effective in building trust and collaborative relationships between EAN staff and the Australian research team. These processes also enabled the Australian research team to give encouragement and support to the M&E team, who often faced considerable challenges in implementing project activities.

A member of the Equal Access International management team conducted a critical review of the project in year 4 of the project. This involved group discussions with the M&E and content teams and interviews with key EAN staff. This produced quite different insights into the challenges and issues that emerged in AC4SC than the Australian team had been able to uncover. During this review the M&E team was encouraged to reflect on the processes used in the project so that they could provide advice to others through a participatory M&E toolkit that we were collaboratively developing. They complained about the way that the AC4SC impact assessment methodology was not predetermined: there was 'too much change and development as we went, no clear vision from start'. While this was deliberate, it also reflected their frustration with the PAR approach, where the research team was facilitating rather than directing developments, and their struggles to adapt to a collaborative learning-based approach, rather than training approach. At the same time, the benefits in terms of capacity building were clearly strong, since the M&E team confidently put forward suggestions for improving the evaluation planning process, and how others might learn from this.

Box 5.2 *Key features of learning organizations*

Based on his extensive experience in international capacity development and organizational development, and those of his colleagues at the NGO Engineers Without Borders Canada, Ashley Raeside has identified the following key features of learning organizations:

> A true learning culture recognises the complexity of any development intervention and the dynamic nature of managing this process. Mistakes are embraced and learnt from. Staff are encouraged and feel safe to be honest and speak out, and the organization itself is flexible and creative. Learning organisations not only ask, but also listen (to communities, staff members, and other stakeholders). They evolve how they operate in response to what they hear. They proactively develop and foster a culture of learning and development among staff members and teams, and develop processes to enable fruitful collaboration. They recognise the importance of decentralised decision-making. In this way they ensure that they have the necessary knowledge, capability and attitude to respond to complex and changing community knowledge and contexts.
>
> (Raeside, 2011: 100)

Developing learning organizations

As Patton (cited in Horton *et al.*, 2003: vi) notes, 'learning how to think evaluatively is learning how to learn'. He makes the important point that:

> ... developing this capacity opens up new possibilities for how evaluations can contribute and be used. It is an experience that the leadership in organizations is coming to value because the capacity to engage in evaluative thinking has more enduring value than a delimited set of findings, especially for organizations interested in ongoing learning and improvement.
>
> (Patton cited in Horton *et al.*, 2003: vi)

C4D organizations can use ECD to become more effective, responsive and appropriate, to ensure they are learning organizations that can effectively respond and adapt in complex and rapidly changing environments.

Box 5.2 highlights the way in which an organization's culture affects how well it can listen, how well it can learn from mistakes and from the outcomes of research and evaluation, and how well it can respond to complex and changing contexts. However, Raeside points out that:

> If learning is not valued at national and international levels, it is unlikely to be supported locally. Equally, if staff at national and international levels do not recognise and understand the dynamics of local-level work, it is unlikely that they will enable spaces or dynamics to emerge to support local learning.
>
> (Raeside, 2011: 100)

Box 5.3 *Key learnings about creative capacity development within organizations*

The essential starting point for effective capacity development is culture

The learning and change required for sustainable capacity development takes place within the ways in which people understand the world, their beliefs, values, attitudes and modes of social interactions.

Learning is a skill that needs to be learned and practised

Not all education systems or approaches teach us how to learn. Learning is a process rather than an event, changing how we have grown up thinking about learning is difficult. Development practitioners need to themselves visibly demonstrate learning practices, if they would like to encourage others to acquire them.

Creativity and learning support relevance and sustainability

Development organizations need to find a balance between, on the one hand, systems, structures and procedures that provide safety through effectiveness, transparency and predictability, with on the other hand, the freedom and flexibility to risk experimentation and innovation.

(Pearson, 2011: 179–184)

Box 5.3 lists some key learnings about creative capacity development identified by Pearson's (2011) work with VBNK in Cambodia. They highlight the need to take the cultural context of ECD into account.

The value of participatory methodologies for evaluation capacity development

Patton (cited in Horton *et al.*, 2003: viii) argues that aiming for multiple levels and kinds of impacts from evaluation is crucial when resources are scarce, such as in the developing world. He notes that those involved in participatory evaluations 'often experience changes in thought and behavior as a result of learning that occurs during the evaluation process' and that 'changes in program or organizational procedures and culture can also be manifestations of an evaluation's impacts' (Patton cited in Horton *et al.*, 2003: v).

Participatory evaluation and action research methodologies are particularly valuable for ECD. The strengths of these approaches include: they use a 'learning by doing' approach that is recommended for adult learners, they enable rapid feedback about the success or failure of an ECD intervention, and they can be a cost-effective method of ECD (Djamankulova *et al.*, 2010; Forss *et al.*, 2006; Taut, 2007; Valery and Shakir, 2005). A key benefit of participatory evaluation approaches is that they can demystify these processes and make them more accessible to a wider range of participants, including community members. Indeed, one of the Expert Panel members in our UN consultations thought that qualitative and participatory methodologies held *'far greater potential in terms of strengthening the research, evaluation and development-capacity of individuals, organizations and communities themselves, in lasting and empowering ways'*, compared with quantitative and survey-based methodologies and methods.

However, as research by Lennie (2005a), Lennie et al. (2009), Forss et al. (2006), Tacchi, Lennie and Wilmore (2010) and Taut (2007) has shown, the use of participatory evaluation methods for ECD raises various challenges, issues and contradictions that need to be taken into account. Those identified by Tacchi et al. (2010: 1) include: 'the power relations between donors, outside evaluation and development specialists and internal M&E staff'; cultural factors that can lead to dependency on research and evaluation specialists; and 'the time required to build relationships and effective communication and engage stakeholders'. We outline other challenges and issues in the next section.

Challenges and issues in evaluation capacity development

There are a number of challenges and issues that have a particular impact on the effectiveness and sustainability of evaluation capacity development in the development and C4D context, including:

- contextual factors in poor, politically unstable, developing countries;
- power relations in ECD projects;
- the complexity of evaluating C4D;
- attitudes to evaluation among donors, C4D organizations and NGOs;
- maintaining and sustaining evaluation capacity;
- facilitating wide participation in evaluation of C4D;
- the wide range of skills required in evaluating C4D.

Contextual factors in poor, politically unstable, developing countries

Developing, implementing and sustaining ECD can present particularly difficult challenges and issues in resource- and capacity-poor developing countries such as Afghanistan and Nepal with high levels of poverty, ill health, illiteracy, gender discrimination, and ongoing political instability or violence. As Valery and Shakir (2005) suggest, the success of ECD is highly context-dependent. While donors and NGOs have been supporting ECD activities for at least three decades, few of these activities occur in conflict or post-conflict settings such as Afghanistan (Valery and Shakir, 2005: 80). Pearson's (2011) work in Cambodia demonstrates the additional challenges that such contexts present.

Among the numerous contextual factors that affected access to and extension of capacity building and health services in Afghanistan, Valery and Shakir (2005) note the erosion of human capacity, the lack of personnel with managerial and technical skills throughout the country, cultural constraints that limit access to health care for rural women, high illiteracy levels, the absence of telecommunications in rural areas, harassment of the international community, violence and political instability. In AC4SC a number of challenges and issues arose which affected the success of our capacity development processes, including language and communication problems, travel restrictions related to political instability, hierarchical social structures that affected the use of PAR processes, regular turnover of M&E coordinators, loss of key leaders, champions and change agents, and other factors related to the complexity of the cultural context (Lennie et al., 2009; Lennie, Tacchi and Wilmore, 2010; Tacchi et al., 2010).

Power relations in ECD

Although power is a central issue in participatory evaluation, it is often ignored (Gregory, 2000). Organizations form networks of people with different agendas and interests and varying levels of power, status, authority, experience and expertise (Cracknell, 2000: 182). The degree of conflict and cooperation among these groups has an impact on ECD and evaluation activities in the C4D area. As our discussion about power–knowledge relations in Chapter 3 suggests, power relations are likely to affect ECD processes, especially as those involved often have different levels of status, knowledge and experience.

As we noted in Chapter 3, the LEARNERS project had a number of unintended and disempowering impacts due to 'inequalities in power and knowledge, the different values and agendas of the participants and researchers, the pre-existing relationships and networks within the communities, and other complex issues' (Lennie, 2005a: 410). Among these other issues was a perceived lack of ownership and control of some aspects of the project along with confusion and misunderstanding about the LEARNERS process. Such issues also emerged within AC4SC, and we became aware of them through our meta-evaluation of the project. For example, we identified a tendency for the M&E team at EAN to defer to the research team as 'the experts' and to agree with our suggested strategies for improvements. This can be understood partly as a result of the educational system in Nepal which has a rigid and conservative structure, in contrast to the participatory processes AC4SC was founded upon (Lennie, Tacchi and Wilmore, 2012).

Complexity of evaluating C4D

As we discussed in Chapter 4, assessing the impacts and outcomes of C4D raises particular methodological challenges and complexities that are less evident in other development areas. Issues here include the need for a better understanding of the communication context (which is often complex and rapidly changing) and the challenges involved in proving impacts to donors and the attribution of impacts to specific C4D elements of larger development initiatives.

Given the difficulty of predicting C4D outcomes and impacts, the use of baseline measures and the development of measurable indicators can be quite problematic. For example, M&E staff involved in AC4SC found it difficult to develop indicators, since the objectives of their radio programmes were constantly changing, based on funding for new radio programme topics. This means that mainstream planning tools such as the logframe are often more difficult to apply to the evaluation of C4D initiatives. ECD projects also need to be based on a good understanding of the particular challenges and issues in the C4D context.

Many C4D initiatives at the country and NGO level are not well equipped to deal with these challenges and complexities, given other constraints and difficult contextual challenges that they face. We saw through AC4SC how attempts to raise awareness and create dialogue, as a contribution to social change, are difficult to evaluate. The tracking of social change requires qualitative and participatory approaches, yet the ability of organizations such as EAN to roll out complex PM&E systems is seriously constrained by a range of factors, including turnover of M&E staff, irregular supply of electricity, and frequent strikes that hamper travel (Lennie *et al.*, 2009).

Attitudes to evaluation

Evaluation of C4D is often donor-driven and undertaken for upward accountability rather than for learning and improvement purposes. It is therefore not always accorded a high level of importance by management and programme staff, beyond a reporting function. Cracknell (2000: 55) suggests that there is a fundamental tension and incompatibility

102 *Evaluation capacity development*

between the two competing objectives of evaluation accountability and lesson learning. It is difficult to adequately satisfy both objectives. In addition, many developing countries complain that evaluation research is 'too costly and too time consuming to be of any use to management' (Khan, 1998: 324). As we have indicated, donors and managers were seen by some of the Expert Panel in our UN consultations as not valuing 'alternative' evaluation approaches that are likely to be more appropriate for C4D. This can affect the amount of time and the adequacy of resources provided for ECD and the effectiveness of strategies that aim to develop an evaluation culture within organizations that implement C4D initiatives. Research shows that a lack of support for evaluation among programme staff and management is a key barrier to effective ECD and evaluation.

Cracknell (2000: 182) also points out that staff attitude to evaluation findings 'will differ according to their role in the organization'. The AC4SC project found that EAN's M&E staff had a lower status than programme production staff, some of whom were high-profile presenters of the very popular SSMK radio programme. Before the AC4SC project began, a few staff, including programme production staff, had received training in EAR. However, there was no system in place to effectively analyse EAR data, provide feedback on it, and make effective use of it beyond the work of the individuals undertaking it. Programme production staff were therefore unable to effectively and systematically utilize this data in reports to donors. While the research helped them to improve some aspects of their work, it did not help them to prove impact. Contrast this with the measurable feedback received through large numbers of listener letters and other feedback about the SSMK programme which indicated that the programme was highly successful, but did not directly help them to understand how or why. The letters were easy to quantify, and the SSMK team therefore felt 'why do we need to evaluate the impact of our work?' As a result, at the beginning of the AC4SC project, most staff thought that EAR was not used very well in their organization and they had not been able to demonstrate its usefulness to stakeholders (Lennie *et al.*, 2009: 4).

One of the most important outcomes of interactive ECD workshops that the Australian research team conducted early on in the AC4SC project was improved 'team building', 'team spirit' and communication and appreciation of the need for a 'culture of sharing' among M&E and radio programme production staff (Lennie *et al.*, 2009). However, at a later point, a critical review of M&E systems identified that:

> While the Naya Nepal program team was cooperating well with the M&E team, the SSMK team was seen as 'resistant' to changing the way it does M&E since they thought their current system was working well. They had also been reluctant to provide content themes to the community researchers in case this affected the number of listeners. M&E staff thought that the SSMK team was very insulated and not open to others entering their group.
>
> (Lennie *et al.*, 2009: 6)

Again, this example highlights the importance of understanding the organizational dynamics and context and attitudes to evaluation before ECD strategies and processes are developed and implemented. It also demonstrates the range of different experiences and knowledge that an organization holds, and that needs to be incorporated.

Maintaining and sustaining evaluation capacity

Maintaining and sustaining evaluation capacity is a key issue when there is high staff turnover in C4D organizations and key 'champions' leave organizations. Employee turnover is a persistent challenge in developing countries where there is often a shortage of people with good evaluation capacities. This can undermine ECD efforts due to problems with maintaining capacity and skills and varying levels of commitment to the ECD process from new staff (Atkinson, Wilson and Avula, 2005; Napp *et al.*, 2002). One of the key challenges which affected the success of the AC4SC project and the ECD process was the regular turnover of M&E coordinators, and loss of key leaders and change agents within EAN. This created problems with continuity, and time was needed to bring each new coordinator up to speed with all the facets of the project. Only the first M&E coordinator took part in the initial ECD workshops with staff, which included developing initial theory of change matrices and practising various participatory tools with community groups. This situation put pressure on remaining staff who then had less time to devote to the project (Lennie *et al.*, 2009).

A holistic approach to capacity development involves the active participation of a broad range of staff and stakeholders in the process, which can cushion the impact of staff turnover (Gibbs *et al.*, 2009). As we have noted, the AC4SC project attempted to use this more holistic approach to ECD. We found that once EAN staff started to talk about EAN as a learning organization the role of evaluation within it became clearer and better valued.

Facilitating wide participation

Effective evaluation of C4D requires a high level of participation from a range of staff, participants and programme or outreach partners. They also need an adequate understanding of C4D and evaluation concepts and a range of relevant evaluation approaches, methodologies and methods, and a willingness to devote time to planning, designing and implementing evaluation processes. Given other demands on their time and energy and other factors, achieving this level of participation and commitment to the process is not easy. Although there are many benefits to involving stakeholders in the evaluation process, Khan (1998: 324) notes that 'where beneficiaries are restricted by unequal power relationships, the ability of evaluators to reach a cross section of beneficiaries will continue to remain a problem'. As Souter (2008) and Slater and Tacchi (2004) point out, it is often difficult for development interventions to reach the most marginalized groups such as the very poor.

Participatory approaches to evaluation and ECD require greater planning and higher levels of participation and engagement than other approaches (Diaz-Puente, Yague and Afonso, 2008). Time and resources are therefore needed for adequate planning, diagnosis of an organization's strengths, weaknesses and capacity building needs, development of trust, and encouraging participation (Diaz-Puente *et al.*, 2008; Horton *et al.*, 2003). A study of self-evaluation capacity building in a large international development organization identified a lack of management support 'through engaged participation' in the ECD workshops (Taut, 2007: 52). However, Forss *et al.* (2006) suggest a need to be realistic about the level of input and involvement in an evaluation that should be expected from senior managers. They also highlight the fact that for deeper learning in evaluation to have occurred they would have had to have 'spent considerable time with programme staff, and to ensure that the interaction between programme staff and the evaluation team made learning possible' (Forss *et al.*, 2006: 138).

Range of skills required

Knowledge and understanding of a range of theories, frameworks, methodologies and methods is needed to undertake effective evaluation of C4D initiatives. A wide range of skills are required to undertake participatory forms of research and evaluation (Greenwood and Levin, 2007; Hearn *et al.*, 2009; Taut, 2007). As well as technical skills, they include: 'strong skills in facilitation, as well as humility, respect for others and the ability to listen' (Narayan, 1993, cited in Boyle, 1999: 143). Other skills include: 'responsiveness to user needs...acceptance of diverse views, [and the] ability to establish rapport and trust' (Green, 1988, cited in Taut, 2007: 49). High-level conflict management and facilitation skills are also needed when stakeholders have contradictory perspectives or there are unequal power relations between participants.

Our research has also found that some popular evaluation methodologies, such as the most significant change (MSC) technique, are not necessarily as simple to use as their handbooks indicate. Indeed, research has shown that the full MSC technique can be quite complex to use effectively (Willetts and Crawford, 2007). We discuss the strengths and limitations of MSC further in Chapter 6.

Effectively using the mixed methods approach to evaluation that we recommend requires a range of skills, knowledge and experience in the collection and analysis of qualitative and quantitative data and in reporting findings. However, as the AC4SC project found, the management, analysis and interpretation of large volumes of qualitative data can be particularly difficult for M&E staff in contexts such as Nepal who lack experience in this area and do not have access to the type of face-to-face training and local support that would more easily and rapidly enhance their capacities in qualitative data analysis. The AC4SC project also demonstrated that, as Jallov (2005, 2012) has shown, community members can be trained to collect useful qualitative data about the impacts of community radio programmes. However, as Lennie *et al.* (2009) note:

> There is a need to ensure that community researchers are very clear about the context and focus of this research work. They also require continuous mentoring and support, and both formal and informal training to increase their capacities and the quality of the data they collect. Effective feedback systems are also needed to maintain motivation and to share learnings and examples of good quality data. This process can take over a year or more.
>
> (Lennie *et al.*, 2009: 8)

Strategies for effective and sustainable evaluation capacity development

This section provides an overview of key learnings about ECD, and reiterates why this is important both for improving the effectiveness of the evaluation of C4D, and improving the likelihood of sustainability. We also suggest strategies for effective and sustainable ECD at the global, national, community and organizational levels, as well as some strategies for the design and evaluation of ECD.

Strategies at the global and national levels

Our research has identified two key strategies for effective and sustainable ECD at the global and national levels:

- engage in and support strong ECD networks and build international and national linkages;
- collaborate with evaluation associations, universities and research institutions.

Engage in and support strong ECD networks and build international and national linkages

It is important to build evaluation communities to support local, national and regional ECD strategies and programmes (Hay, 2010: 229). One of the key strategies for long-term capacity development in the evaluation of C4D suggested in our UN consultations was to establish and build online communities of practice. Box 5.4 provides some good examples of well-established and open C4D and ECD networking initiatives that are providing an effective means of sharing and enhancing learning in this area. In addition, other relevant initiatives are being developed, such as the Media Development Monitoring and Evaluation-Wiki (MediaME) initiative (see http://www.mediame-wiki.net/wiki/).

Such initiatives can provide valuable ways for C4D and evaluation practitioners at different levels to further develop capacities by keeping up to date with the latest ideas, knowledge and practices in the field. They also provide a means for development and C4D agencies, organizations and practitioners to form closer links with each other at international and national levels.

Collaborate with evaluation associations, universities and research institutions

Our own research and the literature highlight the value of collaborating with evaluation associations, universities and research institutions to strengthen evaluation capacities and better practices in this field. For example, Ba Tall (2009) sees the evaluation guidelines, principles and ethical codes of conduct developed by evaluation associations as key tools for developing capacity. She highlights the effectiveness of evaluation associations and networks in building capacity in various developing countries and suggests they can play a key role in organizing national evaluation dialogue amongst development stakeholders and provide a bridge to the international evaluation community (Ba Tall, 2009: 133). Boyle (1999: 141–142) suggests that professional evaluation associations can play a role as facilitators of networks of evaluation practitioners and users. They can promote good practice standards and ethical guidelines, raise methodological awareness, skills and innovations through training, and offer evaluation support. The number of evaluation associations in developing countries has increased dramatically in recent years and some are now well established as strong and effective organizations.

Bamberger (2009) argues that the active involvement of leading national universities and research institutions is critical for ECD in developing countries. Similarly, Balit (2010b: 5) comments on the role of universities in increasing the number of qualified C4D professionals in development institutions and the need for the development of human resources at all levels 'from field workers up to communication planners and managers'. Our research for this book identified a growing number of university programmes in C4D, international development, and related areas, in many different countries around the world, that included courses on research and evaluation. Information on many of these courses can be found on the C4D Network website.

Strategies at the organizational and community levels

We have identified a number of useful strategies for effective and sustainable ECD at the organizational and community levels:

- consider issues of power, knowledge, language and literacy;
- draw on local innovation and experimentation;

106 *Evaluation capacity development*

- take the organizational culture, dynamics and wider context into account;
- foster a learning culture through leadership in organizations;
- empower local staff and communities;
- develop effective knowledge sharing and communication and feedback systems;
- develop appropriate, high quality evaluation processes.

Box 5.4 *Examples of effective online ECD and networking initiatives*

My M&E (http://www.mymande.org) is an interactive Web 2.0 platform to share knowledge on country-led M&E systems worldwide. As well as being a learning source, My M&E facilitates the strengthening of a global community, while identifying good practices and lessons learned about M&E in general, and country-led M&E systems in particular. Registered users can complete their own social profile and exchange experiences and knowledge through blogs and discussion forums. They can also upload documents, webinars and videos. This site is managed by UNICEF and IOCE and supported by several partners.

The Communication Initiative Network (http://www.comminit.com/global) is an online space for sharing the experiences of, and building bridges between, the people and organizations engaged in or supporting communication as a fundamental strategy for economic and social development and change. It does this through a process of initiating dialogue and debate and giving the network a stronger, more representative and informed voice with which to advance the use and improve the impact of C4D. This process is supported by extensive web-based resources of summarized information and several electronic publications, as well as online research, review, and discussion platforms providing insight into communication for development experiences.

The C4D Network (http://www.c4dnetwork.org) is a non-profit organization dedicated to supporting the C4D sector. It aims to facilitate the sharing of knowledge and experience about C4D, and to advocate for an increasingly professional approach and acknowledgement of the C4D sector within development practice. The Network has begun launching a series of online seminars, developed in partnership with the C4D Division of UNICEF. The C4D Network also includes a peer network (www.c4d.org) which is a membership-based online platform that aims to be a place for the lively and useful exchange of knowledge, experience and reflection about C4D.

The Big Push Forward (http://bigpushforward.net) is an informal network of practitioners who are involved in identifying and sharing strategies for encouraging funders and implementers to experiment with and, when appropriate, adopt additional, useful approaches to impact assessment and reporting of international aid programmes and projects. It is creating the space for discussion, debate and the exploration of appropriate approaches for assessing transformative development processes. Initially discussed in September 2010 as the Big Push Back against a narrowing of what is valued and how value is measured, the Big Push Forward initiative seeks constructive ways to advance, conceptually and methodologically, development aid's support of a fairer world, beyond the narrow bureaucratic protocols that assume guaranteed predictable outcomes.

Consider issues of power, knowledge, language and literacy

Vanderplaat (1995: 85) argues that even the more critical models of evaluation have failed 'to deal, in any meaningful way, with... the unequal distribution of discursive power, a central construct in empowerment-based social programming'. McKie (2003: 320) argues that 'Whether we like it or not evaluation has created a language and modus operandi that can be excluding'. This indicates the importance of giving greater attention to the communicative and relational dimensions of participatory ECD, which can affect its outcomes in unintended ways. Including a diversity of community members in participatory evaluation and ECD processes forces us to pay attention to issues related to the appropriateness of language, as well as the perceived value and relevance of participation and evaluation to various groups (Lennie, 2005a: 410).

Valery and Shakir (2005: 93) point out that ECD is 'language-dependent', both in terms of the language of evaluation, and spoken languages. The diversity of local languages and the literacy levels of community participants are key issues that can affect people's participation in certain evaluation activities and was often raised in the AC4SC project. However, many participatory research and evaluation tools have been specifically designed for groups with low levels of written literacy and have been found to be very effective in engaging a wide range of community members in development projects, as the work of Chambers (2008), Liamputtong (2007), Estrella *et al.* (2000) and others has shown. This emphasizes the need for ECD to be adapted to the particular needs of diverse groups.

Draw on local innovation and experimentation

The development of flexible, community-based research and evaluation approaches such as EAR, local adaptations of methodologies such as MSC, and the long history of the use of PAR and other forms of praxis in the field of development highlights the need to look to local knowledge and innovation in order to more effectively and sustainably improve capacities. As Hay (2010: 229) points out: 'Too often models are exported when we know that they are inadequate. Instead of looking to the north for curriculum and methods, field building entails experimentation and indigenous innovation, building on the best ideas available but creating something better'. Hay (2010: 229) further suggests that the on the ground experience of the many thousands of people involved in learning from innovative and locally contextualized development work 'can help stimulate evaluation theory, methods, and applications within a framework of use and practice'.

Take the organizational culture, dynamics and wider context into account

As we have indicated, in order for ECD to be effective an organization needs to be ready for change and open to learning from evaluation, and its environment and culture needs to be conducive to success (Forss *et al.*, 2006; Naccarella *et al.*, 2007; Taut, 2007). As the VBNK example illustrates, in some contexts this can be particularly challenging. However, it is worth working towards through the use of creative and innovative processes. This should be considered as an ongoing, long-term learning and development project.

For an organization to be ready to change in response to evaluation, it needs to be ready to change its habits and practices. This requires a very good understanding of how an organization works and makes decisions; 'how they set objectives; how they resolve internal conflicts; and how they learn' (Cracknell, 2000: 181). ECD needs to reach into all areas of an organization to be effective. When management, programme staff and those responsible for evaluation are part of effective ECD, evaluation is institutionalized, and the impact of key staff members leaving is minimized.

Foster a learning culture through leadership in organizations

A number of organizational factors can hinder learning from evaluation, including 'lack of transparent communication and decision-making, lack of managers as models of learning, lack of reward for innovation and learning from mistakes, and a largely missing collaborative culture' (Forss *et al.*, 2006: 138). Forss *et al.* (2006: 138) suggest that if such contextual prerequisites are not addressed, 'learning from evaluation will encounter too many obstacles to really take off'. As we have already noted, there is a need for leaders to support ECD and evaluation, and to be seen as strong models for learning.

Significant research indicates that leaders in organizations are best placed to foster a learning culture that values individual and collective learning (Forrs *et al.*, 2006; Taut, 2007; Valery and Shakir, 2005). This was also clearly demonstrated in both the AC4SC and the LEARNERS projects (Lennie *et al.*, 2004; Lennie *et al.*, 2009). Our critical reflections on AC4SC suggest that a higher level of engagement with senior EAN staff and greater ownership of AC4SC within EAN would have resulted in the project being given higher priority, especially in the first years when project-related activity, including capacity development, tended to intensify only around visits by the Australian researchers. Our ongoing meta-evaluation of the project highlighted the importance of taking time to form relationships with EAN staff at all levels, based on mutual trust and effective communication and collaboration (Lennie *et al.*, 2012).

Empower local staff and communities

While the leadership of senior management and staff is important, Raeside (2011: 101) stresses the importance of people recognizing their own power to create change in their organizations and the need to empower local staff to act on the knowledge they gain from regularly interacting with communities. Raeside (2011: 101) argues that 'If these staff are not empowered to act on this knowledge, it is unlikely that real power transformation will occur at this level, or that this information will ever trickle into mainstream development debates'.

This was clearly evident in the AC4SC project. At the start of the project the M&E team was in a weak and vulnerable position and had quite a low status within EAN. While the Australian research team encouraged them to be reflexive, they were often criticized by the content production teams who did not think they were collecting data that added value to their programmes. However, over the course of the project the status of the M&E team increased. This was in part due to the richer, more in-depth and useful research and evaluation findings that the M&E team regularly shared and discussed with the content teams. These findings were appreciated because they helped EAN understand community needs, issues, and barriers to communication access, and identify themes for future programming. They also helped EAN to understand ways that programmes could be improved to meet listener and community needs and interests. This data was also useful for formal reports to donors. Similarly, the local researchers in Finding a Voice established their relevance over time, as their research became embedded into the key activities of their organizations (see Box 5.5).

Box 5.5 *Developing and embedding a research culture*

Finding a Voice was essentially a participatory capacity development research project. It had two main aims:

1. to work with community-based media and communications organizations to help them to build strategies and practices to include marginalized people in content creation; and,
2. to build each organization's capacity to research and evaluate these activities through ethnographic action research (EAR), to learn from and improve their effectiveness.

To achieve these aims a team of local researchers and practitioners from Australian Universities, UNESCO, UNDP and local organizations worked together over two years to develop strategies for engaging more people in content creation activities, and to be able to learn from such processes.

One of the key tasks was to build a research culture within the community-based organizations, so that the findings of the local researchers could be fed back into ongoing activities. On their own, EAR researchers often found it hard to develop a research culture, because it was not immediately evident to managers and others in their organization how their research might be useful.

Because of this we started to work with teams from the organizations, and not with individuals. For example, the workshop to develop strategies for local content creation did not only include producers or those responsible for content. We also involved managers and the local researchers. This meant that producers were better able to understand how researchers could bring insights to their strategy development based on their work with local communities. They also better understood how to collaboratively evaluate new strategies and modify them over time, based on research. It also gave the managers ownership, involvement and insight into the content strategy as well as the role of research in its development, and its future evaluation and modification.

Develop effective knowledge sharing and communication and feedback systems

As Cracknell (2000: 186) points out, 'evaluation is all about communication'. Indeed, Preskill and Boyle (2008: 455) suggest that an evaluation culture is reinforced 'through intense and sustained communication about evaluation'. This highlights the importance of good communication and feedback systems and that the language and forms of communication used in ECD need to be appropriate and clear to all staff. Definitions of key concepts need to be clarified and agreed to by all relevant staff as early as possible. This was one of the key activities that we undertook in the early stages of AC4SC and returned to throughout the project as our understandings about the participatory evaluation methodology we were developing became clearer.

Cracknell (2000: 196) notes that although feedback is vitally important, 'ironically this is the branch of evaluation which has so far received least attention'. However, Cracknell (2000: 196) advises that it is now widely recognized that feedback must be planned for and organized 'with as much care and determination as was required for the evaluation itself'.

Box 5.6 *Insights from the 'How wide are the ripples' project*

A recent project commissioned by IKM Emergent aimed to look at how the insights, analysis, evidence and stories generated and documented by international non-governmental organizations (INGOs) during participatory processes can be better used to inform good development policy and planning. Important insights from this project emerged about the significant practical, logistical and ethical challenges of moving information across national and cultural borders, of interpreting and using this information outside of its original context, and about the question of whose knowledge and opinion counts. The project identified accountability and identity issues that affect the ability of INGOs to listen and respond to people on the ground.

It also identified a need to embed the principles and methods that underpin participatory processes throughout the culture and structure of organizations so that information, ideas and insights can flow more effectively and meaningfully. Many of those involved in this project provided examples of the use of various innovative participatory communication and story-based methods that are being effectively used to share learning and knowledge. However, they identified many structural challenges to 'widening the ripples' and the need to engage in development processes that change the 'relationship between INGOs and poor and marginalised communities from one of consultation and implementation, to dialogue and negotiation of plans and activities – and ultimately the kind of world we want to live in'.

(Newman and Beardon, 2011: 18)

Our own work in this area indicates that effective communication and feedback systems are essential to the success of participatory evaluation in C4D organizations. Feedback systems need to be well thought out and timely so that they can be used to improve programmes and evaluation systems. This can help to demonstrate the value of evaluation to programme and management staff, who may be reluctant to spend resources and time on evaluations and ongoing ECD due to pressure to develop or deliver programmes within a set timeframe and budget.

Box 5.6 outlines insights from a recent project that aimed to strengthen and support the role of international NGOs in using knowledge gained from participatory processes to provide better input into development policy and planning.

Develop appropriate, high quality evaluation processes

Weak institutional and methodological capacities affect the quality and credibility of evaluation findings (Khan, 1998: 313). Boyle, Lemaire and Rist (1999: 9) point to the need for 'good reliable data which can be trusted' to enable sound conclusions to be drawn from evaluations. They suggest that if such systems are not available initial efforts need to be put into establishing and developing sound data management and analysis systems. Preskill and Boyle (2008: 455–456) emphasize that sustainable evaluation practice 'is in many ways dependent on the organization's ability to create, capture, store and disseminate evaluation-related data and documents...as well as processes, procedures, and lessons learned from evaluative efforts'. AC4SC used a range of strategies to improve the quality and depth of data gathered by community researchers, including developing a detailed community researcher manual, periodic intensive and refresher training, and regular follow up visits and mentoring by M&E staff.

Strategies for the design and evaluation of ECD

Following the approach of our framework, the design of ECD initiatives needs to be flexible and open to change or revision, based on regular feedback from staff and stakeholders. A key learning from both the LEARNERS and the AC4SC projects is that in the initial phase of ECD initiatives that use participatory research and evaluation methodologies and methods, it is important to keep evaluation methodologies and methods, and M&E systems, as simple and practical as possible. This should help to reduce confusion or lack of motivation and interest among staff and participants, and to increase their usefulness, effectiveness and sustainability. To be effective, this may require spending more time in the initial planning phase on ensuring that the ECD objectives and process are clear to everyone and not too ambitious or unrealistic in their scope. The roles and responsibilities of everyone involved also need to be very clear.

As we have indicated, the ongoing evaluation and meta-evaluation of ECD activities can be very effective in helping to improve evaluation capacity, and in developing evaluative thinking and skills in critical reflection and review within organizations. Ongoing meta-evaluation and critical reviews are also important to gradually increasing the quality and trustworthiness of evaluation findings (Lennie, 2006b; Lennie *et al.*, 2010). In AC4SC, we found that the outcomes of meta-evaluations can also be effectively used to enrich and enliven practical participatory M&E toolkits and to pass on the learnings from ECD projects to others.

Conclusion

There is a significant need to strengthen capacity in evaluation at all levels, from community and field levels to planning and management levels. It is important to take a long-term approach. ECD is an essential part of the process of institutionalizing evaluation and developing learning organizations and an evaluation culture within countries, organizations and initiatives that use C4D. There is a need to consider the following elements of ECD:

- the enabling context of ECD activities and the readiness within organizations for change towards an evaluation culture that is focused on learning, improvement and upwards, downwards and internal accountability;
- the diverse organizational levels and stakeholders groups that need to actively participate in and take ownership of the process and be empowered in order to be most effective;
- the range of capacities and skills that need to be developed, including skills in active listening and learning;
- the need to embed evaluation into all aspects of C4D activities in organizations and initiatives to increase the sustainability of ECD and evaluation practices.

Rather than building the capacities of individuals and parts of an organization, as in traditional approaches, we suggested that it is more effective to build the capacity of organizations as a whole and encourage the active participation of a broad range of staff and stakeholders in the process. Participatory evaluation approaches and PAR methodologies are particularly valuable for ECD. However, using these approaches for ECD raises various challenges and issues. Developing, implementing and sustaining ECD presents particularly difficult challenges and issues for time-, skill- and resource-poor organizations in developing countries.

Strategies for effective and sustainable ECD at the global and national levels include engaging in and supporting strong ECD networks and building linkages through communities of practice. Professional evaluation associations, universities and research institutions are playing important roles in ECD in developing countries. At the organizational and community levels, we need to consider issues of power, knowledge, language and literacy, to draw on local innovation and experimentation, and empower local staff and communities so that their knowledge, ideas and learning can be effectively utilized. It is important to take the organizational culture, dynamics and wider context into account, foster learning cultures through leadership in organizations, and develop effective knowledge sharing and communication and feedback systems, and appropriate, high quality evaluation processes. Valuable learnings about the design of ECD in the C4D context include ensuring that ECD is flexible and open to change, keeping evaluation methodologies and M&E systems as practical and simple as possible, and using ongoing meta-evaluation to improve evaluation capacities and practices and share learnings.

6 Key approaches, methodologies and methods

This chapter describes a number of key research and evaluation approaches, methodologies and methods and critically reviews them in terms of how effective and appropriate they are for evaluating C4D. Most of these approaches and methodologies are seen by Byrne (2009a, 2009b), Byrne and Vincent (2011), Puddephatt, Horsewell and Menheneott, (2009), Parks *et al.* (2005) and participants in our UN consultations as valuable for planning and conducting evaluations of C4D initiatives. Key elements of our framework were used as criteria in making these assessments. We also drew on outcomes of our UN consultations, literature reviews, and our experience in developing, trialling and implementing participatory research and evaluation methodologies in C4D and community-based action research and evaluation capacity building projects. Issues related to identifying and using indicators in C4D evaluations, challenges with using indicators, and alternatives to indicators are also discussed.

Definitions of key terms

Our UN consultations highlighted a need for clear definitions of the terms 'approach', 'methodology', and 'methods' as they relate to evaluation, since they are sometimes used in conceptually confusing ways. We have defined these terms as follows:

By *approach* we mean conceptually distinct ways of thinking about, designing and conducting evaluations. Examples of evaluation approaches are stakeholder-based participatory approaches and the results-based management approach, which is exemplified by the logical framework approach. Other evaluation approaches include developmental evaluation and participatory monitoring and evaluation (PM&E).

By *methodology* we mean the process, design or framework that underpins our choice and use of particular methods, particular approaches to research, monitoring and evaluation, and 'linking the choice and use of particular methods to the desired outcomes'(Hearn *et al.*, 2009: 22). For example, an ethnographic methodology usually includes the use of participant observation, field notes, informant interviews, and other methods that provide rich and in-depth data that enable a better understanding of a particular culture or social context. In some cases an evaluation may use more than one methodology, for example case study and the most significant change (MSC) technique.

By *methods* we mean techniques or tools used to plan an evaluation and to collect and analyse various forms of research, monitoring and evaluation data. We advocate a mixed methods approach in which several methods are included in an evaluation plan. These methods would be selected according to the key evaluation questions, the particular groups who will take part, the resources available, the evaluation methodology, the overall approach and other factors.

For example, our evaluation approach could be participatory evaluation, our methodologies might be empowerment evaluation and case study and we might use a mix of document analysis, interviews, focus group discussions, and surveys as our evaluation methods.

Key approaches and methodologies for evaluating C4D

This section describes and critically reviews various research and evaluation approaches and methodologies that have been identified as effective and appropriate for evaluating C4D and other social change initiatives. It was not possible to review all of the different approaches and methodologies that could be effectively used in the evaluation of C4D but we have selected those that were assessed as particularly useful through our UN consultations and that match our framework well. We have divided these into the following broad categories of research and evaluation approaches and methodologies:

- understanding programme theory and the process of change
- systems and complexity-based
- collaborative and participatory
- action research
- participatory communication and C4D-focused
- feminist and gender-sensitive
- case study
- quantitative survey-based.

There are similarities and differences between these research and evaluation approaches and methodologies. They are mostly participatory, learning- and outcome-oriented. Each has particular strengths and limitations that need to be taken into account when planning an evaluation. This often means that more than one approach or methodology needs to be used since the limitations of one approach or methodology will often be balanced by the strengths of another, as long as they are complementary.

As shown in Table 6.1, our UN consultations found that case study, quantitative survey-based methodologies, participatory rural communication appraisal (PRCA) and outcome mapping (OM) were rated particularly highly by both the UN and Expert Panel for planning C4D evaluations and/or assessing the impacts of C4D. However, as this table indicates, there was a relatively high disparity in the ratings given to a number of approaches

Table 6.1 Ratings for approaches and methodologies considered 'very' or 'fairly' effective for planning C4D evaluations and/or assessing C4D impacts

Approach/methodology	UN Focal Points	Expert Panel
Logical framework approach	80%	58%
Theory of change approach	33%	82%
Outcome mapping	63%	67%
Most significant change technique	75%	58%
Ethnographic action research	38%	64%
Participatory rural communication appraisal	75%	73%
Case study	100%	100%
Quantitative survey-based methodologies	90%	69%

and methodologies, especially the logical framework approach (LFA), the theory of change (ToC) approach, ethnographic action research (EAR) and MSC.

Understanding programme theory and the process of change

One of the first steps in an effective C4D evaluation is to carefully plan the evaluation and to engage key stakeholders in developing a shared understanding of the likely process of change and how change will be assessed. This means working out the underlying theory of change. This section outlines two distinct approaches to doing this: the dominant logical framework (or logframe) approach and the theory of change approach, which is becoming increasingly popular in the international development field. We outline these two approaches and highlight their particular strengths before providing a critique of the LFA and ToC approaches.

The logical framework approach

Since the 1970s the logical framework approach has come to play a central role in planning, monitoring, evaluating and managing international aid and development interventions (Bakewell and Garbutt, 2005; Earle, 2003). Its use is now stronger than ever. The LFA is one of a larger class of tools known as programme logic models that are commonly used in project cycle management and programme evaluation. This approach refers to 'the wider planning procedures of problem analysis, the development of objectives and indicators, and identification of risks and assumptions, which feed into the overall programme plan' (Bakewell and Garbutt, 2005: 3). While there are variations, the logframe matrix is typically constructed of rows listing goals, outcomes or objectives, outputs, activities and inputs, and columns listing indicators, means of verification and assumptions. In theory, the process involved in developing and refining a logframe should involve a number of stakeholders. In practice this is often not the case.

Puddephatt *et al.* (2009: 28) argue that 'a logical model of change should drive any M&E system' and that the logframe 'could be one way to progress impact assessment of C4D initiatives as an interim measure and lay the groundwork for more nuanced evaluation over time'. Proponents of the LFA argue that it provides a 'structured, logical approach to setting priorities and determining the intended results and activities of a project', as well as the basis for evaluating 'the effectiveness, efficiency and relevance of a project' (Dearden, 2001: 3). The LFA has also been praised for encouraging clear and strategic thinking at different levels of a project (Bakewell and Garbutt, 2005; Earle, 2003). It is considered to have learning embedded into the process since it can be used to evaluate programme performance against progress (Johnson and Wilson, 2009).

Similar strengths of the logframe were identified in our UN consultations in which the LFA was assessed as either 'very' or 'fairly effective' by 58 per cent of the Expert Panel and 80 per cent of the UN Focal Points, who made much more use of this approach. The LFA was seen as enabling more effective planning and monitoring by helping people to '*clearly see the linkages of our interventions*', and to '*think things through from the beginning*' in an easy to follow, systematic, step-by-step method. It was also considered to be able to '*give clarity and simplicity to what can be an overly complex design*', and '*essential for identifying what will be tracked, and what baseline data is needed*'. However, as we will discuss shortly, the LFA has also been subject to extensive critique by development practitioners.

The theory of change approach

In order to highlight the difference between the thinking behind the LFA and the theory of change approach, Retolaza (2011) describes two of the kinds of change that occur in our environment:

> *Transformative changes.* Crisis and stagnation prepare the ground for change. This type of change is based on un-learning and liberating oneself from those mindsets, relations, identities, formal and non-formal institutions, etc. which hinder and delay the probability of enacting new realities that are more just and fair in economic, social and political terms.
> *Projectable changes.* Changes based on complicated or simple problems that can be resolved by means of specific projects and actions planned from a linear logic.
> (Retolaza, 2011: 4)

While there are a variety of theory of change approaches, a ToC generally focuses on analysing and proposing actions that lead to transformative changes, which are more complex and 'require flexible thinking-action logic' (Retolaza, 2011: 4). In contrast, projectable changes can be managed using tools such as the LFA (Retolaza, 2011). Understanding the differences between these two approaches to change is important since actions for transformative change are often proposed from the linear, rigid logic of projectable changes rather than from the 'fluid and flexible thought logic' of transformative change (Riso, 2007 in Retolaza, 2011: 4). The aim of a ToC is 'to identify those archipelagos of certainty on which we can feed a thinking-action logic that enables us to navigate through the complex ocean of social change' (Retolaza, 2011: 2). Based on this process, and participants' knowledge and experience, the conditions needed to achieve the desired change can be identified. This is partly done by making our assumptions explicit and by analysing them critically (Retolaza, 2011: 2).

The ToC approach is seen as useful for evaluating complex public policy interventions due to its apparent capacity to accommodate multi-sector activity (diversity), its concern with the relationship between process and outcomes (dynamics) and its emphasis on wholesale change at individual, organizational and system levels (complexity) (Sullivan, Barnes and Matka, 2002: 206). Other strengths of this approach include that it adds value to process–outcome evaluations by 'requiring the link between process and outcomes to be articulated at the beginning of the process', and its capacity to link the 'participation of all relevant stakeholders with a maximization of learning' (Sullivan *et al.*, 2002: 208). Some participants in our UN consultations also thought the ToC approach allows for '*more detailed analysis of different stakeholders, communication flows and processes*' and '*enables targeted project design and M&E*'. It was also seen by one participant as '*good for expressing assumptions about causal changes and for deeper analysis of what is working or not, and for whom etc.*'. As Table 6.1 indicates, there was significant disparity in the assessments of the ToC approach in our UN consultations, with 82 per cent of the Expert Panel rating it as 'very' or 'fairly' effective for planning evaluations of C4D and assessing their impacts, compared with only 33 per cent of the UN Focal Points, who made much less use of this approach than the Expert Panel.

In contrast to the LFA, the ToC approach makes explicit the values that underpin the perspectives of more and less powerful stakeholders (Sullivan *et al.*, 2002). In a ToC, a programme's theory is used to inform the purpose and focus of the evaluation and the key questions to be addressed, and should inform the selection of methods (Blamey and Mackenzie, 2007: 445). A ToC is 'ideally articulated, owned and approved by a wide range of stakeholders' (Blamey and Mackenzie, 2007: 446). Keystone Accountability (2009: 4) suggest that using their structured ToC tool can be 'an exciting and often liberating process of interaction and discovery that helps organizations see beyond their familiar frames and habits... understand the full complexity of the change they wish to see, and imagine new solutions in dialogue with others'. As shown in Box 6.1, we found this to be a useful tool in the AC4SC project. However, we did need to adapt it for our particular purposes.

Critique of the logframe and theory of change approaches

While programme logic models have several strengths and are useful in evaluations that are focused on simple or complicated problems, the LFA and similar logic models have been widely criticized as inflexible and unable to capture change in complex, dynamic contexts. They are bad at accommodating local culture, or capturing unexpected or emergent outcomes or change. Like all models, the logframe represents the simplification of what are often quite complex social processes. It also avoids the importance of process (Earle, 2003) and it has 'handicapped many people and pushed complex systems into linear' (Joseph, 2011: 222). Patton (2011: 18) comments that linear logic models have contributed significantly to clarifying what it is that works or does not work in a programme or initiative. He argues that these models work well 'in simple situations of high certainty and high agreement about what to do', but less well in complex and dynamic situations where the development goal or the social change is less easily defined. These approaches can have a distorting effect when change is 'emergent, evolving and adapting' (Patton, 2011: 18).

A key criticism is that the LFA has an 'overriding concern with accountability, reflecting an audit culture that seeks to reduce uncertainty to measurable goals' (Johnson and Wilson, 2009: 8). This approach is therefore seen as having limited usefulness in situations with complex interactions, unintended or unexpected impacts, and significant differences between stakeholders (Gasper, 2000). The LFA and similar approaches tend to stifle participation, since they 'reinforce relationships of power and control... [embodying] a linear logic associated with things rather than people' (Chambers and Pettit, 2004: 145). An important weakness of the LFA in non-Western contexts is that it does not allow space for styles of communication and working that are more appropriate than Western styles (Marsden, 2004).

As well as a number of strengths, our UN consultations identified serious weaknesses with using the LFA in the evaluation of complex and dynamic C4D initiatives. Their comments reflected several of the limitations identified in the literature. One UN respondent thought that a weakness of the logframe was that they were *'unable to use the full logframe for complex programmes and projects'*, while another UN respondent commented that they *'cannot always account for numerous factors that contribute to social change'*. Comments from the Expert Panel included that the logframe approach was *'generally not participatory, [has] low-levels of flexibility, [made it] hard to talk about dynamic processes, and doesn't express underlying causal theory'*. Similarly, another Expert Panel member suggested that *'it is a delivery plan, not flexible and not impact focused'*. Other comments were that developing a logframe *'can become a box ticking exercise that isn't properly utilized once completed'*, that it is *'easy to gloss over difficulties at the design stage and find at the end that M&E info is actually hard to find'* and that logframes *'can reduce communication creativity'*.

Box 6.1 *Developing an initial theory of change for two C4D radio programmes*

During the AC4SC project, staff of Equal Access Nepal began developing a theory of change for the SSMK and *Naya Nepal* radio programmes. This process was adapted from the Keystone Accountability (2009) tool. Our aim was to develop a shared understanding of the kind of changes that the programmes wanted to achieve and to identify a shared vision of what success would look like. Once this was agreed, the pathways to achieve this vision of success could be thought through and indicators later identified. We emphasized that the radio programmes were only one part of what would make the vision of success happen, that other stakeholders would need to participate in developing the ToCs, and that they needed to be regularly revisited. A one-day workshop was held with management, programme production and M&E staff to begin working through two main steps in the process. This was followed up by meetings of the programme groups, to build on the work undertaken in this workshop.

Step 1: Vision of success

The groups first undertook the 'epitaph' exercise – a way to express how a programme would like to be remembered. The SSMK epitaph was:

> A 'voice' which grew as a 'youth culture' that helped young people of Nepal to believe in what they were capable of by challenging the boundary of traditional society.

Next the groups worked on creating a vision of success: What will they leave behind? What does it look like? The vision of success for SSMK was:

> Youth are aware and empowered through 'life skills' and have created different mediums of sharing ideas and views in society, creating an atmosphere where youths are free to speak their minds and act for the change they believe in.

Step 2: Pathways to success

The two groups then began work on planning for the vision of success. This involved thinking about what the pathways to success would be. Who would be involved? What conditions would need to be in place for this success to happen? The groups made some progress towards identifying the key stakeholders who could help to achieve the vision of success.

While some concerns were raised about the ability of EAN to 'influence' the various stakeholders they identified, workshop participants gained a good appreciation of the value of developing a ToC. They thought the process was a valuable way of bringing the M&E and programme teams together to think through the social change process, and how the radio programmes contributed to that change, in a holistic way.

As Davies (2004: 104) suggests, the challenge is to recognize situations in which the LFA is an appropriate tool. Efforts to bring about change clearly involve many more steps than the logframe allows for and at best 'it is suited to listing parallel processes whose implementation is assumed to be identical from one location to another' (Davies, 2004: 108). Keystone Accountability (2008) further suggests that while logic models such as the LFA are not very useful in developing overall long-term strategies, they can be useful 'to help design specific, short-term strategies where the inputs, activities and objectives can be clearly defined within the overall framework of a theory of change'.

As we noted in Chapter 3, the logframe is based on a 'substantialist' mode of thinking that categorizes things and tends to place secondary importance on relationships among people (Eyben, 2011). The LFA and similar tools do not provide space for analysis of informal interactions and external influences that can be important to successful interventions (Earle, 2003). As Johnson and Wilson (2009: 8–9), citing Biggs and Smith (2003), point out: the 'project management cycle, assumed to promote learning, has taken primacy over organizational settings and cultures and usurped the place of human agency, which can fundamentally influence development programmes and projects'. As Johnson and Wilson (2009) indicate, individuals can have significant influence over the outcomes of development action. Indeed the model for measuring communication for social change (CFSC) developed by Figueroa *et al.* (2002) suggests that particular actors in the development context can be important catalysts for social change. Catalysts, which can be external or internal to the community, are seen in their model as leading to dialogue in a community that can bring about collective action to resolve problems (Figueroa *et al.*, 2002: 6).

The LFA is therefore considered by many to be incompatible with participatory, thinking-action logic and learning-oriented approaches to social change and evaluation (Chambers and Pettit, 2004; Earle, 2003; Johnson and Wilson, 2009; Lacayo, 2006; Retolaza, 2011). Adaptations or improvements to the traditional logframe have been proposed (Bakewell and Garbutt, 2005; Davies, 2004), and Fowler and others (cited in Earle, 2003) have called for more participatory use of the logframe. However, Earle (2003: 14) questions whether 'the problems of language, Western concepts of linearity' and the fundamentally hierarchical nature of the logframe can 'ever be reconciled with goals of empowerment and giving voice to the most marginalized?' Balit (2010a: 7) also points to the problem of applying participatory processes within the rigid timeframes of logframes and results-based management: 'Participatory processes will upset the well defined plan. Donors want quick results. Thus it is easier to implement an information campaign than develop a long-term communication process with the local people'.

Based on these serious shortcomings, we see the LFA as ineffective and inappropriate for the evaluation of long-term, complex and dynamic social change initiatives. In comparison, the more flexible, long-term, participatory, process and context-focused ToC approach is more compatible with the framework presented in this book. However, we need to acknowledge a number of practical, political, theoretical and systemic limitations to applying the ToC approach in practice. They include:

> ...the problem of including 'dissenting voices' in the process, its lack of reference to how power differentials may need to be addressed, and the potential that a bottom up approach to theory could limit other explanations from broader theoretical perspectives.
>
> (Sullivan *et al.*, 2002: 209–210)

Our UN consultations identified other weaknesses of the ToC approach: '*it is often designed to fit the scope and resources of the project (by small NGOs at least) rather than taking in all the external context*' and '*has the same problems as the logframe in that when the context changes the theory has to adjust'*. A further issue encountered in the AC4SC project is the time required to effectively complete all of the steps in the process and for participants to develop a good understanding and appreciation of the holistic ToC approach. We also found that some of the terminology used in the Keystone Accountability tool had to be re-interpreted to make it more understandable to EAN staff. Another issue was the tendency for the logframe approach and the mindset of 'control' associated with this approach to dominate, given the requirements of donors that logframes be used. We discussed the pressure to conform to externally imposed evaluation approaches in more detail in Box 4.2 in Chapter 4.

Systems and complexity-based approaches to evaluation

We now consider two evaluation approaches that are based on systems and complexity theory: outcome mapping (OM) and developmental evaluation (DE). We consider them very useful for planning, developing and evaluating innovative C4D and social change initiatives. We provide a critique of systems and complexity-based approaches and methodologies.

Outcome mapping

Byrne (2009a, b) and Byrne and Vincent (2011) have highlighted the value of outcome mapping for evaluating social change initiatives. The shift from a focus on proving towards developing and improving, which we noted in Chapter 4, is exemplified by the emergence of relatively new planning and evaluation approaches such as outcome mapping, which was developed in response to the 'perceived rigidities' of the logframe (Johnson and Wilson, 2009: 9). The originality of this methodology is seen as its shift from a focus on assessing the impacts of a programme (defined as changes in state – for example, poverty alleviation, or reduced conflict) toward 'changes in the behaviours, relationships, actions or activities of the people, groups, and organizations with whom a development programme works directly' (Earl, Carden and Smutylo, 2001: 1). Drawing on complexity thinking, it recognizes that multiple, non-linear events lead to change. Therefore, instead of focusing on impact, OM focuses on the often subtle changes that are clearly within a programme's sphere of influence, 'without which the large-scale, more prominent achievements in human well-being cannot be attained or sustained' (Earl *et al.*, 2001: 10).

Outcome mapping provides a continuous system for thinking holistically and strategically about how an initiative intends to achieve results. Its focus is on constant improvement, understanding and the creation of knowledge, rather than on proving, reporting and taking credit for results (Earl *et al.*, 2001). It provides a useful conceptual framework for mapping the contributions of people and agencies working together on 'large, complicated/complex, multidimensional, and even multisectoral initiatives' (Patton, 2011: 244). OM has three stages:

1 *Intentional design*, which involves reaching consensus on the macro-level changes that a programme aims to help bring about and planning the strategies to be used. This stage has seven steps which begin with clarifying the vision of what the programme hopes to encourage.
2 *Outcome and performance monitoring*, which provides a four step self-assessment framework for ongoing monitoring of a programme's actions and progress by boundary partners on achieving outcomes.

3   *Evaluation planning*, which helps to identify evaluation priorities and to develop an evaluation plan (Earl *et al.*, 2001: 3).

Outcome mapping is based on the concept of ongoing learning, 'consciousness-raising, consensus-building, and empowerment... for those working directly in the development program' (Earl *et al.*, 2001: 4). It is particularly useful for understanding boundaries and answering questions such as:

- Who are the boundary partners?
- Who touches the boundaries of a program?
- Who is outside the boundaries and how do they impact on program outcomes?

(McKegg and Wehipeihana, 2011)

In our UN consultations outcome mapping was assessed as either 'very' or 'fairly' effective by 63 per cent of the UN Focal Points and 67 per cent of the Expert Panel. Comments on the strengths and weaknesses of this methodology were provided by five Expert Panel members who identified several strengths of OM, including its ability to encourage new ways of thinking about C4D interventions and their evaluation:

> *It encourages outcomes-focused thinking, puts people and behaviours at the heart of the process, and differentiates levels of change.*
> *It broadens the perspective as to the range of stakeholders and 'boundary' partners and the difference in relationship and impact of a C4D intervention from the perspective of these different groups.*
> *OM is useful because it focuses on results that are directly related with a particular programme or project and does it by measuring how peoples' lives have changed and the sense of ownership they acquired over the programme or project.*

Developmental evaluation

As we noted in Chapter 4, developmental evaluation, like EAR, was developed in response to an identified need to move beyond standard approaches to evaluation, and to develop an approach that would help programmes become more effective. DE draws heavily on systems and complexity theory and supports the development of innovations such as social and organizational change initiatives and large-scale system interventions (Patton, 2011). It was designed for use by initiatives with 'multiple stakeholders, high levels of innovation, fast paced decision-making, and areas of uncertainty [that] require more flexible approaches' (Dozois, Langlois and Blanchet-Cohen, 2010: 14).

In this approach, the evaluator is often part of a team whose members 'collaborate to conceptualize, design and test new approaches in a long-term, ongoing process of continuous development, adaptation, and experimentation, keenly sensitive to unintended results and side effects' (Patton, 2011: 1). DE can include any kind of evaluation method, design and type of data and any kind of focus – for example, processes, outcomes, impacts and costs (Patton, 2011: 307). One of the Expert Panel in our consultations used DE to:

> *gather data (situation analysis) and inform critical/creative thinking during an ongoing process of 'developing' a model or project – for example, if there is a big change in context and you have to adapt – or when one has to respond and adjust in complex environments, for example.*

Key approaches, methodologies and methods

Critique of systems and complexity-based approaches and methodologies

While systems and complexity-based evaluation approaches and methodologies have many strengths, and are a key aspect of the framework presented in this book, they also have some limitations and weaknesses that need to be acknowledged. Our UN consultations identified some issues with the complexity, 'overly detailed' and time-consuming nature of the OM methodology and difficulties with the terminology:

> *The terminology can be exclusive and the process can be long. Encourages good understanding among participants, but is less easily communicated from them to others. The tools for collecting evaluation information need more development.*
>
> *It is constrained by its overly detailed methodology. It is difficult to apply, particularly if there are few resources.*

Another respondent highlighted the skills that are needed to use OM well: '*The only weakness is that it all depends on the people who are using the methodology*', while OM's lack of focus on impacts was seen as both a strength and a weakness.

While developmental evaluation has many strengths, McKegg and Wehipeihana (2011) commented in their workshop on DE that 'it's a challenging journey'. They also raised the issue that governments are often not keen to sign up to something new, which may not work, and that developing relationships and trust is important to the successful use of DE. As with OM and other forms of participatory evaluation, some specialized skills are needed to effectively undertake a DE. As well as skills such as communication, facilitation, active listening and flexibility, 'at a *minimum*, a DE needs to have some facility with strategic thinking, pattern recognition, relationship building, and leadership' (Dozois *et al.*, 2010: 22, authors' italics). A further issue is that while DE takes a somewhat critical approach, it lacks an explicit focus on gender and power relations that is important to the effective evaluation of C4D and social change initiatives.

Participatory evaluation approaches and methodologies

In this section we review and critique PM&E and MSC, which were identified in the literature and in our own research as valuable for the evaluation of C4D and other development initiatives. Other relevant collaborative and participatory evaluation approaches and methodologies include: equity and human rights-based evaluation approaches (Bamberger and Segone, 2011), the transformative research and evaluation framework (Mertens, 2009) and empowerment evaluation (Fetterman, 2001; Fetterman and Wandersman, 2005).

Participatory monitoring and evaluation

As we have emphasized, participation is fundamental to C4D and its evaluation. Along with many others, we therefore recommend PM&E as an effective approach to actively engaging stakeholders in all stages of the evaluation of C4D initiatives through two-way communication, feedback, mutual learning and strengthening evaluation capacities and ownership of the process (Byrne *et al.*, 2005; Myers, 2005; Parks *et al.*, 2005). PM&E differs from traditional M&E by 'attempting to include all stakeholders in all aspects of the process' (Holte-McKenzie, Forde and Theobald, 2006: 365). The aim is to build PM&E into the whole project cycle, providing information that can be immediately fed back into a project to improve its performance or better meet its objectives (Vernooy, Qiu and Jianchu, 2003: 29). It also enables local people to develop strategies that provide learning about their own communities and for planning and evaluation purposes (Parks *et al.*, 2005: 11).

The concept of PM&E is not new. It draws from over 30 years of participatory research traditions, including 'participatory action research (PAR), participatory learning and action (including participatory rural appraisal or PRA), and farming systems research (FSR) or farming participatory research (FPR)' (Estrella, 2000: 3). It emerged because of the limitations of conventional M&E, which is seen as mainly serving the needs and interests of project implementers and donors (Vernooy *et al.*, 2003: 29). However, there are many local forms of PM&E 'that go unrecognised, as they are often regarded as common-place practice and part of daily activity' (Estrella, 2000: 3).

PM&E includes a set of principles and a process where 'The process is at least as important as the recommendations and results contained in PM&E reports or feedback meetings' (Parks *et al.*, 2005: 7). PM&E has been defined as:

> ... any process that allows all stakeholders – particularly the target audience – to take part in the design of a project, its ongoing assessment and the response to findings. It gives stakeholders the chance to help define a programme's key messages, set success indicators, and provides them with tools to measure success.
>
> (Myers, 2005: 19)

Two main streams of PM&E have been identified:

1. *Practical PM&E* which is focused on the pragmatic and fostering the use of evaluation. This is seen as similar to developmental evaluation and 'stakeholder-based evaluation'.
2. *Transformative PM&E*, which is based on emancipation and social justice activism. It focuses on the empowerment of oppressed groups and has similarities to transformative versions of 'empowerment evaluation' and 'democratic evaluation' (Parks *et al.*, 2005: 10–11).

In practice, there are overlaps between these two streams (Suárez-Herrera, Springett and Kagan, 2009).

The most significant change technique

The MSC technique has become widely used or recommended in C4D and development contexts (see, for example, Bhattacharya, 2007; Jallov, 2007; Parks *et al.*, 2005; Willetts and Crawford, 2007; Wrigley, 2006). This methodology involves assessing the changes and impacts that have happened as a result of an initiative, through the collection and analysis of stories of significant change. Participants and stakeholders decide what sort of change should be recorded and participate in selecting and analysing the stories of change that are collected. Data from the process can help to improve an initiative and to assess how well an initiative or programme as a whole is working (Davies and Dart, 2005). A key aim is to encourage continuous dialogue through and between the various levels of an organization. When this process works well, it can be a powerful tool for ongoing evaluation and learning (Davies and Dart, 2005; Willetts and Crawford, 2007).

This methodology is highly participatory, especially when all of its steps are undertaken. It is compatible with complexity and systems thinking, capable of taking the complex

> **Box 6.2** Example of a significant MSC story: 'Empowered to protest early arranged marriage'
>
> *I have three brothers, Mum and Dad and myself in my family. My elder sister is already married and living with her family. When I was in grade 8, I started listening to the SSMK radio programme. My elder sister and her friends used to listen to it and discuss about the radio drama. This encouraged me to listen to it regularly. When my sister was in grade 10, my parents told her that her marriage was fixed. Everyone in our family was totally surprised.*
>
> *Later when I was in grade 10, I came to know that my parents had decided my marriage too. I went to my parents and told them that my reproductive health system has not developed yet and I am not mentally and physically ready for it. And most importantly, I haven't completed my studies yet. I told them that I would like to be independent first and then only I will decide when and where should I marry and that this is also my right.*
>
> *I was able to gather all my energy to protest against my parents' decision which is the most significant change for me. Most of the time in our society, our parents decide for us which I was able to protest. I cannot remember the particular episode now but I have heard a story in the SSMK drama about a girl who suffered after early marriage and she was unable to tell her parents that she wasn't prepared for it. This encouraged me to make my own decision and now, as a result, I'm working as a teacher in a boarding school and at the same time completing my Bachelor's level study.*

nature of development and change into account, and of capturing unexpected or unanticipated change. It takes a learning-based approach in which developing skills and shared understanding and identifying shared values among programme staff at different levels and stakeholders is important.

The MSC technique was assessed as either 'very' or 'fairly' effective by 75 per cent of the UN Focal Points and 58 per cent of the Expert Panel. One of the Expert Panel identified a number of important strengths of MSC, including its potential to be empowering and to provide 'group learning':

> *People love telling and hearing stories, if the environment is safe and trust and rapport well established. Caters to the unexpected and unpredictable. Enables people to tell their own stories, in their own words, and to have these listened to by an interested outsider, in a safe environment. The process can be empowering both for the interviewer and the interviewee... MSC can really capture the rich detail of changes in the lives of people, communities and organizations involved.*

The collection and analysis of personal stories of change that could be associated with listening to the SSMK and *Naya Nepal* radio programmes was an effective element of the AC4SC methodology. Box 6.2 provides an example of an MSC story which was collected by community researcher Lila Devkota in the Dang district of Nepal as part of the AC4SC project. This story was selected by a small community group as the most significant story in the domain 'changes in personal development', which was identified as a key domain of change for the SSMK programme. This story highlights the power of storytelling in the evaluation of a C4D programme and how direct programme outcomes can be successfully identified through the MSC process.

Limitations and issues with participatory evaluation approaches and methodologies

The use of participatory evaluation approaches raises a number of challenges and issues including: the funding, time and resources required to build evaluation capacities and rapport; issues with including a diversity of people in the evaluation; and the need to take power, ethical, language and cultural issues into account.

Some complexities and challenges have been found when using the full MSC approach in development contexts. They include: the need for rigorous planning of each stage in the M&E cycle and to ensure adequate representation of data sources; the need for higher-order skills than many conventional M&E methods; problems with conveying the concept of 'most significant change' to villagers; issues with power imbalances and the translation of stories; and the extensive time required for story selection (Willetts and Crawford, 2007). The successful implementation of MSC also requires support from senior management and 'an organizational culture that prioritizes learning and reflection' (Willetts and Crawford, 2007: 377). Several of these challenges and issues were also identified in AC4SC. MSC is not a stand-alone methodology and must be combined with other approaches for an effective evaluation.

All participatory evaluation methodologies are strengthened when they openly address issues of gender, power and control and they acknowledge the complex challenges, contradictions and paradoxes that often emerge in participatory processes that seek empowerment and change. They are also more suitable to long-term community-based projects where there is a commitment to meaningful participation by all stakeholders. Other limitations of participatory approaches are identified later in this chapter.

Action research approaches

We now briefly review and critique participatory action research and highlight its value in C4D research and evaluation. Another relevant action research (AR) approach, which is congruent with our framework, is appreciative inquiry (for more details see Hearn *et al.*, 2009: 53; Patton, 2011: 234).

The term action research describes a wide range of methodologies. Hearn *et al.* (2009: 1) define it as 'a methodology, an overarching process for managing enquiry, and a research culture that can engage all stakeholders in ongoing cycles of planning, acting, observing, and reflecting'. The aim of AR is not only to understand an issue or problem but also to provoke change of some kind. AR is seen as particularly valuable for developing, researching, evaluating, and managing new media initiatives 'that involve constant innovation and change; have unpredictable outcomes; and require flexibility, creativity, and an inclusive, user-centred approach' (Hearn *et al.*, 2009: 9).

Participatory action research is the most widely used participatory research methodology (Hearn *et al.*, 2009). PAR and feminist PAR have been successfully used in community development projects around the world for over 40 years (Brunner and Guzman, 1989; Gatenby and Humphries, 2000; Hearn *et al.*, 2009; Maguire, 1996). These methodologies seek to increase the empowerment and inclusion of people, to build community capacities,

126 *Key approaches, methodologies and methods*

and to produce knowledge and action that is useful in addressing community needs and goals (McTaggart, 1991; Papineau and Kiely, 1996). PAR takes a critical approach that 'begins with a concern for power and powerlessness. It aims to produce knowledge from the perspective of those who are marginalized or disadvantaged' (Hearn *et al.*, 2009: 13). Further, PAR aims to transform theory and practice and to connect the local and the global (Kemmis and McTaggart, 2000).

Communication and dialogue are important to the PAR process, which seeks to include and involve a diversity of community members, to incorporate local knowledge and ideas, and to enhance democracy and individual, group and community empowerment. PAR is a political process because it involves people making changes together that affect others (McTaggart, 1991). PAR seeks to involve all stakeholders in the whole research process. Critical reflection is a crucial step in each PAR cycle. This element of the process is particularly important for ongoing learning and developing strategies for improvement as part of an evaluation.

Critique of action research approaches

The complex and contradictory nature of participation and empowerment discourses and practices and the often idealistic nature of these discourses have been illuminated in numerous critiques (see, for example, Carpentier, 2011; Cooke and Kothari, 2001; Cornwall, 2008; Lennie, 2009; Lennie, Hatcher and Morgan, 2003; Papa, Singhal and Papa, 2006). These critiques suggest a need to give greater acknowledgement to differences between participants, including those related to gender, power and knowledge, and to take both the macro and micro contexts and the politics of participation into account. They also suggest that a rigorous, ongoing meta-evaluation and critical reflection process is required to develop more effective theories and practices in this field (Lennie and Hearn, 2003; Lennie, Tacchi and Wilmore, 2012).

As well as the greater amount of time, energy and commitment required to undertake activities compared with other approaches, a high degree of trust is needed between those involved in AR projects, which can take some time to develop. In addition, when people with different levels of power, status, influence and knowledge come together, the ideal of participation becomes problematic (McTaggart, 1991: 170).

Participatory communication and C4D-focused methodologies

This section describes and critiques three participatory research and evaluation methodologies that were specifically designed for C4D initiatives: ethnographic action research, the AC4SC impact assessment methodology, and participatory rural communication appraisal (PRCA). We have already introduced EAR and the AC4SC methodology in this book but provide more detail here about these methodologies.

Ethnographic action research

Ethnographic action research takes a highly participatory, holistic, learning-based, embedded approach to research and evaluation and capacity building. It is based on systems thinking, especially through the concept of communicative ecology. As we have noted, EAR was mainly designed for use in community-based ICT or media projects and has been applied in a number of major development projects conducted in South and South

East Asia and elsewhere. A key aim of EAR is to develop a research culture through which knowledge and reflection become integral to an initiative's ongoing development (Tacchi, Slater and Hearn, 2003; Tacchi *et al*., 2007).

While EAR is mainly focused on the collection of qualitative data, several participatory EAR tools enable the production of charts, maps and diagrams which can provide valuable quantitative information (see http://ear.findingavoice.org), making it very effective in a mixed methods evaluation of C4D.

EAR was assessed as either 'very' or 'fairly effective' by 38 per cent of the UN Focal Points and 64 per cent of the Expert Panel, who were more likely to use this methodology. Respondents identified many strengths of EAR as a participatory, holistic, learning-oriented methodology that can stimulate new ideas and contribute to the ongoing improvement of community-based ICT or media projects. They included:

> ... *captures relevant data through the active involvement of the researcher with different participant group/s to document their context – geo-physical, cultural, socio-economic and political realities.*
>
> ...*provides timely feedback and ongoing learning. Responsive to programmatic changes. Puts people at the heart of the process.*
>
> ... *the sustained interest of an (informed) outsider can be welcome, can catalyze new ideas and behaviours. Facilitating AR processes can be enriching and fuel significant learning amongst all involved.*

The AC4SC impact assessment methodology

This methodology emerged from a four-year PAR project that the authors were involved in that aimed to develop, implement, and evaluate a participatory impact assessment methodology with and for Equal Access Nepal (see Chapter 1 for more details about the project). The holistic methodology that was developed through the project led to the development of a transferable participatory methodology for use by other Equal Access staff in various countries, and more widely by other C4D initiatives. The *Equal Access participatory monitoring and evaluation toolkit* (Lennie *et al*., 2011) is currently being trialled in Niger.

The AC4SC methodology was built on EAR and PM&E, and the principles and methods of CFSC, which promotes dialogue through participatory and empowering approaches. Taking a pragmatic approach, it aimed to address donor requirements for impact assessment, based on accountability and proving impact, as well as the need for ongoing feedback that could be used to improve C4D radio programmes. A key challenge was to design a participatory impact assessment methodology that was practical and sustainable, but also innovative and rigorous and would provide more useful indicators of social change.

The methodology encourages the development of sustainable C4D programmes, ongoing evaluation capacity development and the ongoing development and improvement of M&E systems and processes through its comprehensive toolkit, which was a key outcome of the project. This toolkit emphasizes the importance of effective planning, communication, feedback and reporting in the PM&E process, with both internal and external stakeholders, and regular critical reflection and analysis of the PM&E process. It includes a module on the effective 'Critical Listening and Feedback Sessions' technique which was developed by EAN to provide rapid feedback to improve their radio programmes. Comprehensive manuals for community researchers and for using the MSC technique were also developed.

As part of the project, a network of trained community researchers was created to gather continuous feedback on two popular radio programmes, contextual information (including information about local issues and concerns), and data on programme impacts and outcomes. Community researchers and M&E staff regularly collected MSC stories and other qualitative and quantitative research and evaluation data, including statistical data collected from short questionnaire surveys. EAR methods such as participant observation, in-depth interviews, and participatory tools and techniques were used that produced maps, diagrams, charts and other information about communities and their problems and issues, their communication systems, and relationships between people, including gender and caste relationships. This participatory, mixed methods approach emphasizes the importance of triangulation to increase the quality and rigour of evaluation outcomes. Triangulation is the process of combining multiple methods and perspectives with various types of data sources in order to cross-check the results of an evaluation (Patton, 2002). This evaluation methodology and the M&E systems established in AC4SC were continued by EAN following the end of the project in March 2011.

The AC4SC methodology aims to develop learning organizations that continually improve what they do and regularly critically reflect on how well they are meeting their vision and goals. This process involves listening to what people think about C4D activities, and engaging them in dialogue about what impacts these activities have had on their lives and communities and what they would like the organization to do in the future. Our meta-evaluation of AC4SC found that the use of this approach resulted in better communication and cooperation between M&E and programme staff in EAN and more effective utilization of M&E data collected from listeners and others to continually develop and improve EAN's radio programmes and related activities (Lennie *et al.*, 2012).

Participatory rural communication appraisal

Participatory rural communication appraisal is a 'quick, multidisciplinary and participatory way to conduct communication research' and to ensure that C4D programmes are 'effective and relevant to them' (Anyaegbunam, Mefalopulos and Moetsabi, 2004: 1). In PRCA community members participate in planning C4D programmes from the beginning. The process involves identifying, defining and prioritizing the needs and problems of the people, identifying segments of the community who are most affected by these problems, and opportunities and solutions that exist in the community. This methodology aims to discover issues that can be resolved through communication and identifies the traditional and modern communication systems in the community that will be used to interact with people during programme implementation (Anyaegbunam *et al.*, 2004: 12). Combined with a baseline study, PRCA is seen as 'a powerful tool to arrive at clear communication objectives in order to plan, implement and manage effective communication activities with the people' (Anyaegbunam *et al.*, 2004: 12).

PRCA is considered to be an innovative methodology that combines participatory approaches with communication methods that aim to investigate issues, especially in rural contexts, while building the capacities of those involved. It also allows stakeholders 'to play an active role in defining their realities and priorities' (Mefalopulos, 2005: 249–250).

In our UN consultations PRCA was assessed as 'very' or 'fairly' effective by 75 per cent of the UN Focal Points and 73 per cent of the Expert Panel. Strengths of PRCA were that it *'stimulates/encourages participation and discussion with stakeholders at all levels'* and enables *'understand[ing] from participants' perspectives, the strengths and weakness of any given program'*. PRCA includes quantitative knowledge, attitudes, behaviours and practices (KABP) baseline surveys for situation and communication analyses. One Expert Panel member thought this made it *'a very powerful and comprehensive approach, especially for BCC [Behaviour Change Communication] benchmarking'*.

Critique of communication and C4D-focused approaches

While EAR has proved effective in a number of major media and development projects, some limitations and issues with this methodology have been identified (see Hearn *et al.*, 2009). A key challenge for community ICT and media centres involved in EAR research (and C4D organizations more broadly) has been obtaining widespread participation, especially from the poorest local communities. Research in Kothmale, Sri Lanka found that both women and Tamil communities had far fewer opportunities to engage with the project, which was intended to be for all the local communities, although participation was possible for some women and for many young people (Tacchi and Kiran, 2008).

MacColl *et al.* (2005) also identified ethical issues in using EAR for understanding and facilitating distributed collaboration in the Australian context that are likely to apply in the development context. These issues include the difficulty in obtaining informed consent from participants due to the wide-ranging nature of the observations conducted by the researchers, and the possibility that the risk of harm to participants and the agents of change may be increased because 'change is fundamentally risky' (MacColl *et al.*, 2005: 3).

Other weaknesses or limitations of EAR that are commonly raised in relation to participatory evaluation methodologies were identified in our UN consultations. EAR was seen as *'resource intensive'*, *'time consuming and requires necessary expertise'* but *'captures depth and nuances of context, over time, which is hard or impossible to do at scale'*. A further issue is that it *'may be merely descriptive without attempts to measure'*. In addition, the *'longitudinal nature of [an EAR] study is not suited to UN's short term allocation of funds for research (usually <6 months)'*. It also requires *'long term planning with defined and agreed benchmarks, the nature of which may shift and change over periods of time sometimes necessitating constant monitoring and adjustment'*. An organizational structure that allows for flexibility and adaptation is also needed to enable EAR to be effectively implemented.

Similar challenges and issues related to achieving widespread community participation in the PM&E process and the extensive time and resources required to conduct these activities and provide effective capacity building emerged during the trial of the AC4SC methodology (Lennie *et al.*, 2008, 2009). Initial data collected by community researchers was of variable quality and relevance and did not provide the type of in-depth qualitative data that was most useful to the impact assessment process. However, this was addressed through ongoing capacity development and mentoring. There was also some resistance from programme staff to changing existing M&E processes, and issues with the perceived complexity of the methodology and the participatory approach. The hierarchical relationships and society in Nepal also presented 'a considerable challenge to the implementation of CFSC and M&E systems and practices based on a participatory methodology and philosophy' (Lennie *et al.*, 2008: 5). Constraints also emerged 'between the "ideal" practice of setting participatory objectives and indicators and the realities of NGOs responding to funders' predefined goals and criteria and requirements of a standardized M&E approach' (Lennie *et al.* 2008: 4).

PRCA uses C4D and a participatory, holistic approach to research that is in keeping with our framework for evaluating C4D. However, a critical analysis of the PRCA handbook by

Anyaegbunam et al. (2004) suggests that it does this in a very uncritical way that neglects potential conflicts and the reality of gender and power relations between diverse groups. It also assumes that participation will automatically lead to empowerment. Moreover, it incorporates ideas and techniques from the logframe approach which have limited compatibility with a participatory approach to research and evaluation. PRCA therefore mixes approaches that come from different paradigms. Rather than emphasizing the need to embed evaluation into the process, the PRCA handbook sets out a step-by-step process for developing a PRCA programme in which evaluation comes at the end, using a traditional baseline study and summative evaluation approach. A quantitative survey questionnaire and observation are the only methods suggested for use in the baseline study, which draws from the outcomes of PRCA research.

Our UN consultations also noted that PRCA '*cannot be generalized to the entire population*' and '*require particular skills and resources*'. The focus on obtaining quick results also raises issues in terms of developing effective rapport and relations of trust with participants and the value of this methodology for sustainable processes of social change. PRCA would therefore need to be adapted to more adequately fit our framework for evaluating C4D.

Feminist and gender-sensitive approaches

This section provides a general overview of various feminist and 'gender-sensitive' approaches to research and evaluation. They are important to include in the process of researching and evaluating C4D since they strongly encompass the principles and framework for evaluating C4D that we have presented in this book. We also consider some of the limitations and issues that arise in this field. There is a large literature in this area and we cannot do justice to it here. Readers are encouraged to seek out the literature we refer to below, which provides more in-depth coverage of feminist approaches and methodologies and the many challenges and issues associated with gender-related research and evaluation.

Feminists have mounted devastating critiques of the concept of objective, value-free research and have reflexively analysed the complex power relations enacted in social research, including feminist research that aims to be empowering and inclusive (Gatenby and Humphries, 1996, 2000; Lennie, 2005b; Lennie et al., 2003). They have also highlighted the need to situate issues of gender within other 'conditions of oppression' such as caste, ethnicity, religious orientation and sexuality (El-Bushra, 2000; Wilkins, 2005: 262).

There are many different forms of feminism, including praxis-oriented, poststructuralist and liberal feminism, and ecofeminism. However, in practice there are commonalities and inter-relationships between them. Several different approaches to feminist research and evaluation can be identified, including feminist PAR (Gatenby and Humphries, 1996, 2000), feminist participatory research (Joyappa and Martin, 1996; Maguire, 1996; Martin, 1994), feminist evaluation (Humphries, 1999) and 'feminist deconstructive ethnography' (Lennie, 2005b, 2009). Various approaches to gender research, analysis and evaluation in the development field have emerged, such as 'gender-sensitive participatory impact assessment' (Ellis, 1997) and 'gender equality and human rights-responsive evaluation' (UN Women, 2010).

Although there is no one unified feminist theory or research methodology, common features of the methodology used by activist feminists, in particular, can be identified.

Collaborative and participatory methods, multidisciplinary approaches and multiple methods are often used in activist feminist research. A 'feminist consciousness' (Stanley and Wise, 1990) is considered central to the research process. Many of the methodologies and methods used by feminists to undertake research and evaluation are similar to those used by non-feminist researchers. However, feminists often find that methodologies and methods need to be redefined or adapted to match their theories and their often more political or activist purposes (Liamputtong, 2007).

Based on her evaluation and critique of the Enhancing Rural Women's Access to ICTs research project, Lennie (2005b, 2006a, 2009) advocated the use of a pragmatic, pluralist, critical and open inquiry approach to feminist research and evaluation that incorporates praxis and poststructuralist feminist theories and methodologies. This was considered to produce effective strategies for meeting women's communication and interaction needs and to enable honest and trustworthy accounts of evaluations to be presented. Various strengths of participatory feminist evaluation methodology were identified in this research. It enabled a diversity of women's knowledge, ideas and experiences to be represented, validated and included in the evaluation and the outcomes of the ongoing evaluation to inform the redesign of project activities to better meet women's needs.

While there are differences between various feminist approaches and methodologies, with some being more pragmatic and grounded in lived experiences and others being more theory-driven, a common focus of feminist research in the development area is in providing critiques of development discourse and practice. This has resulted in alternative ways of thinking about development and its effects, new solutions to the complex challenges and issues they have raised, and more effective and culturally appropriate strategies for doing gender-oriented evaluation, as shown in the example in Box 6.3.

Challenges, limitations and issues with feminist and gender-sensitive approaches

As well as the various challenges, limitations and issues that we have already identified with participatory evaluation and AR approaches, Lennie (2005b, 2009) identified some limitations of participatory feminist evaluation methodology. They include the tendency for such evaluations to maintain a binary logic that can reinforce the status quo rather than challenge it, and to gloss over issues of power and knowledge. However, feminist deconstructive ethnography was effective in countering these limitations by 'enabling taken-for-granted assumptions about important feminist concepts such as "empowerment" to be problematized, and the sometimes unintentionally oppressive effects of projects with emancipatory aims to be illustrated' (Lennie, 2005b: 133). This indicates the value of taking an open approach to feminist research and evaluation that draws on multiple feminist theories and approaches and multiple methodologies.

We were interested to find that gender-sensitive approaches and gender analysis were not suggested as effective methodologies for C4D research and evaluation in our UN consultations. The only mention of gender was in relation to the use of community/village mapping for comparing different groups and genders. Clearly there are many difficulties with openly advocating feminist frameworks in the development context and feminism is often seen as emanating from Western liberation movements. Wilkins (2005: 269) notes how difficult female development professionals across organizations have found it to 'use the vocabulary or framework of "feminism"'. As the example from Newton (2011) and the work of Cornwall (1998), El-Bushra (2000), Ellis (1997) and Wilkins (2005) suggests,

> **Box 6.3** *New evaluation solutions to the 'problem' of gender and development*
>
> A recent critical review by Karen Newton indicates that advancing gender equality through strategies such as the Millennium Development Goals is at odds with mainstream development strategies such as the Paris Declaration on Aid Effectiveness and the aims of developing countries. She argues that this is because 'the promotion of gender equality is an inherently political activity that challenges existing gender relations – with the intention of realigning the distribution of social, political and economic power between men and women'. As a consequence, the goal of gender equality and the 'gender mainstreaming' strategy appears to have dropped off the mainstream development agenda. Drawing on the work of various researchers and evaluators in the development field, Newton puts forward a range of innovative evaluation solutions to the 'problem' of gender and development, including:
>
> - Carrying out 'gender work' but calling it something different so that it's more acceptable to aid recipients and evaluations can look at other differences that may be important to a particular context.
> - Using local-context specific terms other than 'gender' that are more appropriate. For example, participants in a gender-mainstreaming workshop in Fiji found it important to distinguish between 'gender equality', which was seen as a Western construct, and 'gender respect', which was a more appropriate term in the Fijian context.
> - Conducting gender work in a way that captures the lived realities, on the ground, of gender and gender relations.
> - Going beyond the 'templated' approach to gender analysis by using a more flexible and sensitive approach that enables transformative moments between men and women to occur from the ground up, rather than being imposed from the top-down.
> - Including women in evaluations, not because they are women, but because they often do not benefit from development assistance and are frequently excluded from evaluations. This strategy is expected to increase the validity of evaluation results, since the results of many development evaluations would look much less positive if women were included.
>
> (Newton, 2011)

despite the rhetoric about 'gender mainstreaming', there is ongoing resistance to openly addressing issues of gender in the development and C4D field. Cornwall (1998) notes:

> Those men who would become involved in bringing about change can feel excluded from gender work by virtue of their sex. Those who retain their prejudices can feel affronted by a perceived totalizing assault on masculinity, become defensive and angry, and resist. Rather than addressing issues that should be everyone's issues, 'gender' becomes a battleground on which other struggles are waged.
>
> (Cornwall, 1998: 46)

Newton (2011), El-Bushra (2000), Cornwall (1998) and many others have highlighted the complexity of gender politics and practices and the problems that arise when complex gender issues are oversimplified in development work. Moving beyond these simplifications requires a 'more nuanced and sophisticated understanding of the roots of human behavior' (El-Bushra, 2000: 60). Cornwall (1998: 47) also suggests that gender-aware participatory research needs to work 'with the differences that affect local people's lives and livelihoods, rather than with blanket notions of difference that fail to do justice to the complexities of most people's lived realities'.

Case study approaches

Case study is defined as 'an in-depth exploration from multiple perspectives of the complexity and uniqueness of a particular project, policy, institution or system in a "real-life" context. It is research based, inclusive of different methods and is evidence-led' (Simons, 2009: 21). Complexity theorists favour a case study approach to evaluation since it enables the study of a phenomenon 'as an integrated whole' (Lacayo, 2006: 11). A case study frequently involves the use of a wide range of participatory, qualitative and quantitative methods and is appropriate for exploratory, descriptive, or explanatory purposes (Lacayo, 2006; Simons, 2009). 'Democratic case study' engages participants and stakeholders in the process, considers how different people interpret and value a programme, offers participants the opportunity to check how their data is used and disseminates the outcomes to audiences within and beyond the case (Simons, 2009).

Khagram (2009) suggests that case studies are the best method, empirically, for looking at causal pathways about the effects of an intervention. However, he notes that they are often poorly done. Case studies enable us to focus on context, multiple outcomes from the same initiative, and unintended causes. Khagram (2009) sees the comparative case study approach as a rigorous method that provides learning and knowledge development from impact evaluations.

In our UN consultations, case study was considered the most highly effective of all the methodologies listed in our surveys for assessing the impacts of C4D programmes – it was assessed as either 'very' or 'quite' effective by all of the UN Focal Points and the Expert Panel. It is also the methodology that was most often used by both groups – 80 per cent of the UN respondents and 85 per cent of the Expert Panel 'often' used case studies in their C4D research and evaluation activities.

Strengths of case studies identified in our consultations included that they '*have the potential to capture complexities, messy realities and nuances of context that so many other approaches do not*'; they '*provide in-depth analysis of a specific issue, and allow holistic description of process and outcomes of a given milieu*'; they can allow you to '*compare various scenarios to find out "why"*'. Also, they '*not only record in detail the process for achieving results but also the type of dynamics required to get there*' and '*enables us to track and describe small process changes on the way to longer-term change*'. However, various limitations were also noted, including: the '*quality depends on the qualities of the documenter and sources of information*'; they can '*illustrate what is happening but do not prove large-scale results*'; they '*require necessary expertise, time and support*'; and they are '*often poorly done with poor link to theory*'.

One of the advantages of case study research is 'its uniqueness, its capacity for understanding complexity in particular contexts' but a corresponding disadvantage that is often cited (and was raised in our UN consultations) is 'the difficulty of generalizing from the single case' (Simons, 1996: 225). However, Simons (1996: 225) highlights a paradox of case study – 'by focusing in depth and from a holistic perspective, a case study can generate both unique and universal understandings'. This requires new ways of seeing and new forms of understanding that the paradox of case study can provide. She argues that:

> ...case study research is needed now more than ever before to challenge orthodox thinking, to get beneath the surface of policy implementation to reveal in depth understanding and, most importantly, to take a quantum leap in how we come to understand complex educational situations.
>
> (Simons, 1996: 231)

Similar arguments could be made about the need for rigorous, in-depth participatory case study evaluations that capture the complexity of C4D.

Quantitative survey-based methodologies

A number of quantitative and survey-based techniques are frequently used in the evaluation of development programmes. They have some application in the evaluation of C4D when used in combination with qualitative and participatory methodologies. Commonly used methods in C4D evaluations include: behaviour change comparison surveys, behavioural surveillance surveys and KABP surveys (Puddephatt *et al.*, 2009). Chambers (2008: 14) notes that mixed methods and 'qual–quant [qualitative/quantitative] sequences' are the most significant improvements to survey-based approaches in the development context. However, in an important critique of survey-based approaches, he argues that large questionnaires 'belong to a paradigm of things rather than a paradigm of people' and are therefore a 'paradigmatic misfit for complexity' (Chambers, 2008: 19).

In our UN consultations quantitative survey-based methodologies were assessed as either 'very' or 'fairly' effective by 69 per cent of the Expert Panel and 90 per cent of the UN Focal Points, who made much more use of these methodologies in developing and evaluating C4D programmes. Some respondents commented that KABP surveys can be useful for setting C4D indicators, are *'more people-centred'* than other types of survey methods, and *'allow the researcher to cross-check subjects' responses'*. However, they also noted several weaknesses of KABP surveys: they *'do not capture underlying causes of behaviour and issues around social norms'*; *'they may not include enough background to place responses in context'*; and they *'require research skills normally acquired through PhD studies, thereby limiting the pool of researchers available to carry them out'*. In addition, Papa *et al.* (2006: 21–22) found that this method 'did not address the complexity of the social change phenomena that we saw unfold on the ground'.

Singhal and Rogers (2003: 349) suggest that quantitative methods can be useful in HIV prevention programmes for describing behaviours that are known risk factors, monitoring changes in behaviour, and helping to evaluate the effects of interventions. However, as we noted in Chapter 3, these methods are often unable to capture the complexity of AIDS-related issues and behaviours (Singhal and Rogers, 2003). Other weaknesses include: the proxy measures used in quantitative surveys are often unreliable, especially self-reports about stigmatized behaviours; minor variations in the wording of survey questions can 'negatively impact a measurement'; there may be problems with recruiting and retaining participants; and the focus of such surveys is on measuring individual-level behaviour change rather than on developing a broader understanding of individual, group and social-level changes (Singhal and Rogers, 2003: 350–351).

Table 6.2 Ratings for methods considered 'very' or 'fairly' effective for assessing C4D impacts

Method	UN Focal Points	Expert Panel
In-depth interviews	100%	91%
Focus group discussions	89%	83%
Community/village mapping	88%	78%
Channel/media usage and preference analysis	75%	64%
Communication environment analysis	44%	64%
Participant/audience analysis	50%	67%
KABP surveys	60%	58%

Key C4D evaluation methods

We now briefly review a variety of research and evaluation methods that are seen as effective and appropriate for evaluating C4D. As shown in Table 6.2, our UN consultations found that commonly used qualitative methods such as in-depth interviews and focus group discussions and participatory tools such as community/village mapping were considered particularly effective for assessing the impacts of C4D.

Methods for understanding the local context

Key methods that we have identified as useful for understanding a local context and its communication systems and environment are:

- communicative ecology mapping (see Chapter 3 for more information);
- communication environment analysis, which was described by one of the UN Focal Points as '*a holistic approach to addressing political, socio-cultural, economic, geo-physical determinants of communication environment at family, community and national levels that uses quantitative and qualitative methods*';
- ethnographic methods such as participant observation and field notes are useful for understanding the everyday lives and cultural and communication practices of people from the perspectives of a range of different people (see http://ear.findingavoice.org/).

Media usage and audience analysis methods

Our UN consultations identified the following methods as useful for understanding and analysing the audiences of C4D programmes and their media usage and preferences:

- channel/media usage and preference analysis, which '*can pinpoint the selecting of media and interpersonal channel support*'; and
- participant/audience analysis, which can '*provide a background for further questioning*'.

Interview methods

In-depth interviews and focus group discussions were both rated very highly for the evaluation of C4D in our UN consultations. There are many types of in-depth interviews, including:

- *Household interviews* – literally, interviewing people in their homes, where they are comfortable. They can be quite intimate and personal and include discussions about interviewees' feelings, their family relationships, their aims, and so on.

136 *Key approaches, methodologies and methods*

- *Interviews with 'key informants'* or community figures such as staff from a local radio station, teachers, business people, religious figures, health workers and political figures. These interviews will probably be less personal and might aim to find out how they understand the community and its problems from their professional perspective and experience, or what changes they have observed (see http://ear.findingavoice.org/).

Focus group discussions are designed to generate discussion among a group of participants around certain topics or issues. They should therefore be made up of people who are likely to talk easily with one another. This means that issues such as gender, class, caste or religion need to be considered when using this method.

Creative, visual and technology-based methods

We discussed the growing use of creative, innovative and visual research and evaluation methods in Chapter 4. These methods include digital storytelling, photovoice, drawing and painting methods, video diaries and participatory video (see Liamputtong, 2007, for a good overview of these techniques). These methods combine well with interview methods and are particularly useful for vulnerable and less literate groups (Liamputtong, 2007). In recent times, rapid feedback from audiences and programme participants has also been gathered through the use of technologies such as mobile phones and websites.

Maps, diagrams and charts

Community/village mapping, gender charts, and other participatory tools and techniques that involve the creation of maps, diagrams and charts are useful for representing local conditions and relationships (see http://ear.findingavoice.org/ and Chambers, 2008). Developed with participants through these techniques, these representations often provide a clear and simple way to communicate complex issues to others and provide researchers with a good tool for discussing and representing local realities. Participatory techniques are also useful for understanding barriers to communication and information access, identifying issues and solutions to local problems, and providing feedback on C4D initiatives by, for example, ranking the most popular radio programme segments. Gender division of labour charts can also help to identify such things as gender-related barriers to accessing information. These charts were found to be effective in the AC4SC project.

Survey methods

Survey-based techniques have an application in the evaluation of C4D when they are used in combination with qualitative and participatory methodologies. We have already noted a number of limitations of KABP surveys. For these reasons they are not highly recommended in C4D evaluations that use our framework. However, short questionnaire surveys can be useful. They enable the generation of less detailed information from larger numbers of people, and can provide useful statistical information for evaluation reports and for making comparisons between outcomes at different points in time. They are particularly useful for testing ideas emerging from qualitative and participatory research and evaluation activities or for verifying how widespread the themes and issues in qualitative data such as interviews and group discussions are.

Strengths and limitations of the key methods

A number of strengths and limitations of key research and evaluation methods that were identified in our UN consultations as particularly useful for evaluating C4D are set out in Lennie and Tacchi (2011a). Other information on the strengths and limitations of many of the methods we have outlined in this section can be found in various evaluation guides, toolkits and compendiums, such as those by Clark and Sartorius (2004), Gosling and Edwards (2003), Heeks and Molla (2009) and Westat (2002).

Indicators

Indicator setting is considered by some to be 'the most difficult step in establishing a reliable evaluative approach' (Guijt, 1998 and Mikkelsen, 1995, in Classen, 2003: 24). In this final section we define what indicators are, discuss some of the challenges concerning indicators in relation to complexity and systems thinking and participation, and suggest some alternatives to indicators in the evaluation of social change and C4D initiatives.

Indicators are 'objective ways of measuring (indicating) that progress is being achieved', with 'progress' determined by the aims and objectives of a particular initiative (Gosling and Edwards, 2003: 338). They are commonly used to measure the impact of development interventions and to monitor the performance of projects in relation to predetermined targets (Bennett and Roche, 2000). Quantifiable and 'objectively verifiable' indicators are a key element of the results-based management approach to evaluation, which includes the use of logframes. We have already noted the incompatibility of this approach with the complexity of assessing the outcomes of C4D.

In C4D, indicators should be developed through dialogue and negotiation between key stakeholders, so that they are chosen based on local assessments of what participants want to know and why (Balit, 2010b; Byrne *et al.*, 2005; DANIDA, 2005). This helps to identify what information is critical, and to clarify goals, views on change, information needs and values. This process is considered to be empowering 'as it allows local views to dictate what constitutes success or change' (Guijt, 2000: 204). However, Guijt (2000: 204) continues on to note that 'for indicator development to be empowering is an impressive feat and one that few M&E efforts can correctly claim to have achieved'.

Holism and complexity thinking

Indicator setting is a complex and time-consuming process since it attempts to provide indications of change in complex contexts. Parks *et al.* (2005) suggest that indicators:

> ...can measure the tangible (e.g. service uptake), the intangible (e.g. community empowerment) and the unanticipated (i.e., results that were not planned). Ideally indicators reveal changes related to a specific phenomenon that in itself represents a bigger question or problem.
>
> (Parks *et al.*, 2005: 17)

While quantitative indicators are emphasized in mainstream evaluation approaches, for C4D initiatives they often need to be qualitative to be most effective and appropriate. The most important indicators are often not quantifiable. For example, the number of people

138 *Key approaches, methodologies and methods*

participating in a social network is relatively unimportant compared to the quality of relationships and dialogue within that network. Indicators for assessing C4D also need to provide data that can be divided by gender and other relevant differences. The Communication for Social Change Consortium has proposed the following broad qualitative indicators for measuring social change communication:

- expanded public and private dialogue and debate;
- increased accuracy of the information that people share in the dialogue/debate;
- supported the people centrally affected by issue(s) voicing their perspective in the debate and dialogue;
- increased leadership role by people disadvantaged by the issues of concern;
- resonates with the major issues of interest to people's everyday interests;
- linked people and groups with similar interests who might otherwise not be in contact.

(Parks *et al.*, 2005: 31)

Servaes *et al.* (2012) have proposed a new framework for assessing C4D that uses 'sustainability' as the main focus of analysis. This framework is a hybrid model that draws on established indicator frameworks within both the participatory and expert-led paradigms. The framework covers four categories: health, education, environment and governance, and includes eight qualitative indicators: actors, factors, level, type of communication, channels, process, methods and message. The idea behind this model is that it 'allows for a flexible interpretation of sustainability and the components supporting it', thus allowing for the 'diversity (cultural, social, economic) of projects while still being able to evaluate their sustainability' (Servaes *et al.*, 2012: 118). This framework fits quite well with the complexity-based approach that we have advocated and the focus on creating lasting change in organizations and communities.

A complexity-based approach also recognizes the need to understand rather than measure social change processes (Lacayo, 2006). This requires looking for different ways to do things, asking different questions to get different answers, trying different strategies, and understanding the importance of context and how and why social change happens (Lacayo, 2006: 48). As one of the Expert Panel in our UN consultations commented: '*However strong certain indicators might be, their ability to meaningfully capture complex, dynamic processes of social change, over time and in multiple and diverse contexts, will always be limited*'.

Indicators are therefore needed that are flexible and encompass complexity, or alternatives to indicators need to be considered. Creative approaches such as those using pictures or stories of significant change can be particularly useful when working with community groups that include people with low levels of literacy.

Alternatives to indicators

Guijt (2000) provides two suggested alternatives to indicators: 'significant change' and 'verifying assumptions'. As an example of the significant change approach, Guijt cites Davies (1998) who describes a development initiative in Bangladesh. A network of credit groups provided monthly reports, which detailed the single most significant change that occurred amongst the group members. These changes related to people's well-being, the sustainability of people's institutions, people's participation, and open-ended change. This project informed the development of the MSC technique, which was previously described as 'monitoring-without-indicators' (Davies and Dart, 2005: 8). In a critique of indicators, one of the Expert Panel for our UN consultations emphasized the benefits of this alternative approach:

> *If capacity is low, time and essential support and resources for research and evaluation are minimal/inadequate, we have found that stories of change for example can reveal far more, more accurately and in timely ways, than can indicators.*

In the AC4SC project, we found that identifying domains of change based on an analysis of the themes of MSC stories was an effective means of developing more useful and meaningful qualitative indicators of change.

An example of 'verifying assumptions' is provided in Harnmeijer (1999), who promotes a flexible and creative approach to evaluation that prioritizes participation. In the Small Dam Rehabilitation Project, implemented by CARE International in Zimbabwe, an in-depth review was considered more appropriate than a conventional evaluation. This evaluation included a series of workshops with dam users. The evaluation team had identified ten assumptions about expected changes, including '*Perceived impacts:* Improved nutrition and income security are the main benefits perceived by users of the project dams' (Harnmeijer, 1999: 2, author's italics). The idea was to work with local dam users to find evidence to support, refine or reject these assumptions. Findings from the evaluation led to the revision of key assumptions that were found to be untenable. Simply measuring impact against predetermined indicators, based on those assumptions, would have failed to have allowed the initiative to adjust its assumptions and improve its practices, which would have made it more likely to succeed in the future.

In their paper on principles for evaluating mode-2 programmes (which address complex social and environmental problems), Regeer *et al.* (2009) redefine the purpose of indicators as moving from assessment to 'sensitizing'. In explaining this they refer to the process of dialogue and deliberation in Dutch sustainability programmes that resulted in new understandings about sustainable development. These new understandings contained sensitizing concepts that captured a 'specific quality of mode-2 indicators' (Regeer *et al.*, 2009: 527). The function of such indicators 'is not to assess but rather to perceive, or make visible, aspects that are or seem relevant to sustainable development', which in turn 'stimulates sustainable development through discursive activity' (Regeer *et al.*, 2009: 527). They suggest that this is similar to the idea in systems evaluation that 'deeper meaning-making is more likely to promote valuable action than better data' (Imam, LaGoy and Williams, 2006: 8). The MSC technique is based on a similar concept.

Regeer *et al.* (2009) suggest that, in mode-2 programmes, indicators are context-dependent and dynamic. This means that they need to change over the course of a project 'as a result of evolving insights on the part of a mode-2 intermediary and due to an increased number of stakeholders and perspectives entering the interpretative space over time' (Regeer *et al.*, 2009: 527). This highlights the need for flexibility in the process of indicator setting.

Participatory approaches

Selecting indicators is one of the most difficult steps in setting up a PM&E approach as it 'highlights, more than any other, the different information needs and expectations that the different stakeholders have of the monitoring work' (Parks *et al.*, 2005: 17). Participatory approaches to C4D and evaluation require that the development of indicators focus 'not just on what is measured, but also on how it is measured, and especially on who decides which indicators are important' (Bennett and Roche, 2000: 26). Guijt (2000) provides various examples of participatory indicator identification and states that 'in each of these experiences indicators were identified by primary stakeholders, often local people who live with the changes being tracked'.

We agree with Parks *et al.* (2005: 22) who suggest that it may well be that 'combinations of locally-generated measurements and PM&E processes and externally derived indicators and M&E approaches are at times the most appropriate way of monitoring and evaluating CFSC initiatives'. However, externally derived indicators should only be used to stimulate discussion. Identification of indicators is best begun after dialogue about the community's concerns, goals, issues and obstacles and their vision of the change they seek.

An alternative to the dominant SMART indicator approach (specific, measurable, attainable and action-oriented, relevant, and time-bound), which tends to suit quantitative indicators, is the SPICED approach: 'subjective, participatory, interpreted, communicable, empowering and disaggregated' (Estrella, 2000: 9). Compared with the SMART approach, the SPICED approach places more emphasis on developing indicators that stakeholders can define and use for their own purposes of interpreting and learning about change, rather than simply measuring or attempting to demonstrate impact to meet donor requirements (Estrella, 2000). Souter (2008: 168) considers that SMART describes the properties of the indicators themselves, while SPICED relates more to how indicators should be used. The SPICED approach is likely to be more appropriate for participatory evaluations of C4D initiatives, which would draw heavily on qualitative and descriptive definitions of change.

Conclusion

There is a need for greater openness, freedom and flexibility in selecting and using different evaluation approaches, methodologies and methods to ensure that they are appropriate and fit well with the underlying aims, principles and values of C4D. We strongly advocate using a range of participatory and innovative research and evaluation approaches, methodologies and methods. Benefits include strengthened evaluation capacities, greater utilization of findings and learnings, empowerment of participants and the development and improvement of initiatives in ways that better meet community needs and aspirations.

We emphasize the need to take a critical, realistic, 'big picture' view that considers the various challenges, contradictions and issues in using participatory, feminist and alternative research and evaluation approaches. This is particularly so in the current context, in which development agencies have mainstreamed participation. Participatory approaches can be co-opted to give the appearance that a range of stakeholders' views have been taken into account when this is not actually the case. They are also often used in standardized, step-by-step ways that are anathema to the goals of empowerment and inclusion in PM&E, PAR, feminist and other participatory and learning-oriented approaches. A wide range of skills are needed to effectively use participatory and complexity-based evaluation approaches and methodologies. This requires effective capacity development to ensure that outcomes meet the needs of a broad diversity of stakeholders and that findings are useful, of high quality and rigorous.

Based on our critical reviews of the logframe and theory of change approaches, we argue that the ToC approach is more appropriate for the evaluation of C4D initiatives due to its capacity to imagine new solutions to development problems, from new perspectives, and to analyse and plan action related to transformative change, using 'flexible thinking-action logic' (Retolaza, 2011: 4). In contrast, the linear logic of the logframe approach is more suited to the evaluation of short-term initiatives that are focused on simple problems.

Indicator setting is often challenging, complex, time-consuming and unable to capture complex realities and relationships or the reasons behind social change. We suggest that alternatives to indicators, such as significant change stories and verifying assumptions, can be more useful. In the evaluation of complex C4D initiatives it may be useful to redefine the purpose of indicators as moving from measurement and assessment to developing new understandings of the concept of social change that contain 'sensitizing concepts' (Regeer, *et al.*, 2009: 527). This process can facilitate dialogue that can lead to sustainable social change.

In the next, concluding chapter we include an outline of some of the factors that need to be considered in selecting the most appropriate approaches, methodologies and methods to use in the evaluation of C4D initiatives, as well as other practical ideas and processes for implementing the framework presented in this book.

7 Conclusion and implementation

The framework for evaluating communication for development presented in this book comprises seven inter-related components: *participatory, holistic, complex, critical, emergent, realistic, and learning-based*, with a set of principles underlying each component. The framework draws on work that promotes innovative and creative approaches to research and evaluation, and alternative paradigms of development. Based on the latest thinking and research in the fields of development, C4D, and evaluation, the framework proposes critical approaches to understanding development, social change, and the evaluation of C4D. These approaches can help us to conceptualize development interventions in realistic ways, clarify messy solutions to complex social problems, and improve mutual understanding and relationships among diverse stakeholders involved in C4D and its evaluation.

Key features and benefits of the framework for evaluating C4D

Four conceptualizations of evaluation and shifts in evaluation practice underpin the framework, and are significant in understanding and evaluating development and C4D:

1. Evaluation is best considered and most usefully practised as an ongoing action learning and organizational improvement process.
2. There is a shift from proving impacts to developing and improving development practices.
3. Evaluative processes can effectively support the development of innovations.
4. There is a shift from external to internal and community accountability.

The framework is based on concepts and principles derived from systems and complexity theory, action research and feminist methodologies, new approaches to social change, and holistic approaches to community development, organizational change, and evaluation capacity development (ECD) (see Figure 7.1). These approaches promote ongoing learning from research, monitoring and evaluation and continuous listening to a broad diversity of participants and stakeholders in development initiatives.

In the framework, evaluation is conceptualized as an ongoing, participatory action learning and capacity development process that continuously develops and improves initiatives and helps to create learning organizations and communities. This approach to evaluation effectively supports collaborative development of emerging innovations in C4D and development. It requires keeping evaluation methodologies and systems as practical and simple as possible and using strategies such as ongoing meta-evaluation to improve evaluation capacities and practices.

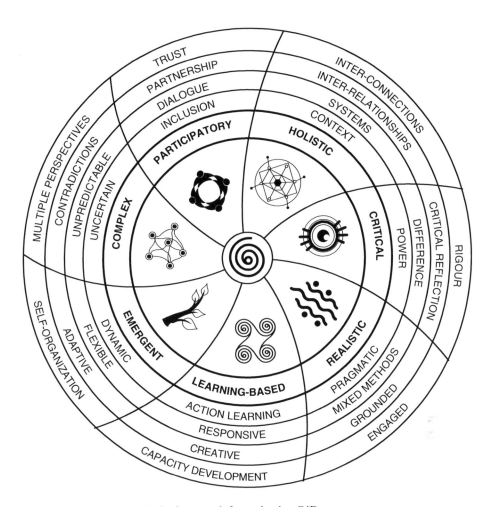

Figure 7.1 Key concepts in the framework for evaluating C4D

Continuous participation, dialogue and ownership of development processes, visions and goals are essential to effective development initiatives. A participatory approach to evaluation is therefore an essential component of our framework. This means developing a partnership between stakeholders to collaboratively design and implement an evaluation, and share issues, experiences and learnings. Such processes aim to include all relevant stakeholders in all aspects of evaluation, while acknowledging the challenges of wide participation that brings people with diverse agendas, backgrounds and perspectives together. This approach aims to meet goals of stakeholder empowerment and inclusion, which are unlikely to be achieved by using participatory processes in standardized, step-by-step ways.

While greater time and resources are often required to effectively use participatory evaluation approaches, our framework takes the position that a long-term view of the benefits of participatory approaches is required. As Servaes *et al.* (2012: 118) suggest in relation to C4D and social change projects, 'Sustainability requires continuous and long-term evaluation and monitoring'. Along with a growing number of others working in this field, such as

144 *Conclusion and implementation*

Byrne and Vincent (2011), Jallov (2012), Patton (2011) and Servaes *et al.* (2012), we contend that effective C4D and alternative approaches to development and evaluation are the best route to sustainable C4D and development. They are also less costly than the failure of expensive development initiatives due to lack of participation and ownership on the part of the communities concerned (Balit, 2010a).

Challenges, issues and contradictions

As well as presenting the framework and its possibilities, we identified many complex challenges, issues, tensions and contradictions. These are contextual, structural, institutional and organizational. They affect the long-term sustainability and success of social change and development initiatives. They affect the evaluation of C4D and have implications for the effective implementation of our framework. These issues challenge us to put people back at the centre of development, and to use evaluation to help to achieve real outcomes and positive change in people's lives rather than perform development accountancy. This is the larger challenge that sits behind the challenges and issues we discuss in this book. At the same time, they point to a need for the framework for evaluating C4D, and its need to encompass complexity.

The key challenges and issues that we outline below align with the seven inter-related components of our framework:

- *Participatory*: The need to address the contradictions arising from participatory and dominant approaches to C4D.
- *Holistic*: The need for a holistic approach to evaluation capacity development at all levels.
- *Complex*: The need to better understand the complex context of development and C4D.
- *Critical*: The need to take a critical approach that considers gender, power and inclusion issues.
- *Emergent*: The lack of support for alternative, emergent evaluation approaches.
- *Realistic*: The need for realistic approaches to assessing the outcomes of C4D.
- *Learning-based*: The need for openness, freedom and flexibility in using different evaluation approaches to enable better understandings of the process of social change and better ongoing learning from evaluation.

We present key differences between dominant and participatory approaches to C4D, evaluation, and evaluation capacity development in a series of tables below. While the dichotomies we present are, to some extent, based on generalizations, they help us to summarize key differences and to highlight the contradictions and tensions in this field. We acknowledge the need to draw on all approaches to development and evaluation that are effective, appropriate and complementary, but our framework does insist on the centrality of a participatory, holistic approach.

Addressing the contradictions arising from different approaches to C4D

Long-term research highlights a recurring problem with decision-makers in development organizations. They often do not appreciate what C4D means, or its important role in development. Our research found that decision-makers in the United Nations often do not understand that C4D includes two-way communication systems that enable dialogue,

Table 7.1 Tensions between dominant and participatory approaches to C4D

Dominant approaches	Participatory approaches	Tensions and issues
Vertical, top-down models, sending messages or disseminating information via one-way communication or public relations.	Horizontal models based on meaningful participation, engaging people in dialogue, sharing knowledge and learning from each other, in a multi-way process.	Many C4D approaches refer to both perspectives in contradictory ways. This results in confusion and inappropriate compromises.
Communication is seen as marginal in the development process. There is a lack of high-level support and understanding in some agencies of C4D as dialogue, and of community participation in decisions that affect their lives.	Communication is seen as a major pillar for development and change. Some agencies strongly support horizontal communication for social change and participatory development approaches.	Institutions are often structurally unsuited for listening to the community. Many C4D units are located in corporate communication and external relations departments. The wide range of C4D approaches and meanings suggest a need to reduce confusion about the meaning of C4D.
'Participation' in development is often rhetoric, not put into practice, or is implemented in top-down ways.	Takes the view that people on the ground need to be included in all stages of development processes. Participation and ownership are seen as vital for sustainability.	Full and direct participation is incompatible with dominant organizational cultures and practices. Participation challenges entrenched power structures and is difficult to achieve, given issues of power and inclusion of a diversity of stakeholders, politics and perceptions of the greater time and resources required.

'allow communities to speak out, express their aspirations and concerns and participate in the decisions that relate to their development' (UN Resolution 51/172, 1997). Table 7.1 summarizes the key challenges, contradictions and tensions related to C4D that we identified in our UN consultations and other research.

Addressing these issues requires advocacy with organizations, donors and others to highlight the importance of C4D and its ongoing evaluation and to develop a greater appreciation of C4D's contribution to achieving important development outcomes.

The need for a holistic approach to evaluation capacity development at all levels

Our research identified a clear need to implement participatory, holistic, learning-based evaluation and capacity development at all levels, from community members, to development and evaluation specialists, to managers. This will improve the design and outcomes of C4D. We consider that ECD is an essential part of the process of institutionalizing evaluation and developing learning organizations and an evaluation culture within countries, organizations and initiatives that use C4D.

146 *Conclusion and implementation*

Table 7.2 Tensions between dominant and alternative approaches to evaluation capacity development

Dominant approaches	Alternative approaches	Tensions and issues
Narrow, short-term focus on training in key tools such as the logframe and development of individual staff members. A one-off 'workshop culture' dominates, as opposed to longer term capacity development and sustained support over time.	Holistic, participatory, long-term approach to capacity development that seeks to develop learning organizations and strengthen capacities, including in a wide range of evaluation-related skills, at all levels. These processes are long-term.	A participatory approach to ECD is often effective and appropriate, but can require greater time and planning. Developing evaluation capacities and achieving a high level of participation in ECD can be particularly difficult in pressured and resource-constrained organizational contexts.
M&E is separated from other functions in organizations and often lacks status and power. There are issues with communications and programme staff not seeing the value of M&E. This reduces the overall effectiveness of evaluation and discourages the development of a learning culture.	The effective development of learning cultures in organizations requires good communication, cooperation, collaboration and trust between M&E and other staff and the integration of evaluation into the whole project or programme cycle.	There is a need for management to act as models of learning and organizational change, and greater funding and support for long-term, sustainable capacity development. However, this is often difficult to achieve, particularly for organizations with highly bureaucratic structures.

Learning organizations engage in constant reflection and learning to continually develop and improve systems and initiatives in ways that meet community and stakeholder needs, goals and aspirations. However, in order to achieve effective and sustainable ECD there is a need to take into account the organizational culture, dynamics and wider context, and issues of power, knowledge, language and literacy. There is also a need to draw on local innovation and experimentation, and to empower local staff and communities so that their knowledge, ideas and learnings can be utilized.

A key challenge is the pressure from donors to conform with standardized upward accountability-focused evaluation approaches that are generally unable to provide the type of ongoing learning needed for effective C4D, and for ongoing development and improvement purposes. A wide range of skills are needed to effectively use participatory and complexity-based evaluation approaches and methodologies. However, developing, implementing and sustaining ECD presents particularly difficult challenges and issues for time-, skill- and resource-poor organizations in developing countries. Table 7.2 highlights some of the tensions between dominant and alternative approaches to ECD.

The need to better understand the complex context of C4D

Complex social, economic, political, cultural, environmental and technological factors are at play in the fields of development and C4D, including issues of power, gender and other differences. The context of C4D includes communities, organizations and institutions as well as geography, history, culture, political and economic systems, rapidly changing information and communication technologies, and media systems and institutions. The evaluation of C4D is also affected by the funding rules and requirements of donor organizations and development decision-makers. In addition, the context of C4D includes particular challenges and issues that emerge in many developing countries that are associated with geography, the political situation, gender, caste, class, ethnicity, communication and social structures, institutions, culture and social norms. Such an environment can significantly affect communication and relationships among the stakeholders involved in an evaluation. There is a need to better understand the implications and effects of wider systems and local environments in the evaluation of C4D.

The need to consider gender, power and inclusion issues

Issues of power are an inevitable aspect of participatory approaches to development, C4D and evaluation. Our framework therefore stresses the need to be alert to power dynamics and issues of inclusion and exclusion, empowerment and disempowerment. C4D will always, to some extent, involve challenging power relationships and structures because it depends on actively engaging a diverse range of people, with multiple, often conflicting perspectives and agendas. In the development context, gender issues raise particularly important challenges to effective participatory evaluation of development initiatives, which need to be adequately addressed. This highlights the political nature of both development and evaluation.

Lack of support for alternative, emergent evaluation approaches

Our research identified a lack of appreciation, funding and support for alternative, innovative, emergent evaluation approaches among management and mainstream evaluation specialists in major development agencies. Commitment to participatory processes often remains rhetoric rather than meaningful or appropriate practice. Funders tend to place greater value on narrow, quantitative measurement-oriented approaches and indicators that better fit their own management systems and tools, but that take insufficient account of the complexity of the wider systems and social and cultural context of particular C4D and development initiatives.

We highlighted some of the paradoxes and contradictions that C4D organizations have to contend with in their work. For example, our research identified NGOs such as Puntos de Encuentro and Equal Access Nepal which are using complexity-based and participatory approaches to C4D but are required to use evaluation approaches based on linear logic models and pre-defined indicators that do not fit their values and their more complex and inclusive approaches to social change. However, we recognized a need to better demonstrate the benefits and rigour of alternative, participatory and complexity-based approaches to evaluation. Table 7.3 sets out some of the key challenges, issues and tensions that we identified between dominant and alternative approaches to the evaluation of C4D.

The need for a realistic approach to assessing the outcomes of C4D

A crucial step in C4D achieving greater prominence in the development agenda and fostering greater appreciation of the value of participatory approaches to C4D, is demonstrating the outcomes of C4D. However, this is often more complex and difficult than for other

148 *Conclusion and implementation*

Table 7.3 Tensions between dominant and alternative approaches to evaluation of C4D

Dominant approaches	*Alternative approaches*	*Tensions and issues*
Narrow focus on individual behaviour change, short-term changes; use of linear cause–effect models of social change that do not foster understanding of the complexity of the wider systems and context of development initiatives.	The complexity of social change is seen as requiring a participatory, holistic approach, incorporating insights from systems thinking and complexity theories and including a focus on gender, power and wider social norms. This approach draws attention to the underlying dynamics of social change.	There is a lack of funding and support for alternative evaluation approaches that are often more appropriate for C4D. Since policy-makers and managers often have a hard science background, they tend to lack an understanding and appreciation of the potential of alternative approaches and question their rigour.
Dominance of quantitative, measurement-oriented approaches that limit the ability to ask important questions about social and behaviour change, or capture the unexpected.	A pragmatic, participatory, mixed methods approach, guided by appropriate principles and key evaluation questions would move us beyond unhelpful qualitative/quantitative dichotomies and increase the strength and rigour of evaluation and impact assessment findings.	Funders typically have a preference for numerical data but often do not appreciate the value of participatory tools for eliciting information that is more credible and useful to communities themselves. A participatory, mixed methods approach requires a wider range of skills and knowledge to use effectively.

development initiatives that are addressing relatively simple problems such as increasing the rate of vaccination against disease.

There are often unrealistic demands, targets and timeframes for cause and effect impact assessments, with donors expecting to see measurable results in an unreasonably short timeframe, most likely determined through measurable, pre-set indicators. This can lead to the creation of 'results' that may have little connection with outcomes that are actually happening on the ground. The requirements of standard approaches to impact assessment, including the imperative to directly attribute 'success' and positive impacts, further challenges an approach to development that is based on relationships, values, dialogue and collaboration. Some of the key challenges, issues and tensions in assessing the outcomes and impacts of C4D are shown in Table 7.4.

Addressing these challenges and issues will require donors and those implementing C4D to provide sufficient budgets and time for the evaluation of C4D, including for longitudinal studies of outcome and impacts.

The need for openness, freedom and flexibility in using different evaluation approaches to enable learning from evaluation

Dominant quantitative and measurement-oriented evaluation methodologies are limited in their ability to ask important questions about the social, cultural and political context within which development problems are embedded and to enable learning from evaluation. They are unable to capture the level of detail required to understand the nuances of the

Table 7.4 Tensions between dominant and alternative approaches to assessing the outcomes of C4D

Dominant approaches	Alternative approaches	Tensions and issues
Dominance of instrumental, upward accountability-based approaches that focus on proving impacts, using linear cause–effect logic and formal reporting of results. Alternative approaches are not adequately resourced or supported and are often critiqued for lacking 'objectivity', 'rigour' and 'validity'.	Flexible, holistic interdisciplinary approach based on ongoing learning, improvement and understanding. Takes the complexity of social change and the particular context into account and focuses on outcomes that an initiative can realistically influence.	Demonstrating the impact of C4D is complex and difficult. Dominant approaches discourage ownership of the evaluation process and learning from evaluation. Results are often biased towards positive outcomes, failures are not captured or learned from, and evaluations are not independent from donor influences.
Pressure to produce short-term results within rigid and unrealistic timeframes. This results in a focus on more tangible, short-term changes that are not good indicators of long-term social change.	Seen as more important to focus on *progress towards* long-term social change and the *contribution* made by C4D. This is a more realistic measure of effectiveness and provides practical recommendations for the implementation of policies and initiatives.	Longitudinal studies are required but they are costly and one of the most difficult challenges in evaluation. Donors are reluctant to fund them. This means that there is a lack of strong evidence on which to build C4D research, which fuels scepticism.
Indicators are often pre-defined, set without input from key participants, are quantitative and unrealistic and do not fit C4D outcomes.	Indicators need to be selected and developed through dialogue with key stakeholders, to be most useful and appropriate. Qualitative C4D indicators are often most effective and appropriate.	Indicators are unable to capture complex realities and relationships and the reasons behind social change. In some C4D evaluations it may be more useful to use alternatives to indicators such as stories of significant change.

outcomes of C4D, which can often involve indirect, ripple effects that are important to the process of social change. Dominant approaches do not allow for qualitative analysis and change over time in a given context, and are more suited to short-term activities. However, each of the (mainly) participatory approaches, methodologies and methods that we consider effective for evaluating C4D have some limitations or constraints that need to be considered.

This emphasizes the need to draw on a range of complementary approaches, methodologies and methods in the evaluation of C4D. We have demonstrated in this book that there is a clear need for greater openness, freedom and flexibility in the selection and use of different evaluation approaches, methodologies and methods to ensure that they are appropriate and fit the underlying aims and values of different C4D initiatives. C4D initiatives and their evaluation also need to be flexible enough to respond and adapt to the needs and values of different communities and cultures. They also need to take into account various constraints such as time, resources and organizational challenges. As we have emphasized, there is a

Conclusion and implementation

crucial need to strengthen capacities in using participatory, qualitative and mixed methods approaches, so as to enhance the success of C4D and the effectiveness and rigour of the evaluation of C4D. This can help to ensure the trustworthiness of evaluation findings and the inclusion of multiple perspectives in the evaluation process.

Strategies proposed to address these challenges and issues

We have identified the following strategies that can help to address many of these challenges and issues:

- using our framework to improve the effectiveness and sustainability of C4D;
- valuing the contributions of feminist and gender-sensitive approaches;
- demystifying and valuing participatory evaluation;
- using creative and innovative approaches, methodologies and methods;
- incorporating meta-evaluation into C4D initiatives;
- developing online communities and networks.

Using our framework to improve the effectiveness and sustainability of C4D

We see our framework as offering part of the solution to several of the challenges and issues that we have identified in this book. It can help to bridge the gap between various ideas, theories, concepts and practices that can be usefully incorporated into the evaluation of C4D. It can help participants and stakeholders in C4D initiatives and their evaluation to better understand and realistically address the complex social change issues that development and C4D seek to address. It advocates a mixed methods approach to evaluation that strengthens evaluation outcomes by enabling a diversity of perspectives and different forms of data and information (including creative and visual forms of data) to be included in an evaluation.

Our framework reinforces the case for effective two-way communication and dialogue as a central and vital component of participatory forms of development and evaluation that seek positive and sustainable social change. It highlights the important role of evaluation in the ongoing development and improvement of C4D. In the approach we advocate, the aim of evaluation is to develop innovations, and to improve the effectiveness, quality and sustainability of C4D initiatives by learning from research and evaluation in an ongoing way. This approach identifies and helps explain unexpected outcomes, and learns from 'failures' to better develop new initiatives, projects and innovations and to improve future activities, trust and relationships between different stakeholder groups. As well as greater openness to learn from weaknesses and failures, this requires transparency and honesty, which is only possible with the removal of the current imperative to ignore failures.

The emphasis of our framework is on people, relationships, processes, principles and values, particularly participation, inclusion, open communication, trust, continuous learning and powerful listening. When it is well-planned and facilitated, this approach enables the inclusion of diverse perspectives in an evaluation, and can have significant effects in terms of the empowerment, inclusion and capacity development of participants and stakeholders.

Valuing the contributions of feminist and gender-sensitive approaches

Throughout this book we have emphasized the significant, yet often under-acknowledged, contributions of feminist research to development and to the evaluation of community development, C4D and social change initiatives. This is exemplified by the work of researchers such as Lacayo (2006), Lennie (2005b, 2006a, 2009), Newton (2011) and Rattine-Flaherty and Singhal (2009). Feminists have provided important critiques of development discourses and practices. They have highlighted the complexity of gender politics and practices and the problems that arise when complex gender issues are oversimplified in development work.

Along with action research practitioners and others, feminists have highlighted the need to pay more attention to gender, power–knowledge relations, culture and social norms in the evaluation of social change. They have highlighted the need to take gender discrimination and inequalities in the development context into account and to recognize that participation in evaluation can have disempowering, as well as empowering, effects on participants. Feminist researchers have also demonstrated the need to encompass the understanding and analysis of other 'conditions of oppression' such as caste, ethnicity, and sexuality (El-Bushra, 2000; Wilkins, 2005: 262).

This work has resulted in: alternative ways of thinking about development and its effects; new and innovative solutions to the complex challenges and issues they have raised; and more gender-sensitive, creative, flexible, and culturally appropriate strategies for doing evaluation that is firmly grounded in people's complex lived realities. It has clearly demonstrated the vital importance of understanding and addressing complex gender issues in development and social change in order to better achieve development goals, including the key goal of sustainable development.

Demystifying and valuing participatory evaluation

There is a need to demystify evaluation, promote its many benefits, and to encourage participants to think in an evaluative way. Including a diversity of people in an evaluation forces us to pay attention to the appropriateness of the language used in the evaluation, as well as the perceived value and relevance of participation and evaluation to various groups (Lennie, 2005a: 410).

We advocate the use of various participatory and innovative forms of research and evaluation as a key strategy that can effectively create new understandings of the value of continuous, embedded research and evaluation. Participatory approaches are particularly effective at the community level. When well-planned and facilitated, these approaches can develop evaluation capacities, and enable collaborative planning, analysis, problem solving and critical reflection, and a better understanding of different perspectives, agendas and issues. These processes can lead to appropriate and effective action to address identified problems and issues. Other benefits of participatory and action-oriented approaches to evaluation include greater utilization of evaluation findings and learnings, and the empowerment of participants. They are also open approaches that can be adapted locally.

Using creative and innovative approaches, methodologies and methods

As well as using well-established approaches such as case study and participatory action research, we emphasized the value of innovative evaluation methodologies such as developmental evaluation, outcome mapping and ethnographic action research for the evaluation of C4D. In addition, we value the use of creative and visual methods, such as digital storytelling, photovoice and various mapping, grouping, ranking, comparing and sequencing techniques, as ways of visualizing or expressing important relationships, needs, problems and solutions at the community level. These methods can be used to powerfully drive home messages to key stakeholders and donors about important development and social change issues identified by community members. The use of visual and creative methods can highlight the value of these approaches for the evaluation of C4D, including their ability to give a voice to largely excluded women and men and their capacity building benefits.

Incorporating meta-evaluation into C4D initiatives

Through our work on AC4SC in particular, we demonstrated the value of using concurrent meta-evaluation (Hanssen, Lawrenz and Dunet, 2008) to develop new approaches to evaluation, to identify challenges and issues in the evaluation of C4D and ECD processes, and to develop and share valuable learnings. When used as a tool for ECD and learning, meta-evaluation can be an important means of improving the quality of evaluations and increasing organizational learning and the utilization of evaluation results (Lennie, Tacchi and Wilmore, 2012). This can lead to innovative and sustainable solutions to the challenges and issues that arise in the evaluation of C4D. However, meta-evaluation of this kind requires an organizational culture in which 'critical comments are well-accepted, people are willing to learn from evaluations, and leaders actively practice and support this "learning organization" ideal' (Lennie *et al.*, 2012: 22).

Developing online communities and networks

Another key strategy is forming or joining online networks and communities of practice to connect people who are working in this field and interested in using alternative approaches to researching and evaluating C4D. In Chapter 5 we provided some good examples of well-established C4D and evaluation capacity development and networking initiatives. These initiatives can provide an effective means of sharing information, forming international linkages and collaborations, and enhancing ongoing learning in this area.

Implementing the framework for evaluating C4D

The framework is flexible and can be adapted to many different forms of C4D research, monitoring and evaluation. As we have noted, it is particularly well-suited to the evaluation of communication for social change (CFSC) initiatives. The principles and key components of the framework can also be effectively used to guide the implementation process. This means that the processes used should be participatory, holistic, critical, emergent, realistic, learning-based, and based on the concepts and ideas of complexity and systems thinking. We list some key questions later in this section that provide a means of critically assessing various evaluation approaches, methodologies and methods, based on our framework. The following are some practical ideas and processes that can be useful for implementing the framework (several of these ideas were adapted from Lennie and Tacchi, 2011b).

Assess the context and seek support

Effectively implementing the framework requires a receptive organizational and community context and culture. Staff of organizations at all levels and relevant community members need to be willing to engage in constant reflection and learning from evaluations in order to continually develop and improve organizational systems and C4D initiatives in ways that meet community, organizational and stakeholder needs, goals and visions of the future. The support of management and a commitment to long-term engagement in the evaluation process is particularly important. Consideration needs to be given to how well the approach advocated by the framework will engage primary stakeholders in the evaluation process. This includes asking questions such as:

- How receptive is the culture of your organization or funding body to the use of participatory and alternative evaluation approaches?
- Can you identify key champions in your organization or funding body who can advocate for the framework and help to increase interest in and acceptance of these approaches?
- What kind of approaches and methods will most interest and engage the primary stakeholders and participants/users?

According to Parks *et al.* (2005: 14), the essential ingredients needed for effective participatory monitoring and evaluation (PM&E) include: an open and democratic context, commitment to participation, recognition that PM&E cannot be rushed, people skills (particularly facilitation skills), a focus on capacity building, and structuring the process to ensure participation by different interest groups.

Conduct an evaluability assessment

It may be useful to conduct an evaluability assessment as part of the process of implementing the framework. This is 'a systematic process that helps to identify whether a programme is in a condition to be evaluated, and whether an evaluation is justified, feasible and likely to provide useful information' (UN Women, 2010). Those who are designing an evaluation need to be aware of the key elements involved in assessing the evaluability of C4D initiatives. These usually relate to the design of the initiative, availability of information, and the conduciveness of the context. Without these elements, an evaluation is unlikely to be useful and more work will be required to 'generate all the necessary conditions to be evaluated' (UN Women, 2010). This process could include assessing the simple, complicated and complex aspects of an initiative that will require different approaches to evaluation.

Identify key stakeholders

A key stage in the implementation of the framework is to identify the key stakeholders or boundary partners (Earl, Carden and Smutylo, 2001) in the evaluation process. These are the people whose active participation is contingent to achieving the changes or outcomes that are sought from the C4D initiative. This process includes:

- undertaking an initial process of identifying these groups through various stakeholder and boundary partners analysis methods, including the use of tools such as the theory of change (ToC) approach and outcome mapping;
- identifying the most effective and appropriate ways to engage stakeholders in the evaluation process;
- considering primary and secondary ways of being involved, based on factors such as different capacities, interests and skills, and the level of time and energy they are able to commit.

Clarify expectations and outcomes

It is important to clarify what the key participants and stakeholders (including funders) expect from an evaluation and what its purpose is. The aim is that the evaluation produces useful outcomes and learnings for all involved in the initiative, including funders, staff, volunteers, managers, participants, stakeholders and communities. Evaluation findings and feedback should be used to develop and improve the initiative, and provide understanding of the process of social change and the role of C4D in bringing about change. Questions to be considered include:

- Who is the evaluation for?
- What is it for?
- Who are the intended users of the evaluation?
- What are the intended uses?
- What expectations do various groups have for the evaluation?
- How will the process itself empower those involved and strengthen wider C4D processes?

Develop an initial theory of change

We suggest that developing a dynamic, moving ToC is more appropriate for the evaluation of complex C4D initiatives compared with the logframe approach. The ToC approach can help us to imagine new solutions to development problems from new perspectives, and to analyse and plan action related to transformative change, using 'flexible thinking-action logic' (Retolaza, 2011: 4). Key steps in creating a ToC include:

- establish the time span of change;
- create the story that would explain the change in the particular context;
- study conflict areas and their causes;
- ensure underlying assumptions of the ToC are valid and accurate;
- determine the pathway of change;
- understand the factors that oppose or support the change process;
- determine who collects, selects and analyses the change indicators, and establish their purpose;
- establish who participates in the design and implementation of monitoring and accountability systems, integrate lessons learnt for future actions, and find ways of achieving deeper and more contextualised social learning process.

(Governance and Social Development Resource Centre, 2012)

Clarify the boundaries and scope of the evaluation

Depending on the particular C4D initiative, it may be necessary to define the geographical and time boundaries of the initiative so that everyone is clear about the limits to the areas in which outcomes have occurred and the time period over which C4D activities are being assessed. As we have noted, there is a need to be realistic about what kinds of outcomes can be expected within certain timeframes. This part of the process also needs to consider the type of outcomes to be assessed, which groups or organizations are the focus of the evaluation, and what levels the evaluation will focus on (i.e. individuals, households, groups, organizations, whole communities). However, this process should be seen as open to revision as the evaluation proceeds and new learnings emerge that have implications for the focus of the evaluation.

An evaluation should be proportionate to the scale of the initiative. Key questions to consider in relation to the scale and scope of the evaluation and in obtaining the most trustworthy and meaningful results are:

- How many participants are needed?
- Which particular groups of people need to be involved at various stages?
- How can we engage a wide diversity of people in the evaluation and make it as inclusive as possible?
- What criteria and methods should we use to select particular case study sites?
- How many communities or sites need to be involved?

Conduct scoping and communicative ecology research

Undertaking scoping research and/or communicative ecology research in selected communities is an important part of understanding the context of a C4D initiative. It helps us to understand the inter-relationships and inter-connections between various groups and organizations involved in the initiative, and the complex contextual factors that can affect outcomes. If conducted in a participatory way, this type of research helps to generate community interest in and ownership of an evaluation. Processes such as communicative ecology mapping enable participants and evaluators to understand and explore communication systems, patterns and issues in a community and identify barriers to information and communication access among different groups such as poor housebound women with limited education and more educated women with outside careers.

Establish effective communication and feedback systems

The effective implementation of the framework requires the establishment of good two-way communication and feedback systems to communicate findings to different stakeholders (both internal and external to an organization) and enable continuous sharing, discussion and critical reflection on evaluation learnings and outcomes. This process aims to achieve continuous learning and downward, upward and internal accountability. It also requires identifying the most effective and appropriate ways to present results to different stakeholder groups. This includes using creative or innovative methods to assist those involved to advocate for alternative forms of evaluation, and, for C4D, to mainstream evaluation specialists in development agencies. Based on learnings from AC4SC, key strategies and steps that can assist in developing effective communication, feedback and reporting systems in C4D organizations include:

- identifying who is currently involved in your M&E work;
- determining the level of involvement of each stakeholder group in the PM&E process and the best way to work together;
- identifying what is being communicated, how this is done, and any potential barriers to the flow of communication;
- identifying any relationships where there is no existing means of communication in order to enhance connections;
- considering the best style and form of communication to use for different stakeholder groups;

156 *Conclusion and implementation*

- assessing new communication, research and evaluation skills that may be needed;
- ensuring that the various communications used in PM&E fit into organizational work schedules and time pressures so that findings are shared in a timely way.

(adapted from Module 1 in Lennie *et al.*, 2011)

Select the most appropriate approaches, methodologies and methods

The implementation process also needs to consider the many factors involved in selecting the most appropriate approaches, methodologies and methods to use in the evaluation. Further information about this process can be found in Clark and Sartorius (2004), Gosling and Edwards (2003), Heeks and Molla (2009) and Westat (2002). We advocate taking an approach that is participatory and involves openness, freedom, flexibility and realism, and is based on a good understanding of the strengths and limitations of different approaches, methodologies and methods.

Congruence with the framework

A useful way of critically assessing various evaluation approaches, methodologies and methods is to ask the following key questions, which are based on our framework:

1. Does it enable the active, meaningful and inclusive participation of a diversity of stakeholders, including marginalized or typically excluded groups such as women and the very poor?
2. Does it take a holistic approach that provides an understanding of the wider context and the networks and inter-relationships between relevant people, groups and organizations?
3. Does it allow you to take the complex and contradictory nature of development and social change and multiple perspectives and agendas about change into account?
4. Does it take a critical approach that enables you to explicitly and openly address issues of unequal power, local social norms, gender and other differences among the people and organizations involved?
5. Does it enable a holistic, participatory, learning-oriented approach to evaluation capacity building to be taken?
6. Does it take a learning-based approach to research and evaluation and enable the development of learning organizations?
7. Is it dynamic and flexible, able to be adapted, and capable of capturing unexpected, unpredictable and self-evolving changes and emergent outcomes?
8. Does it take a realistic approach to evaluation and social change that is grounded in local realities and considers what is actually achievable in a particular timeframe?
9. Does it enable a mixed methods approach to evaluation to be taken?

Consistency with the principles underpinning the framework

The process of selecting approaches, methodologies and methods should be consistent with the principles of the framework. Some general questions that could be considered are: Do the approaches, methodologies and methods selected:

- fit the underlying values and aims of the initiative?
- fit the initial ToC for the initiative?
- enable the active participation and input from a diversity of stakeholders?

- provide an opportunity to develop evaluation capacities?
- provide some understanding of the wider context and larger structural issues that have an effect on the initiative and are of concern and interest to users of the initiative?
- enable you to go beyond a focus on individual behaviour to consider local social norms, current policies, culture and the wider development context?
- enable you to understand how and why social change happens?
- allow you to look at the issues of concern from multiple perspectives, to understand the micro and macro context and issues, and their inter-relationships?

Engaging primary stakeholders and audiences

Consideration also needs to be given to how well the approaches, methodologies and methods selected will engage primary stakeholders and audiences in the evaluation process. This includes asking questions such as:

- What type of approaches, methodologies and methods will most interest and readily engage the primary stakeholders and participants?
- What sort of approaches, methodologies and methods would be most appropriate for the particular groups involved (i.e. taking into account issues such as culture and social norms, and differences such as gender, age, caste, and literacy and educational levels)?
- What sort of approaches, methodologies and methods will lead to findings and outcomes that primary stakeholders and participants will see as useful, trustworthy and credible and will lead to utilization of results for the ongoing development and improvement of initiatives?

Deciding the best mix of approaches, methodologies and methods

Once the above issues have been clarified, the evaluation team should consider which particular mix of approaches, methodologies and methods will best fit the evaluation outcomes being sought. This requires becoming familiar with the main purpose of each approach, methodology and method and understanding their strengths and limitations or constraints. It also requires considering the extent to which any limitations or constraints outweigh the strengths of the methodology or method and how well different approaches, methodologies and methods balance or complement each other. For example, the strengths of feminist and gender-sensitive research and evaluation approaches can balance the limitations of developmental evaluation, which tends to lack a critical approach to issues of gender and power relations.

Flexibility and robustness of the design

The design of an evaluation needs to be flexible and open to revision and adaptation as information and data is gathered, those involved learn from the process, and new issues and understandings emerge. If some methodologies or methods prove unsuitable or do not yield the results that were sought, other methodologies and methods need to be readily available for use. An evaluation design should allow for further exploration of key questions or identification of gaps in the information that is being collected.

Time, resources and support available

Constraints such as time factors and various resource issues need to be considered before finalizing the evaluation questions and selecting the approaches, methodologies and methods for your evaluation. A key question here is: Will the particular approach, methodologies and methods provide the type of information that we want, when we want it, and help to answer our particular evaluation questions? Other factors that need to be considered include:

- The complexity and quality of the data to be gathered – this affects the time needed for data collection, analysis and reporting. Participatory and qualitative methods often require more time than quantitative methods. However, as we have emphasized in this book, when the many benefits of taking a participatory approach are considered, the time and other costs involved can be easily justified.
- The capacities of staff, community-based researchers, community participants and other stakeholders to effectively undertake the evaluation and use particular methodologies and methods.
- Budget constraints and the costs involved in tasks such as capacity building, organizing evaluation activities, data collection, analysis, gathering feedback and reflections on the evaluation, and reporting to various audiences.
- The support of management, programme development and communication staff in an organization is very important to the success of an evaluation, especially if you are using alternative approaches. If your organization or initiative is not very open to alternative approaches, you need to consider what strategies could be used to help foster greater support.

Assess capacity development needs and delivery

Assessing the capacity development and support needs of organizations and key stakeholders involved in the evaluation will help to increase the effectiveness, quality and rigour of the overall evaluation process and effective utilization of evaluation outcomes. This requires taking a holistic and participatory approach and asking questions such as:

- What type of capacity development is needed, for whom, and at what level?
- How can capacity development be most effectively built into the activities of our organization and its evaluation systems and processes?
- How will evaluation capacity be sustained, especially if key staff leave our organization?
- What sort of ongoing training, support or mentoring might be needed? How can this best be delivered?
- What online communities of practice should we tap into in order to enhance capacities and strengthen our networks?

Establish meta-evaluation processes

Another important component of the implementation process is the establishment of appropriate meta-evaluation processes that enable ongoing critical reflection and reviews of the effectiveness of evaluations and evaluation capacity development strategies. The aim here is to continually strengthen and improve these processes so that they better meet the needs of the people and organizations involved and help to create more sustainable, learning-oriented C4D organizations and initiatives. The multiple methods used in the meta-evaluation of AC4SC included:

- preparing a detailed 'baseline' report on existing and past M&E practices of EAN, and the organisation of EAN's project and program activities;
- an initial survey of key EAN staff at all levels to understand existing M&E knowledge and capacities, and capacity development needs;
- regular critical review and reflection meetings;
- group and individual interviews;
- feedback questionnaires completed after capacity building activities;
- participant observations of project-related activities;
- informal feedback during field visits and via email and the project website;
- providing detailed feedback on research reports prepared by the M&E team and materials such as research plans.

(Lennie et al., 2012)

Looking to the future

We have acknowledged that there are many challenges and issues in successfully implementing this framework, given the current dominance of the results-based management approach, which tends to work against the approach we have advocated. A particularly difficult challenge is finding ways to implement the alternative approach to the evaluation of C4D that we have proposed, while at the same time meeting current donor requirements for upward accountability and evidence of impact. We need to take a long-term view of this process and the significant value of adopting the approach we have advocated, which can be less costly when its many benefits in terms of the sustainability of social change and capacity development are considered.

Achieving change towards this approach will require collaboration and cooperation between of a wide range of key stakeholders in this field, including UN and other development agencies, NGOs, university specialists, consultants and practitioners, to reach mutual understanding and agreement on more appropriate and effective ways of evaluating C4D. This will require integrating complementary evaluation approaches in order to develop a new paradigm that moves beyond the dichotomies and divisions that have hindered progress in this field.

The framework we have presented in this book is open to revision, as we receive feedback from people working in this area and we learn from the outcomes of further research that uses the framework to design and implement C4D evaluations and evaluation capacity development initiatives. We encourage readers and reviewers of this book to send us feedback on our framework and how useful it has been in understanding social change and evaluating C4D.

References

Anyaegbunam, C., Mefalopulos, P. and Moetsabi, T. (2004) *Participatory rural communication appraisal: Starting with people. A handbook* (2nd ed.), Rome: FAO. Online. Available HTTP: http://www.fao.org/sd/dim_kn1/docs/y5793e00.pdf (accessed 27 May 2012).

Appadurai, A. (2002) 'Deep democracy: Urban governmentality and the horizon of politics', *Public Culture*, 14 (1): 21–47.

Appadurai, A. (2004) 'The capacity to aspire: Culture and the terms of recognition', in V. Rao and M. Walton (eds) *Culture and Public Action*, Stanford, CA: Stanford University Press.

Arnstein, S. (2011) 'A ladder of citizen participation', in A. Cornwall (ed.) *The Participation Reader*, London: Zed Books.

Atkinson, D. D., Wilson, M. and Avula, D. (2005) 'A participatory approach to building capacity of treatment programs to engage in evaluation', *Evaluation and Program Planning*, 28 (3): 329–334.

Ba Tall, O. (2009) 'The role of national, regional and international evaluation organisations in strengthening country-led monitoring and evaluation systems', in M. Segone (ed.) *Country-led Monitoring and Evaluation Systems. Better Evidence, Better Policies, Better Development Results*, Geneva: UNICEF. Online. Available HTTP: http://www.ceecis.org/remf/Country-ledMEsystems.pdf (accessed 28 May 2012).

Bailur, S. (2007) 'The complexities of community participation in ICT for development projects', paper presented at the *9th International Conference on Social Implications of Computers in Developing Countries*, Sao Paulo, Brazil, 28–30 May, 2007.

Bakewell, O. and Garbutt, A. (2005) *The use and abuse of the logical framework approach*, Stockholm: Swedish International Development Cooperation Agency. Online. Available HTTP: http://www3.interscience.wiley.com/cgi-bin/fulltext/72506844/PDFSTART (accessed 28 May 2012).

Balit, S. (2010a) 'Communicating with decision makers', *Glocal Times* 14. Online. Available HTTP: http://webzone.k3.mah.se/projects/gt2/viewarticle.aspx?articleID=181&issueID=21 (accessed 28 May 2012).

Balit, S. (2010b) 'Communicating with decision makers (continued)', *Glocal Times* 14. Online. Available HTTP: http://webzone.k3.mah.se/projects/gt2/viewarticle.aspx?articleID=183&issueID=21 (accessed 28 May 2012).

Bamberger, M. (2009) *Institutionalizing impact evaluation within the framework of a monitoring and evaluation system*, Washington DC: World Bank. Online. Available HTTP: http://siteresources.worldbank.org/EXTEVACAPDEV/Resources/4585672-1251461875432/inst_ie_framework_me.pdf (accessed 28 May 2012).

Bamberger, M. and Segone, M. (2011) *How to design and manage equity-focused evaluations*, New York: UNICEF Evaluation Office. Online. Available HTTP: http://www.mymande.org/?q=content/how-design-and-manage-equity-focused-evaluations (accessed 28 May 2012).

Bamberger, M., Rugh, J. and Mabry, L. (2006) *Real World Evaluation*, Thousand Oaks, CA: Sage.

Bamberger, M., Rao, V. and Woolcock, M. (2010) *Using mixed methods in monitoring and evaluation: Experiences from international development*, Manchester: The World Bank

Development Research Group. Online. Available HTTP: http://www-wds.worldbank.org/servlet/WDSContentServer/WDSP/IB/2010/03/23/000158349_20100323100628/Rendered/PDF/WPS5245.pdf (accessed 28 May 2012).

Barahona, C. (2011) 'Participatory numbers', in A. Cornwall and I. Scoones (eds) *Revolutionizing Development: Reflections on the Work of Robert Chambers*, London: Earthscan.

Baulch, E. (2008) 'Sustainability' in J. Tacchi and M.S. Kiran (eds) *Finding a Voice: Themes and Discussions*, Delhi: UNESCO.

Beattie, J. (1964) *Other Cultures: Aims, Methods and Achievements in Social Anthropology*, London: Routledge and Keegan Paul.

Bennett, F. and Roche, C. (2000) 'Developing indicators: The scope for participatory approaches', *New Economy*, 7 (1): 24–28.

Bhattacharya, N. (2007) *Stories of significance: Redefining change. An assortment of community voices and articulations. A report based on an evaluation of the program 'Community driven approaches to address the feminisation of HIV/AIDS in India' by means of the 'Most Significant Change' technique*, New Delhi: The India HIV/AIDS Alliance. Online. Available HTTP: http://www.aidsallianceindia.net/Material_Upload/document/Stories_of_Significance_Redefining_Change.pdf (accessed 28 May 2012).

Blamey, A. and Mackenzie, M. (2007) 'Theories of change and realistic evaluation: Peas in a pod or apples and oranges?', *Evaluation*, 13 (4): 439–455.

Boyle, R. (1999) 'Professionalising the evaluation function: Human resource development and the building of evaluation capacity', in R. Boyle and D. Lemaire (eds) *Building Effective Evaluation Capacity. Lessons from Practice*, New Brunswick, NJ: Transaction Publishers.

Boyle, R., Lemaire, D. and Rist, R. C. (1999) 'Introduction: Building evaluation capacity', in R. Boyle and D. Lemaire (eds) *Building Effective Evaluation Capacity. Lessons from Practice*, New Brunswick, NJ: Transaction Publishers.

Brown, D. (2004) 'Participation in poverty reduction strategies: Democracy strengthened or democracy undermined?', in S. Hickey and G. Mohan (eds) *Participation: From Tyranny to Transformation*, London: Zed Books.

Brunner, I. and Guzman, A. (1989) 'Participatory evaluation: A tool to assess projects and empower people', *International Innovations in Evaluation Methodology: New Directions for Program Evaluation*, 42: 9–17.

Burns, D. (2007) *Systemic Action Research: A Strategy for Whole System Change*, Bristol: The Policy Press, University of Bristol.

Byrne, A. (2008) 'Evaluating social change and communication for social change: New perspectives', *MAZI*, 17. Online. Available HTTP: http://www.communicationforsocialchange.org/mazi-articles.php?id=385 (accessed 28 May 2012).

Byrne, A. (2009a) 'Pushing the boundaries: New thinking on how we evaluate', *MAZI*, 19. Online. Available HTTP: http://www.communicationforsocialchange.org/mazi-articles.php?id=399 (accessed 28 May 2012).

Byrne, A. (2009b) *Evaluating social change communication. Expert group meeting*, Brighton, England: Institute of Development Studies. Online. Available HTTP: http://www.communicationforsocialchange.org/pdfs/evaluating%20social%20change%20communication%20brighton%20may%2009%20-%20unaids.pdf (accessed 28 May 2012).

Byrne, A. and Vincent, R. (2011) *Evaluating Social Change Communication for HIV/AIDS: New Directions*, Discussion paper produced by Communication for Social Change Consortium for UNAIDS: Geneva. Online. Available HTTP: http://www.unaids.org/en/media/unaids/contentassets/documents/unaidspublication/2009/20111101_JC2250_evaluating-social-change_en.pdf (accessed 14 May 2012).

Byrne, A., Gray-Felder, D., Hunt, J. and Parks, W. (2005) *Measuring change: A guide to participatory monitoring and evaluation of communication for social change*, South Orange, NJ: Communication for Social Change Consortium. Online. Available HTTP: http://www.communicationforsocialchange.org/pdf/measuring_change.pdf (accessed 28 May 2012).

Carpentier, N. (2011) 'The concept of participation: If they have access and interact, do they really participate?', *Communication Management Quarterly*, 21: 13–36.

Chambers, R. (2008) *Revolutions in Development Inquiry*, London: Earthscan.

Chambers, R. (2009a) 'Making the poor count: Using participatory methods for impact evaluation', in H. White (ed.) *Designing impact evaluations: Different perspectives*, Working Paper 4: The International Initiative for Impact Evaluation. Online. Available HTTP: http://www.3ieimpact.org/admin/pdfs_papers/50.pdf (accessed 28 May 2012).

Chambers, R. (2009b) 'Using participatory methods to assess impacts', Expert lecture presented at the *Perspectives on Impact Evaluation: Approaches to Assessing Development Effectiveness International Conference*, Cairo, 29 March – 2 April 2009.

Chambers, R. and Pettit, J. (2004) 'Shifting power to make a difference', in L. Groves and R. Hinton (eds) *Inclusive Aid: Changing Power and Relationships in International Development*, London: Earthscan.

Chavis, D., Lee, K. and Jones, E. (2001) *Principles for Evaluating Comprehensive Community Initiatives*, Washington DC: The Association for the Study and Development of Community. Online. Available HTTP: http://www.evaluationtoolsforracialequity.org/evaluation/resource/doc/CVP062001.pdf (accessed 29 May 2012).

Clark, M. and Sartorius, R. (2004) *Monitoring and evaluation: Some tools, methods and approaches*, Washington DC: World Bank. Online. Available HTTP: http://lnweb90.worldbank.org/oed/oeddoclib.nsf/24cc3bb1f94ae11c85256808006a0046/a5efbb5d776b67d285256b1e0079c9a3/$FILE/MandE_tools_methods_approaches.pdf (accessed 28 May 2012).

Classen, L. S. (2003) 'Assessing sustainable rural development: A participatory impact assessment of the IPCA project in Honduras', unpublished Master of Arts thesis, University of Guelph, Ontario.

Cooke, B. (2004) 'Rules of thumb for participatory change agents', in S. Hickey and G. Mohan (eds) *Participation: From Tyranny to Transformation*, London: Zed Books.

Cooke, B. and Kothari, U. (eds) (2001) *Participation: The New Tyranny*, London: Zed Books.

Cornwall, A. (1998) 'Gender, participation and the politics of difference', in I. Guijt and M. K. Shah (eds) *The Myth of Community: Gender Issues in Participatory Development*, London: Intermediate Technology Publications.

Cornwall, A. (2000) *Making a difference? Gender and participatory development*, IDS Discussion Paper 378, Brighton, England: Institute of Development Studies. Online. Available HTTP: http://www.ntd.co.uk/idsbookshop/details.asp?id=597 (accessed 29 May 2012).

Cornwall, A. (2008) 'Unpacking "participation": Models, meanings and practices', *Community Development Journal*, 43 (3): 269–283.

Cornwall, A. (ed.) (2011)*The Participation Reader*, London: Zed Books.

Cornwall, A. and Brock, K. (2005) *Beyond buzzwords "poverty reduction", "participation" and "empowerment" in development policy*, Overarching Concerns Programme Paper 10, Geneva: United Nations Research Institute for Social Development.

Cornwall, A. and Coelho, V. (2007) *Spaces for Change? The Politics of Citizen Participation in New Democratic Arenas*, London: Zed Books.

Cracknell, B. E. (2000) *Evaluating Development Aid: Issues, Problems and Solutions*, Thousand Oaks, CA: Sage.

Crewe, E. and Harrison, E. (1998) *Whose Development? An Ethnography of Aid*, New York: Zed Books.

Dag Hammarskjöld Foundation (1975) *What Now? Another Development Dialogue 1 (2)*, Uppsala: Dag Hammarskjöld Foundation.

DANIDA (2005) *Monitoring and indicators for communication for development*, Copenhagen: Technical Advisory Service, Royal Danish Ministry of Foreign Affairs. Online. Available HTTP: http://webzone.k3.mah.se/projects/comdev/_comdev_PDF_doc/Danida_ComDevt.pdf (accessed 29 May 2012).

David, R. and Mancini, A. (2011) 'Participation, learning and accountability: The role of the activist academic', in A. Cornwall and I. Scoones (eds) *Revolutionizing Development: Reflections on the Work of Robert Chambers*, London: Earthscan.

Davies, R. (2004) 'Scale, complexity and the representation of theories of change', *Evaluation*, 10 (1): 101–121.

Davies, R. and Dart, J. (2005) *The 'Most Significant Change' (MSC) technique. A guide to its use*. Online. Available HTTP: http://www.mande.co.uk/docs/MSCGuide.pdf (accessed 29 May 2012).

Deane, J. (2004) 'The context of communication for development', paper presented at the *9th United Nations Roundtable on Communication for Development*, Rome, 6–9 September, 2004. Online. Available HTTP: http://www.communicationforsocialchange.org/pdf/roundtable.pdf (accessed 29 May 2012).

Dearden, P. (2001) 'Programme and project cycle management (PPCM): Lessons from DFID and other organisations', paper presented at the *Foundation for Advanced Studies for International Development*, Tokyo, 2001. Online. Available HTTP: http://www.informaworld.com/smpp/content~db=all~content=a714883398 (accessed 29 May 2012).

Diaz-Puente, J. M., Yague, J. L. and Afonso, A. (2008) 'Building evaluation capacity in Spain: A case study of rural development and empowerment in the European Union', *Evaluation Review*, 32 (5): 478–506.

Dick, B. (1999) 'Sources of rigour in action research: Addressing the issues of trustworthiness and credibility', paper presented at the *Association for Qualitative Research Conference*, Melbourne, 6–10 July, 1999. Online. Available HTTP: http://www.aral.com.au/resources/rigour3.html (accessed 25 May 2012).

Djamankulova, K., Temirova, N. and Sobirdjonova, M. (2010) *Using action learning sets methodology in an NGO capacity building programme*, Praxis Note No. 53, INTRAC.

Dozois, E., Langlois, M. and Blanchet-Cohen, N. (2010) *DE 201: A practitioner's guide to developmental evaluation*, Victoria, BC: IICRD. Online. Available HTTP: http://mcconnellfoundation.ca/assets/Media%20Library/Publications/DE%20201%20EN.pdf (accessed 29 May 2012).

Earl, S., Carden, F. and Smutylo, T. (2001) *Outcome mapping: Building learning and reflection into development programs*, Ottawa: IDRC. Online. Available HTTP: http://www.idrc.ca/en/ev-9330-201-1-DO_TOPIC.html (accessed 29 May 2012).

Earle, L. (2003) 'Lost in the matrix: The logframe and the local picture', paper presented at the *INTRAC's 5th Evaluation Conference: Measurement, Management and Accountability?*, The Netherlands, 31 March – 4 April, 2003. Online. Available HTTP: http://www.intrac.org/data/files/resources/154/Lost-in-the-Matrix-The-Logframe-and-the-Local-Picture.pdf (accessed 29 May 2012).

Easterly, W. (2006) *The White Man's Burden: Why the West's Efforts to Aid the Rest Have Done so Much Ill and So Little Good*, Oxford: Oxford University Press.

El-Bushra, J. (2000) 'Rethinking gender and development practice for the twenty-first century', *Gender & Development*, 8 (1): 55–62.

Ellis, P. (1997) 'Gender-sensitive participatory impact assessment: Useful lessons from the Caribbean', *Knowledge and Policy. The International Journal of Knowledge Transfer and Ulitization*, 10 (1/2): 71–82.

Escobar, A. (1995) *Encountering Development: The Making and Unmaking of the Third World*, Princeton Studies in Culture/Power/History, Princeton, NJ: Princeton University Press.

Escobar, A. (2007) '"World and knowledges otherwise": The Latin American Modernity/Coloniality Research Program', *Cultural Studies*, 21 (2/3): 179–210.

Estrella, M. (2000) 'Introduction: Learning from change', in M. Estrella with J. Blauert, D. Campilan, J. Gonsalves, I. Guijt, D. Johnson et al. (eds) *Learning from Change: Issues and Experiences in Participatory Monitoring and Evaluation*, London: Intermediate Technology Publications. Online. Available HTTP: http://www.idrc.ca/openebooks/895-3/#page_201 (accessed 29 May 2012).

Estrella, M. with Blauert, J., Campilan, D., Gonsalves, J., Guijt, I., Johnson, D. et al. (eds) (2000) *Learning From Change: Issues and Experiences in Participatory Monitoring and Evaluation*, London: Intermediate Technology Publications. Online. Available HTTP: http://www.idrc.ca/openebooks/895-3/#page_201 (accessed 29 May 2012).

Eyben, R. (2011) 'Relationships matter: The best kept secret of international aid?', *CDRA An Annual Digest for Practitioners of Development 2010/2011*, Community Development Resource

Association, Cape Town, 2011. Online. Available HTTP: http://www.capacity.org/capacity/export/sites/capacity/documents/topic-readings/fa_cdra_digest.pdf (accessed 5 December 2011).

Feek, W. and Morry, C. (2009) Fitting the glass slipper! Institutionalising communication for development within the UN – A discussion document, *11th UN Inter-Agency Round Table on Communication for Development*, Washington DC, 11–13 March, 2009. Online. Available HTTP: http://www.c4d.undg.org/files/fitting-glass-slipper-institutionalising-communication-development-within-un (accessed 29 May 2012).

Fetterman, D. (2001) *Foundations of Empowerment Evaluation*, Thousand Oaks, CA: Sage.

Fetterman, D. and Wandersman, A. (eds) (2005) *Empowerment Evaluation Principles in Practice*, New York: The Guilford Press.

Figueroa, M. E., Kincaid, D.L., Rani. M. and Lewis, G. (2002). 'Communication for social change: An integrated model for measuring the process of its outcomes', in B. I. Byrd. (ed.) *Communication for Social Change*. Working Paper Series, No.1. New York: The Rockefeller Foundation. Online. Available HTTP: http://www.communicationforsocialchange.org/pdf/socialchange.pdf (accessed 30 May 2012).

Forss, K., Kruse, S., Taut, S. and Tenden, E. (2006) 'Chasing a ghost? An essay on participatory evaluation and capacity development', *Evaluation*, 12 (1):128–144.

Fraser, C. and Restrepo-Estrada, S. (1998) *Communicating for Development: Human Change for Survival*, London: I.B. Tauris Publishers.

Fraser, C. and Villett, J. (1994) *Communication: A Key to Human Development*, Rome: FAO. Online. Available HTTP: http://www.fao.org/docrep/t1815e/t1815e00.htm (accessed 29 May 2012).

Funnell, S. and Rogers, P. (2010) *Purposeful Program Theory: Effective Use of Logic Models and Theories of Change*, San Francisco, CA: Jossey-Bass.

Garaway, G.B. (1995) 'Participatory evaluation', *Studies in Educational Evaluation*, 21 (1): 85–102.

Gardner, K. and Lewis, D. (1996) *Anthropology, Development and the Post-Modern Challenge*, London: Pluto Press.

Gariba, S. (1998) 'Participatory impact assessment as a tool for change: Lessons from poverty alleviation projects in Africa', in E. Jackson and Y. Kassam (eds) *Knowledge Shared: Participatory Evaluation in Development Cooperation*, Sterling, VA: Kumarian Press. Online. Available HTTP: http://www.idrc.ca/openebooks/868-6/ (accessed 17 June 2012).

Gasper, D. (2000) 'Evaluating the "logical framework approach" towards learning-oriented development orientation', *Public Administration and Development*, 20 (1):17–28.

Gatenby, B. and Humphries, M. (1996) 'Feminist commitments in organisational communication: Participatory action research as feminist praxis', *Australian Journal of Communication*, 23 (2): 73–87.

Gatenby, B. and Humphries, M. (2000) 'Feminist participatory action research: Methodological and ethical issues', *Women's Studies International Forum*, 23 (1): 89–105.

Gaventa, J. (2006) *Triumph, deficit or contestation? Deepening the 'deepening democracy' debate*, IDS Working Paper 264, Brighton: IDS.

Gergen, K. (2009) *An Invitation to Social Construction* (2nd ed.), Los Angeles, CA: Sage Publications.

Geyer, R. (2003) 'Europeanization, complexity, and the British welfare state', paper presented at the *UACES/ESRC Study Group on The Europeanization of British Politics and Policy-Making*, Department of Politics, University of Sheffield, 19 September, 2003.

Gibbs, D. A., Hawkins, S. R., Clinton-Sherrod, A. M. and Noonan, R. K. (2009) 'Empowering programs with evaluation technical assistance. Outcomes and lessons learned', *Health Promotion Practice*, 10 (1): 385–445.

Gosling, L. and Edwards, M. (eds) (2003) *Toolkits: A practical guide to monitoring, evaluation and impact assessment*, London: Save the Children Fund.

Gould, J. (ed.) (2005) *The New Conditionality: The Politics of Poverty Reduction Strategies*, London: Zed Books.

Governance and Social Development Resource Centre (2012) *Summary of A Theory of Change: A Thinking and Action Approach to Navigate in the Complexity of Social Change Processes*,

University of Birmingham. Online. Available HTTP: http://www.gsdrc.org/go/display&type=Document&id=4095 (accessed 22 March 2012).

Greene, J. (2002) 'Mixed-method evaluation: A way of democratically engaging with difference', *Evaluation Journal of Australasia*, 2 (2): 23–29.

Greenwood, D. and Levin, M. (2007) *Introduction to Action Research: Social Research for Social Change*, Thousand Oaks, CA: Sage.

Gregory, A. (2000) 'Problematising participation. A critical review of approaches to participation in evaluation theory', *Evaluation*, 6 (2): 179–199.

Greiner, K. and Singhal, A. (2009) 'Communication and invitational social change', *Journal of Development Communication*, 20 (2): 31–44.

Grubb, B. and Tacchi, J. (2008) 'Reaching out to communities: Creatively engaging the excluded in Sri Lanka', in J. Watkins and J. Tacchi (eds) *Participatory Content Creation for Development: Principles and Practices*, New Delhi: UNESCO.

Guba, E. and Lincoln, Y. (1989) *Fourth Generation Evaluation*, Newbury Park, CA: Sage.

Guijt, I. (2000) 'Methodological issues in participatory monitoring and evaluation', in M. Estrella with J. Blauert, D. Campilan, J. Gonsalves, I. Guijt, D. Johnson *et al.* (eds) *Learning from Change: Issues and Experiences in Participatory Monitoring and Evaluation*, London: Intermediate Technology Publications. Online. Available HTTP: http://web.idrc.ca/openebooks/895-3/#page_201 (accessed 29 May 2012).

Guijt, I., Brouwers, J., Kusters, C., Prins, E. and Zeynalova, B. (2011) *Evaluation revisited: Improving the quality of evaluative practice by embracing complexity*, Wageningen: Centre for Development Innovation, Wageningen University. Online. Available HTTP: http://capacity.org/capacity/export/sites/capacity/documents/topic-readings/110412-evaluation-revisited-may-2010_small-version.pdf (accessed 29 May 2012).

Gumucio Dagron, A. (2008) 'Vertical minds versus horizontal cultures: An overview of participatory process and experiences', in J. Servaes (ed.) *Communication for Development and Social Change*, London: Sage.

Gumucio Dagron, A. (2009) *Promoting the development of free, independent and pluralistic media and community participation in sustainable development through community media*, Uruguay: UNESCO.

Hall, B. (1993) 'Introduction', in P. Park, M. Brydon-Miller, B. Hall and T. Jackson (eds) *Voices of Change: Participatory Research in the United States and Canada* (vol. xi–xii), London: Bergin & Garvey.

Hanssen, C., Lawrenz, F. and Dunet, D. (2008) 'Concurrent meta-evaluation. A critique', *American Journal of Evaluation*, 29 (4): 572–582.

Harnmeijer, J. (1999) *From terms of reference to participatory learning: Using an evaluation's creative space*, PLA Notes 36, London: IIED.

Hartley, J. and McWilliam, K. (eds) (2009) *Story Circle: Digital Storytelling Around the World*, Oxford: Wiley-Blackwell.

Hay, K. (2010) 'Evaluation field building in South Asia: Reflections, anecdotes, and questions', *American Journal of Evaluation*, 31 (2): 222–231.

Hearn, G., Tacchi, J., Foth, M. and Lennie, J. (2009) *Action Research and New Media: Concepts, Methods and Cases*, Cresskill, NJ: Hampton Press.

Heeks, R. and Molla, A. (2009) *Compendium on impact assessment of ICT-for-development projects*, Development Informatics Working Paper Series No. 36, University of Manchester: Development Informatics Group, Institute for Development Policy and Management. Online. Available HTTP: http://ict4dblog.wordpress.com/2008/12/03/impact-assessment-of-ict4d-projects/ (accessed 29 May 2012).

Hickey, S. and Mohan, G. (eds) (2004) *Participation: From Tyranny to Transformation*, London: Zed Books.

Holte-McKenzie, Forde, S. and Theobald, S. (2006) 'Development of a participatory monitoring and evaluation strategy', *Evaluation and Program Planning*, 29 (4): 365–376.

Horton, D., Alexaki, A., Bennett-Lartey, S., Brice, K. N., Campilan, D., Carden, F. *et al.* (2003) *Evaluating capacity development: Experiences from research and development organizations around the world*, The Hague: International Service for National Agricultural Research. Online. Available HTTP: http://web.idrc.ca/openebooks/111-6/ (accessed 29 May 2012).

Hummelbrunner, R. (2006) 'Systemic evaluation in the field of regional development', in B. Williams and I. Imam (eds) *Systems Concepts in Evaluation : An Expert Anthology*, Fairhaven, MA: American Evaluation Association. Online. Available HTTP: http://preval.org/files/Kellogg%20enfoque%20sistematico%20en%20evaluacion.pdf (accessed 24 May 2012).

Humphries, B. (1999) 'Feminist evaluation', in I. Shaw and J. Lishman (eds) *Evaluation and Social Work Practice*, London: Sage.

Imam, I., LaGoy, A. and Williams, B. (2006) 'Introduction', in B. Williams and I. Imam (eds) *Systems Concepts in Evaluation: An Expert Anthology*, Fairhaven, MA: American Evaluation Association. Online. Available HTTP: http://preval.org/files/Kellogg%20enfoque%20sistematico%20en%20evaluacion.pdf (accessed 24 May 2012).

Inagaki, N. (2007) *Communicating the impact of communication for development. Recent trends in empirical research*, Working Paper Series No. 120, Washington DC: World Bank. Online. Available HTTP: http://wwwwds.worldbank.org/external/default/WDSContentServer/WDSP/IB/2007/08/10/000310607_20070810123306/Rendered/PDF/405430Communic18082137167101PUBLIC1.pdf (accessed 29 May 2012).

Jallov, B. (2005) 'Assessing community change: Development of a "bare foot" impact assessment methodology', *Radio Journal: International Studies in Broadcast & Audio Media*, 3 (1): 21–34.

Jallov, B. (2007) 'Most Significant Change: A tool to document community radio impact. Measuring change. Planning, monitoring and evaluation in media and development cooperation', in A. S. Jannuschm (ed.) *3rd Symposium Forum on Media and Development*: Bad Honnef: Catholic Media Council. Online. Available HTTP: http://www.cameco.org/files/measuring_change_1.pdf (accessed 29 May 2012).

Jallov, B. (2012) *Empowerment Radio. Voices Building a Community*, Gudhjem: Empowerhouse.

Jennings, L. and Graham, A. (1996) 'Exposing discourses through action research', in O. Zuber-Skerritt (ed.) *New Directions in Action Research*, London: The Farmer Press.

Johnson, H. and Wilson, G. (2009) *Learning for Development*, London: Zed Books.

Johnson, R. and Onwuegbuzie, A. (2004) 'Mixed methods research: A research paradigm whose time has come', *Educational Researcher*, 33 (7): 14–26.

Jones, H. (2011) *Taking responsibility for complexity: How implementation can achieve results in the face of complex problems*, ODI Working Papers 330, June 2011, London: Overseas Development Institute. Online. Available HTTP: http://www.odi.org.uk/resources/details.asp?id=5275&title=complex-problems-complexity-implementation-policy (accessed 30 May 2012) .

Joseph, S. (2011) 'Changing attitudes and behaviour', in A. Cornwall and I. Scoones (eds) *Revolutionizing Development: Reflections on the Work of Robert Chambers*, London: Earthscan.

Joyappa, V. and Martin, D. (1996) 'Exploring alternative research epistemologies for adult education: Participatory research, feminist research and feminist participatory research', *Adult Education Quarterly*, 47 (1): 1–14.

Kabeer, N. (2011) *Contextualising the economic pathways of women's empowerment: Findings from a multi-country research programme*, Pathways Policy Paper, October 2011, Brighton: Pathways of Women's Empowerment RPC.

Kemmis, S. and McTaggart, R. (2000) 'Participatory action research', in N. Denzin and Y. Lincoln (eds) *The Handbook of Qualitative Research* (2nd ed.), Beverly Hills, CA: Sage.

Keystone Accountability (2008) *Tool 2: Developing a theory of change*. Online. Available HTTP: http://www.keystoneaccountability.org/node/215 (accessed 24 May 2012).

Keystone Accountablility (2009) *Developing a theory of change. A guide to developing a theory of change as a framework for inclusive dialogue, learning and accountability for social impact*, IPAL Guide 2, London: Keystone. Online. Available HTTP: http://www.keystoneaccountability.org/sites/default/files/2%20Developing%20a%20theory%20of%20change.pdf (accessed 29 May 2012).

Khagram, S. (2009) 'Comparative (case study) evaluation', presentation in a workshop on 'Impact Evaluation for Improving Development' at the *Perspectives on Impact Evaluation: Approaches to Assessing Development Effectiveness International Conference*, Cairo, 29 March – 2 April, 2009.

Khan, M. (1998) 'Evaluation capacity building', *Evaluation*, 4 (3): 310–328.

Lacayo, V. (2006) 'Approaching social change as a complex problem in a world that treats it as a complicated one. The case of Puntos de Encuentro, Nicaragua', Master of Arts thesis (Communication and Development), Ohio University, Athens, Ohio.

Lacayo, V. (2007) 'What complexity science teaches us about social change', *MAZI*, 10. Online. Available HTTP: http://www.communicationforsocialchange.org/mazi-articles.php?id=333 (accessed 30 May 2012).

Leal, P. (2007) 'Participation: The ascendancy of a buzzword in the neo-liberal era', *Development in Practice*, 17 (4): 539–548.

Leeuw, F. and Vaessen, J. (2009) *Impact evaluations and development. NONIE guidance on impact evaluation*, Washington DC: The Network of Networks on Impact Evaluation. Online. Available HTTP: http://siteresources.worldbank.org/EXTOED/Resources/nonie_guidance.pdf (accessed 29 May 2012).

Lennie, J. (2002) 'Including a diversity of rural women in a communication technology access project: Taking the macro and micro contexts into account', in G. Johanson and L. Stillman (eds) *Proceedings, Electronic Networks – Building Community: 5th Community Networking Conference*, Monash University, Melbourne, 3–5 July.

Lennie, J. (2005a) 'An evaluation capacity-building process for sustainable community IT initiatives. Empowering and disempowering impacts', *Evaluation*, 11 (5): 390–414.

Lennie, J. (2005b) 'An eclectic feminist framework for critically evaluating women and communication technology projects', in K. Kwansah-Aidoo (ed.) *Topical Issues in Communications and Media Research*, Nova Science Publishers: New York.

Lennie, J. (2006a) 'Critically evaluating rural women's participation and empowerment: An interdisciplinary feminist framework for research and analysis', in M.C. Behera (ed.) *Globalising Rural Development: Competing Paradigms and Emerging Realities*, New Delhi: Sage.

Lennie, J. (2006b) 'Increasing the rigour and trustworthiness of participatory evaluations: Learnings from the field', *Evaluation*, 6 (1): 27–35.

Lennie, J. (2009) *Troubling Empowerment: A Feminist Critique of a Rural Women and Communication Technology Project*, Saarbrucken: VDM.

Lennie, J. and Hearn, G. (2003) 'The potential of PAR and participatory evaluation for increasing the sustainability and success of community development initiatives using new communication technologies', *Proceedings of the Action Learning, Action Research & Process Management and Participatory Action Research Congress*, University of Pretoria, South Africa, 21–24 September, 2003.

Lennie, J. and Tacchi, J. (2011a) *Researching, monitoring and evaluating communication for development: Trends, challenges and approaches*. Report on a literature review and consultations with Expert Reference Group and UN Focal Points on C4D. Prepared for the United Nations Inter-Agency Group on Communication for Development, New York: UNICEF. Online. Available HTTP: http://www.unicef.org/cbsc/index_44255.html (accessed 24 May 2012).

Lennie, J. and Tacchi, J. (2011b) *Outline of a guide to designing the research, monitoring and evaluation process for communication for development in the UN*. Prepared for the United Nations Inter-Agency Group on Communication for Development, New York: UNICEF. Online. Available HTTP: http://www.unicef.org/cbsc/index_42377.html (accessed 24 May 2012).

Lennie, J., Hatcher, C. and Morgan, W. (2003) 'Feminist discourses of (dis)empowerment in an action research project involving rural women and communication technologies', *Action Research*, 1 (1): 57–80.

Lennie, J., Hearn, G., Simpson, L., Kennedy Da Silva, E., Kimber, M. and Hanrahan, M. (2004) *Building community capacity in evaluating IT projects: Outcomes of the LEARNERS project*. Final Report, Creative Industries Research and Applications Centre and Service Leadership and

Innovation Research Program, Brisbane: Queensland University of Technology. Online. Available HTTP: http://eprints.qut.edu.au/archive/00004389/ (accessed 13 February 2012).

Lennie, J., Skuse, A., Tacchi, J. and Wilmore, M. (2008) 'Challenges, issues and contradictions in a participatory impact assessment project in Nepal', paper presented at the *Australasian Evaluation Society International Conference*, Perth, 12 September, 2008. Online. Available HTTP: http://www.aes.asn.au/conferences/2008/papers/p14.pdf (accessed 29 May 2012).

Lennie, J., Skuse, A., Koirala, B., Rijal, N. and Wilmore, M. (2009) 'Developing a participatory impact assessment approach and action research culture within a communication for social change organisation in Nepal', paper presented at the *Perspectives on Impact Evaluation: Approaches to Assessing Development Effectiveness International Conference*, Cairo, 2 April, 2009. Online. Available HTTP: http://www.3ieimpact.org/cairo_conference.html (accessed 29 May 2012).

Lennie, J., Tacchi, J. and Wilmore, M. (2010) 'Critical reflections on the use of meta-evaluation in the "Assessing Communication for Social Change" project', paper presented at the *Australasian Evaluation Society International Conference*, Wellington, 3 September, 2010. Online. Available HTTP: http://www.aes.asn.au/conferences/ (accessed 29 May 2012).

Lennie, J., Tacchi, J., Koirala, B., Wilmore, M. and Skuse, A. (2011) *Equal Access participatory monitoring and evaluation toolkit*, Queensland University of Technology, University of Adelaide, and Equal Access Nepal.

Lennie, J., Tacchi, J. and Wilmore, M. (2012) 'Meta-evaluation to improve learning, evaluation capacity development and sustainability: Findings from a participatory evaluation project in Nepal', *South Asian Journal of Evaluation in Practice*, 1 (1): 13–28.

Liamputtong, P. (2007) *Researching the Vulnerable. A Guide to Sensitive Research Methods*, London: Sage.

Lundgren, H. and Kennedy, M. (2009) 'Supporting partner country ownership and capacity in development evaluation. The OECD evaluation network', in M. Segone (ed.) *Country-led Monitoring and Evaluation Systems. Better Evidence, Better Policies, Better Development Results*, Geneva: UNICEF. Online. Available HTTP: http://www.ceecis.org/remf/Country-ledMEsystems.pdf (accessed 29 May 2012).

McCall, E. (2011) *Communication for development: Strengthening the effectiveness of the United Nations*, New York and Oslo: FAO, ILO, UNAIDS, UNDP, UNESCO, UNICEF and WHO. Online. Available HTTP: http://www.unicef.org/cbsc/files/Inter-agency_C4D_Book_2011.pdf (accessed 29 May 2012).

MacColl, I., Cooper, R., Rittenbruch, M. and Viller, S. (2005) 'Watching ourselves watching: Ethical issues in ethnographic action research', *Proceedings of the OZCHI Conference*, Canberra, 23–25 November, 2005.

McKegg, K. and Wehipeihana, N. (2011) 'Developmental evaluation: A practitioner's introduction', Australasian Evaluation Society workshop, 17 June 2011, Brisbane.

McKie, L. (2003) 'Rhetorical spaces: Participation and pragmatism in the evaluation of community health work', *Evaluation*, 9 (3): 307–324.

McTaggart, R. (1991) 'Principles for participatory action research', *Adult Education Quarterly*, 41 (3): 168–187.

Maguire, P. (1996) 'Proposing a more feminist participatory research: Knowing and being embraced openly', in K. De Koning and M. Martin (eds) *Participatory Research in Health: Issues and Experiences*, London: Zed Books.

Mansell, R. (2011) 'Power and interests in information and communication and development: Exogenous and endogenous discourses in contention', *Journal of International Development*, 11: 19–22.

Marsden, R. (2004) 'Exploring power and relationships: A perspective from Nepal', in L. Groves and R. Hinton (eds) *Inclusive Aid: Changing Power and Relationships in International Development*, London: Earthscan.

Martin, M. (1994) 'Developing a feminist participative research framework: Evaluating the process', in B. Humphries and C. Truman (eds) *Re-thinking Social Research: Anti-discriminatory Approaches in Research Methodology*, Aldershot: Avebury.

Martin, M. (1996) 'Issues of power in the participatory research process', in K. de Koning and M. Martin (eds) *Participatory Research in Health. Issues and Experiences*, London: Zed Books.

Martin, M. (2000) 'Critical education for participatory research', in C. Truman, D. Mertens and B. Humphries (eds) *Research and Inequality*, New York: UCL Press.

Mathie, A. and Greene, J. (1997) 'Stakeholder participation in evaluation: How important is diversity?', *Evaluation and Program Planning*, 20 (3): 279–285.

Mayne, J. (1999) *Addressing attribution through contribution analysis: Using performance measures sensibly*, Discussion paper produced by Office of the Auditor General of Canada.

Mayoux, L. and Chambers, R. (2005) 'Reversing the paradigm: Quantification, participatory methods and pro-poor impact assessment', *Journal of International Development*, 17 (2): 271–298.

Mebrahtu, E., Pratt, B. and Lönnqvist, L. (2007) *Rethinking Monitoring and Evaluation: Challenges and Prospects in the Changing Global Aid Environment*, Oxford: INTRAC.

Mefalopulos, P. (2005) 'Communication for sustainable development: Applications and challenges', in O. Hemer and T. Tufte (eds) *Media and Glocal Change: Rethinking Communication for Development*, Suecia: Nordicom.

Mertens, D. (2009) *Transformative Research and Evaluation*, New York: The Guilford Press.

Mertens, D. and Chilisa, B. (2009) 'Mixed methods and social transformation', Workshop presented at the *Perspectives on Impact Evaluation: Approaches to Assessing Development Effectiveness International Conference*, Cairo, 29 March – 2 April, 2009.

Midgley, G. (2006) 'Systems thinking for evaluation', in B. Williams, I. Imam and American Evaluation Association (eds.) *Systems Concepts in Evaluation: An Expert Anthology*, Fairhaven, MA: American Evaluation Association. Online. Available HTTP: http://preval.org/files/Kellogg%20enfoque%20sistematico%20en%20evaluacion.pdf (accessed 24 May 2012).

Miskelly, C., Hoban, A. and Vincent, R. (2009) *How can complexity theory contribute to more effective development and aid evaluation?* Dialogue at the Diana, Princess of Wales Memorial Fund, London: Panos. Online. Available HTTP: http://panos.org.uk/wp-content/files/2011/03/Panos_London_Complexity_and_Evaluation_dialogueCK5gVc.pdf (accessed 30 May 2012).

Mongella, G. (1995) 'Moving beyond rhetoric', in *Women: Looking Beyond 2000*, New York: United Nations Publications.

Morariu, J., Reed, E., Brennan, K., Stamp, A., Parrish, S. and Pankaj, V. (2009) *Pathfinder Evaluation Edition. A Practical Guide to Advocacy Evaluation*, Washington DC: Innovation Network. Online. Available HTTP: http://www.innonet.org/client_docs/File/advocacy/pathfinder_evaluator_web.pdf (accessed 29 May 2012).

Morgan, G. and Ramirez, R. (1983) 'Action learning: A holographic metaphor for guiding social change', *Human Relations*, 37 (1): 1–27.

Myers, M. (2005) *Monitoring and evaluating information and communication for development (ICD) programmes: Guidelines*, London: DFID. Online. Available HTTP: http://www.idrc.ca/uploads/user-S/11592105581icd-guidelines.pdf (accessed 29 May 2012).

Naccarella, L., Pirkis, J., Kohn, F., Morley, B., Burgess, P. and Blashki, G. (2007) 'Building evaluation capacity: Definitional and practical implications from an Australian case study', *Evaluation and Program Planning*, 30 (3): 231–236.

Napp, D., Gibbs, D., Jolly, D., Westover, B. and Uhi, G. (2002) 'Evaluation barriers and facilitators among community-based HIV prevention programs', *AIDS Education and Prevention*, 14 (Supplement A): 38–48.

Newman, K. (2008) 'Whose view matters? Using participatory processes to evaluate *Reflect* in Nigeria', *Community Development Journal*, 43 (3): 382–394.

Newman, K. and Beardon, H. (2011) 'Overview: How wide are the ripples? From local participation to international organisational learning', in H. Ashley, N. Kenton and N. Milligan (eds) *How Wide are the Ripples? From Local Participation to International Organisational Learning, Participatory Learning and Action*. London: The International Institute for Environment and Development. Online. Available HTTP: http://pubs.iied.org/pdfs/14606IIED.pdf (accessed 13 February 2012).

Newton, K. (2011) 'The "problem" of gender and development evaluation in the Pacific', *Evaluation Journal of Australasia*, 11 (1): 26–37.

O'Donnell, P., Lloyd, P. and Dreher, T. (2009) 'Listening, path building and continuations: A research agenda for the analysis of listening', *Continuum*, 23 (4): 423–439.

Oleari, K. (2000) 'Making your job easier: Using whole-system approaches to involve the community in sustainable planning and development', *Public Management*, 82 (12): 4–10.

O'Meara, P., Chester, J. and Han, G.S. (2004) 'Outside – looking in: Evaluating a community capacity building project', *Rural Society*, 14 (2): 126–141.

Panos (2008) *Spark discussion: Evaluating social change communication*, London: Panos. Online. Available HTTP: http://panos.org.uk/2008/09/25/spark-evaluating-social-change-communication/ (accessed 9 March 2012).

Papa, M., Singhal, A. and Papa, W. (2006) *Organizing for Social Change: A Dialectical Journey of Theory and Praxis*, New Delhi: Sage.

Papineau, D. and Kiely, M. (1996) 'Participatory evaluation in a community organization: Fostering stakeholder empowerment and utilization', *Evaluation and Program Planning*, 19 (1): 79–93.

Parker, W. (2004) *Rethinking conceptual approaches to behaviour change: The importance of context*, South Africa: Centre for Aids Development, Research and Evaluation. Online. Available HTTP: http://cadre.pnnt.predelegation.com/files/CANBehaviour.pdf (accessed 5 May 2012).

Parks, W., Gray-Felder, D., Hunt, J. and Byrne, A. (2005) *Who measures change: An introduction to participatory monitoring and evaluation of communication for social change*, South Orange, NJ: Communication for Social Change Consortium. Online. Available HTTP: http://www.communicationforsocialchange.org/pdf/who_measures_change.pdf (accessed 29 May 2012).

Patton, M.Q. (2002) *Qualitative Research and Evaluation Methods* (3rd ed.), Thousand Oaks, CA: Sage.

Patton, M.Q. (2008) *Utilization-Focused Evaluation* (4th ed.), Thousand Oaks, CA: Sage.

Patton, M.Q. (2011) *Developmental Evaluation: Applying Complexity Concepts to Enhance Innovation and Use*, New York: The Guilford Press.

Pearson, J. (2011) *Creative Capacity Development: Learning to Adapt in Development Practice*, Sterling, VA: Kumarian Press.

Pink, S. (2007) *Doing Visual Ethnography: Images, Media and Representation in Research* (2nd ed.), Thousand Oaks, CA: Sage.

Postill, J. (2011) *Localizing the Internet: An Anthropological Account*, Oxford: Berghahn.

Pratt, B. (2007) 'Rethinking monitoring and evaluation'. *INTRAC Newsletter* 37: 1–2.

Preskill, H. and Boyle, S. (2008) 'Multidisciplinary model of evaluation capacity building', *American Journal of Evaluation*, 29 (4): 443–459.

Puddephatt, A., Horsewell, R. and Menheneott, G. (2009) Discussion paper on the monitoring and evaluation of UN-assisted communication for development programmes. Recommendations for best practice methodologies and indicators, *11th UN Inter-Agency Round Table on Communication for Development*, Washington DC, March 11–13, 2009. Online. Available HTTP: http://www.communicationforsocialchange.org/pdfs/monitoring%20and%20evaluation%20of%20un-assisted%20cfd%20programmes.pdf (accessed 29 May 2012).

Quarry, W. and Ramirez, R. (2009) *Communication for Another Development: Listening Before Telling*, London: Zed Books.

Raeside, A. (2011) 'Are INGOs brave enough to become learning organisations?', in H. Ashley, N. Kenton and N. Milligan (eds) *How Wide are the Ripples? From Local Participation to International Organisational Learning, Participatory Learning and Action*, London: The International Institute for Environment and Development, 63: 97–102. Online. Available HTTP: http://pubs.iied.org/pdfs/14606IIED.pdf (accessed 30 May 2012).

Rajbhandari, B. (2006) 'Sustainable livelihood and rural development in South Asia. Issues, concerns and general implications', in M. C. Behera (ed.) *Globalising Rural Development: Competing Paradigms and Emerging Realities*, New Delhi: Sage.

Ramalingam, B and Jones, H. with Reba, T. and Young, J. (2008) *Exploring the science of complexity: Ideas and implications for development and humanitarian efforts*, ODI Working Paper

(2nd ed.), London: Overseas Development Institute. Online. Available HTTP: http://www.odi.org.uk/resources/download/583.pdf (accessed 21 March 2012).

Rattine-Flaherty, E. and Singhal, A. (2009) 'Analyzing social-change practice in the Peruvian Amazon through a feminist reading of participatory communication research', *Development in Practice*, 17 (6): 726–736.

Reason, P. (ed.) (1988) *Human Inquiry in Action: Developments in New Paradigm Research*, London: Sage.

Regeer, B., Hoes, A., Sanne, M., Caron-Flinterman, F. and Bunders, J. (2009) 'Six guiding principles for evaluating mode-2 strategies for sustainable development', *American Journal of Evaluation*, 30 (4): 515–537.

Retolaza, I. (2011) *Theory of change. A thinking and action approach to navigate in the complexity of social change processes*, The Hague: HIVOS (Humanist Institute for Development Cooperation). Online. Available HTTP: http://www.hivos.nl/%20content/download/70159/602460/version/1/file/2011RetolazaToCENG.pdf (accessed 22 March 2012).

Rice, R. and Foote, D. (2001) 'A systems-based evaluation planning model for health communication campaigns in developing countries', in R. E. Rice and C. Atkin (eds) *Public Communication Campaigns* (3rd ed.), Thousand Oaks, CA: Sage.

Rihani, S. (2002) *Complex Systems Theory and Development Practice. Understanding Non-linear Realities*, London: Zed Books.

Rodriguez, C. (2005) 'From the Sandanista revolution to telenovelas: The case of Puntos de Encuentro', in O. Hemer and T. Tufte (eds) *Media and Glocal Change: Rethinking Communication for Development*, Suecia: Nordicom.

Rogers, E. (ed.) (1976) *Communication and Development: Critical Perspectives*, Thousand Oaks, CA: Sage.

Rogers, P. (2009) 'Matching impact evaluation designs to the nature of the intervention and the purpose of the evaluation', in E. White (ed.) *Designing impact evaluations: Different perspectives*, Working Paper 4, New Delhi: The International Initiative for Impact Evaluation. Online. Available HTTP: http://www.3ieimpact.org/admin/pdfs_papers/50.pdf (accessed 29 May 2012).

Rogers, P. (2011) 'Evaluation's influence – the dream, the nightmare, and some waking thoughts', Keynote address presented at the *Australasian Evaluation Society International Conference*, Sydney, 1 September 2011.

Sankar, M. and Williams, B. (2007) 'Editorial – Evaluation matters', in B. Williams and M. Sankar (eds) *Evaluation South Asia*, Kathmandu: UNICEF. Online. Available HTTP: http://unicef.org/rosa/ROSA_Evaluation_Journal.pdf (accessed 29 May 2012).

Schiavo-Campo, S. (2005) *Building country capacity for monitoring and evaluation in the public sector: Selected lessons of international experience*, Evaluation Capacity Development, ECD Working Paper Series No. 13: The World Bank Operations Evaluation Department. Online. Available HTTP: http://preval.org/files/2086.pdf (accessed 29 May 2012).

Servaes, J. (ed.) (2008) *Communication for Development and Social Change*, London: Sage.

Servaes, J. and Malikhao, P. (2005) 'Participatory communication: The new paradigm?', in O. Hemer and T. Tufte (eds) *Media and Glocal Change: Rethinking Communication for Development*, Suecia: Nordicom.

Servaes, J., Polk, E., Shi, S., Reilly, D. and Yakupitijage, T. (2012) 'Towards a framework of sustainability indicators for "communication for development and social change" projects', *The International Communication Gazette*, 74 (2): 99–123.

Simons, H. (1996) 'The paradox of case study', *Cambridge Journal of Education*, 26 (2):225–240.

Simons, H. (2009) *Case Study Research in Practice*, Los Angeles, CA: Sage.

Singhal, A. and Lacayo, V. (2007) *Engaging and mobilizing society through edutainment. Experience-sharing and cross-learning among four pioneering organizations*, Oxfam-Novib, KIC Project. Online. Available HTTP: http://utminers.utep.edu/asinghal/technical%20reports/CLEAN-FINALsinghal-lacayo-KIC-workshop_report-March-8-_2008.pdf (accessed 23 November 2011).

Singhal, A. and Rogers, E. (2003) *Combating AIDS: Communication Strategies in Action*, New Delhi: Sage.

Skuse, A. (2006) *Voices for change: Strategic radio support for achieving the Millennium Development Goals*, London: DFID. Online. Available HTTP: http://www.bnnrc.net/resouces/voices-of-change.pdf (accessed 30 May 2012).

Slater, D. and Tacchi, J. (2004) *Research: ICT Innovations for Poverty Reduction*, New Delhi: UNESCO.

Slater, D., Tacchi, J. and Lewis, P. (2002) *Ethnographic monitoring and evaluation of community multimedia centres: A study of Kothmale Community Radio Internet Project*, Sri Lanka, London: DFID.

Souter, D. (2008) *Investigation 4: Impact assessment. In BCO impact assessment study. The final report*: Building Communication Opportunities Alliance. Online. Available HTTP: www.bcoalliance.org/system/files/BCO_FinalReport.pdf (accessed 30 May 2012).

Stanley, L. and Wise, S. (1990) 'Method, methodology and epistemology in feminist research process', in L. Stanley (ed.) *Feminist Praxis: Research, Theory, and Epistemology in Feminist Sociology*, London: Routledge.

Stevenson, T. and Lennie, J. (1995) 'Emerging designs for work, living and learning in the communicative age', *Futures Research Quarterly*, 11 (3): 5–36.

Stiefel, M. and Wolfe, M. (1994) *A Voice for the Excluded: Popular Participation in Development – Utopia or Necessity?*, London: Zed Books.

Suárez-Herrera, J. C., Springett, J. and Kagan, C. (2009) 'Critical connections between participatory evaluation, organizational learning and intentional change in pluralistic organizations', *Evaluation*, 15 (3): 321–342.

Sullivan, H., Barnes, M. and Matka, E. (2002) 'Building collaborative capacity through "theories of change"', *Evaluation*, 8 (2): 205–226.

Tacchi, J. (2009) 'Finding a Voice: Digital storytelling as participatory development', in J. Hartley and K. McWilliams (eds) *Story Circle: Digital Storytelling Around the World*, Oxford: Wiley-Blackwell.

Tacchi, J. (2012a) 'Open content creation: The issues of voice and the challenges of listening', *New Media and Society*, 14 (4): 652–668.

Tacchi, J. (2012b) 'Digital engagement: Voice and participation in development', in H. Horst and D. Miller (eds) *Digital Anthropology*, Oxford: Berg.

Tacchi, J. and Grubb, B. (2007). 'The case of the e-Tuktuk', *Media International Australia incorporating Culture and Policy*, 125: 71–82.

Tacchi, J. and Kiran, M. S. (eds) (2008) *Finding a Voice: Themes and Discussions*. New Delhi: UNESCO. Online. Available HTTP: http://www.findingavoice.org/files/finding_a_voice_themes_and_discussions.pdf (accessed 30 May 2012).

Tacchi, J., Slater, D. and Hearn, G. (2003) *Ethnographic action research: A user's handbook*. New Delhi: UNESCO.

Tacchi, J., Fildes, J., Martin, K., Mulenahali, K., Baulch, E. and Skuse, A. (2007) *Ethnographic action research training handbook*. Online. Available HTTP: http://ear.findingavoice.org/ (accessed 30 May 2012).

Tacchi, J., Lennie, J. and Wilmore, M. (2010). 'Critical reflections on the use of participatory methodologies to build evaluation capacities in international development organisations', *Proceedings of the 8th World Congress on Participatory Action Research and Action Learning*, Melbourne, Victoria, 6–9 September 2010. Online. Available HTTP: http://www.alara.net.au/wc2010/proceedings (accessed 20 June 2012).

Taut, S. (2007) 'Studying self-evaluation capacity building in a large international development organization', *American Journal of Evaluation*, 28 (1): 45–59.

Tenhunen, S. (2008) 'Mobile technology in the village: ICTs, culture, and social logistics in India', *Journal of the Royal Anthropological Institute (N.S.)*, 14 (3): 515–534.

Thomas, L. (2000) 'Bums on seats; or "listening to voices": Evaluating widening participation initiatives using participatory action research', *Studies in Continuing Education*, 22 (1): 95–113.

UKCDS (2011) *Note from UKCDS workshop 'Exploring the potential of complexity sciences in international development'*, London: Wellcome Trust. Online. Available HTTP: http://ukcds.org.uk/_assets/file/UKCDS%20Complexity%20Workshop%20meeting%20report.pdf (accessed 26 May 2012).

UN Resolution 51/172 (1997) *Communication for development programmes in the United Nations system*. Online. Available HTTP: http://portal.unesco.org/ci/en/files/21351/11712967771A-RES-51-182.pdf/A-RES-51-182.pdf (accessed 30 May 2012).

UN Women (2010) *A manager's guide to gender equality and human rights responsive evaluation*, New York: UN Women. Online. Available HTTP: http://unifem.org/evaluation_manual/ (accessed 30 May 2012).

UNESCO (2007) 'Towards a common UN systems approach: Harnessing communication to achieve the Millennium Development Goals', Background paper prepared for the *10th UN Inter-Agency Round Table on Communication for Development*, Addis Ababa, Ethiopia. Online. Available HTTP: http://unesdoc.unesco.org/images/0014/001496/149687e.pdf (accessed 30 May 2012).

Uusikyla, P. and Virtanen, P. (2000) 'Meta-evaluation as a tool for learning. A case study of the European structural fund evaluations in Finland', *Evaluation*, 6 (1): 50–65.

Valery, R. and Shakir, S. (2005) 'Evaluation capacity building and humanitarian organization', *Journal of Multidisciplinary Evaluation*, 2 (3): 78–112.

Vanderplaat, M. (1995) 'Beyond technique. Issues in evaluating for empowerment', *Evaluation*, 1 (1): 81–96.

Vernooy, R., Qiu, S. and Jianchu, X. (2003) *Voices for change. Participatory monitoring and evaluation in China*, Ottawa: International Development Research Centre. Online. Available HTTP: http://www.idrc.ca/openebooks/994-1/ (accessed 30 May 2012).

Wadsworth, Y. (1997) *Everyday Evaluation on the Run*, St Leonards, NSW: Allen & Unwin.

Wadsworth, Y. (2010) *Building in Research and Evaluation: Human Inquiry for Living Systems*, Sydney: Allen & Unwin.

Waisbord, S. (2001) *Family tree of theories, methodologies and strategies in development communication*, South Orange, NJ: Communication for Social Change. Online. Available HTTP: http://www.communicationforsocialchange.org/pdf/familytree.pdf (accessed 30 May 2012).

Waisbord, S. (2005) 'Five key ideas: Coincidences and challenges in development communication', in O. Hemer and T. Tufte (eds) *Media and Glocal Change: Rethinking Communication for Development*, Suecia: Nordicom.

Waisbord, S. (2008) 'The institutional challenges of participatory communication in international aid', *Social Identities*, 14 (4): 505–522.

Waisbord, S. (2011) 'The global promotion of media diversity: Revisiting operational models and bureaucratic imperatives', in M. E. Price, S. Abbott and L. Morgan (eds) *Measures of Press Freedom and Media Contributions to Development: Evaluating the Evaluators*, New York: Peter Lang.

Watkins, J. and Tacchi, J. (2008) *Participatory Content Creation for Development: Principles and Practices*, New Delhi: UNESCO. Online. Available HTTP: http://unesdoc.unesco.org/images/0015/001586/158624e.pdf (accessed 30 May 2012).

Webb, D. and Elliott, L. (2002) *Learning to live: Monitoring and evaluating HIV/AIDS programmes for young people*, London: Save the Children Fund. Online. Available HTTP: http://resourcecentre.savethechildren.se/content/library/documents/learning-live-monitoring-and-evaluating-hivaids-programmes-young-people (accessed 30 May 2012).

Wehipeihana, N. and McKegg, K. (2009) 'Developmental evaluation in an indigenous context: Reflections on the journey to date', paper presented at the *American Evaluation Association Conference*, Orlando, FL, 11–14 November, 2009.

Westat, J. (2002) *The 2002 user friendly handbook for project evaluation*, Arlington VA: The National Science Foundation. Online. Available HTTP: http://www.nsf.gov/pubs/2002/nsf02057/nsf02057.pdf (accessed 30 May 2012).

White, H. (2009) 'Designing theory-based impact evaluations', Workshop presented at the *Perspectives on Impact Evaluation: Approaches to Assessing Development Effectiveness International Conference*, Cairo, 29 March – 2 April, 2009.

White, S. (1996) 'Depoliticising development: the uses and abuses of participation', *Development in Practice*, 6 (1): 6–15.

Wilkins, K. (ed.) (2000) *Redeveloping Communication for Social Change: Theory, Practice and Power*, Boulder, CO: Rowman & Littlefield.

Wilkins, K. (2005) 'Out of focus: Gender visibilities in development', in O. Hemer and T. Tufte (eds) *Media and Glocal Change: Rethinking Communication for Development*, Suecia: Nordicom.

Wilkins, K. (2009) 'What's in a name? Problematizing communication's shift from development to social change', *Glocal Times*, 13. Online. Available HTTP: http://webzone.k3.mah.se/projects/gt2/viewarticle.aspx?articleID=173&issueID=20 (accessed 30 May 2012).

Willetts, J. and Crawford, P. (2007) 'The most significant lessons about the Most Significant Change technique', *Development in Practice*, 17 (3): 367–379.

Williams, B. and Imam, I. (eds) (2006) *Systems Concepts in Evaluation. An Expert Anthology*, Fairhaven, MA: American Evaluation Association. Online. Available HTTP: http://preval.org/files/Kellogg%20enfoque%20sistematico%20en%20evaluacion.pdf (accessed 24 May 2012).

World Congress on Communication for Development (WCCD) (2006) *The Rome Consensus. Communication for Development. A Major Pillar for Development and Change*, Rome: WCCD. Online. Available HTTP: http://www.uneca.org/africanmedia/documents/Recommendations_Rome_Consensus.pdf (accessed 30 May 2012).

Worthen, B., Sanders, J. and Fitzpatrick, J. (1997) *Program Evaluation: Alternative Approaches and Practical Guidelines* (2nd ed.), New York: Longman.

Wrigley, R. (2006) *Learning from capacity building practice: Adapting the 'Most Significant Change' (MSC) approach to evaluate capacity building provision by CABUNGO in Malawi*, Praxis Paper 12, Oxford: INTRAC. Online. Available HTTP: http://www.eldis.org/go/home&id=24529&type=Document (accessed 30 May 2012).

Index

AC4SC methodology *see* Assessing Communication for Social Change methodology

AC4SC project *see* Assessing Communication for Social Change project

access: to communication and information 51–6; to ICTs 7, 48–9; **59**, **67**, 72, **80**; differences in, to communication and information 49, 51, 56

accountability, shift to internal and community forms of 89, 147, 148; *see also* downward accountability; upward accountability-based evaluation approaches

Accountability, Learning and Planning System (ALPS) 89–90

action learning 23–4, 49, 58; importance of skills in 37; as key element of framework for evaluating C4D 8, 17, 23

action learning cycle 93

action research (AR) 14; critiques of 126; definition of 125; as key methodology for evaluating C4D 125–6; synergies with systems thinking 50

Action Research and New Media framework, compared with framework for evaluating C4D **39**, 41

activist E–E (entertainment–education) 44

Afghanistan, capacity building in 100

age 8, 32, **65**, **80**, 157

ALPS *see* Accountability, Learning and Planning System

alternative approaches in ECD: need for 94–5; tensions between dominant approaches and **146**

alternative approaches to evaluation 2–3, 25, 45, 83–5, 140–1, **148**, **149**; advocating for 155; attitudes and policies of funders and managers to 74–5, 79, 90, 102, 147, **148**; challenges with 77; cost-effectiveness of 12, 26, 77, 83, 99, 144, 158; criticisms of, in Puntos de Encuentro 46; lack of support for 74–6, 147, **149**; tensions between dominant and, to evaluation of C4D, **148**, **149**; value of

for impact assessment 9, 24, 38, 46, 49, **50**, 83, 88, **148**, **149**; *see also* developmental evaluation; EAR; evaluation; feminist approaches to research and evaluation; innovative and creative approaches; learning-based approaches; methodologies and approaches for evaluating C4D; PM&E

appreciative inquiry 125

approach (to evaluation), definition of term 113

appropriateness: cultural 8, 18, 22, 26, 29, 36, 85, 117, **132**, 151; of dominant approaches to evaluating C4D 4, 48, 69, 119; of language in evaluation and ECD 107, 151; *see also* dominant approaches to evaluation

AR *see* action research

Assessing Communication for Social Change (AC4SC) methodology **39**, 40–1, 127–8; comparison with framework for evaluating C4D **39**, 41; critiques of 129; principles of 40, 127

Assessing Communication for Social Change (AC4SC) project: background 14–15, 45–6; communicative ecology concept and mapping in 48, 51, 56, **80**; contextual factors 72–3; critical reflections on **97**, 108, 129; developing a ToC in **76**, **118**; development of PM&E toolkit 15, **97**, 127; ECD in 15, 96–7, **97**, 102, 104, 108, 110–11; empowering local staff and communities 108; key challenges and issues 72, **76**, 100, 101, 103, 104, 107, 120; meta-evaluation of **97**, 101, 108, 111, 152, 158–9; methodology and principles **39**, 40–1; methodology critiques 129; methodology for impact assessment 127–8; mixed methods PM&E approach in **32**, 40–1; MSC technique in 123–5, 139; PAR process in 26, **97**; pressure to conform to externally imposed evaluation approaches **76**; understanding community context **80**; value of community feedback forums 90

assessing context 152–3

assessing evaluability 153

assessing impacts *see* impact assessment

Index

assessing outcomes 2–3, 6, 8, 21, 25–9, 34, 67, 82, **84**, **149**; challenges in 71, 79–83, 93, 101; importance of context 4, 9, 17, 27, 38, 47, 49, 72, 82, 83, 101; need for realistic approach 147–8; tensions between dominant and alternative approaches **149**; use of visual participatory methods **84**, 84–5, 136; *see also* impact assessment
assumptions, verifying 138, 139
attitudes and policies of funders and managers 74–5, 77, **78**, 79, 90, 102, 147, **148**; to alternative evaluation approaches 74–5; to evaluation of C4D, 79, 101–2, 129
attitudes of managers and staff to evaluation 26, **76**, **78**, **146**
attribution problem 81–2
audience analysis methods **135**
audience engagement 40, 123, 157
audience feedback 8, 40, 136
audit culture 117

Balit, S. 5, 6, 12, 36, 72, 73, 81, 105, 119, 137, 144
Bamberger, M. 29, 86, 87, 94, 105, 122
behaviour change communication (BCC) theories 44, 63–4
behaviour change comparison surveys 114
behaviour change evaluation, limitations of 45
behavioural surveillance surveys 114
Big Push Forward 76–7, **106**
both/and approach, need for 42, 48
bottom-up approach 42, **49**, 62
boundaries and scope of evaluations 154–5
boundary partners 120, 121, 153
Burns, D. 27, 47, 48, 50, 51, 56, 62, 63, 65, 68, 84, 85, 88
Byrne, A. 24, 27, 43, 46, 47, 50, 56, 64, 72, 75, 85, 88, 94, 113, 120, 122, 137, 144

C&IT *see* communication and information technology
C4D *see* communication for development
C4D Network **106**
capacity development 16, 25, 63, 95, 158; in Cambodia 92–3; challenges and issues 67, 92, 100; creative 92–3, **99**; in Finding a Voice **109**; flaws of traditional approach to 95; holistic approach to 43, 96, 103, 142, **146**; need for, in C4D 6, 145; of organizations 28, 37, 96, **99**, **109**; sustainable **99**; *see also* creative capacity development; ECD
CARE International 139
CAS *see* complex adaptive systems
case study approach: definition of 133; democratic 133; paradox of 133–4; ratings for **114**, 133; strengths and limitations of 133–4
caste 32, 49, **80**, 85, 130, 147
catalysts for change **84**, 119; role in leading to dialogue 119; role of women 4
CFSC *see* communication for social change
challenges and issues: in AC4SC 72, **76**, 103; in assessing impacts and outcomes 79–83; of complexity theory 56–7; in conceptualizing, outsourcing and managing research and evaluation 77–9; in development 91; in ECD 100–4; in evaluating C4D 70–1, 81, 144–50; framework for evaluating C4D as solution to 150; of incorporating EAR **75**; at institutional and country level 73–4; in moving beyond dominant approaches 45–6; strategies to address 150–2
Chambers, R. 25, 27, 34, 42, 47, 48, **49**, 56, 64, 85, 88, 107, 117, 119, 134, 136
change: focus on different forms of 43; need to move beyond the 'social' 69; readiness for 107, 111; resistance to 61, 92–3, 102, 129; sustainable 7, 21, 141; *see also* social change
channel/media usage and preference analysis 135
chaos 58; self-organizing systems on edge of 64–5
class 8, 23, 32, **65**, **75**, 147
communication, importance of to development 3, 5–6, 7, 110, 150
communication and feedback systems 104, 106, 109–10, 155–6
communication and information flows 10, 13, 27, 48–9, 51, 58, 65, **110**, 155
communication and information technology (C&IT) 13, 15–16, 67
communication and media studies 9, 10, 13–14, 44–5, **50**, 72, 74, 81, **109**, 129; *see also* Finding a Voice; ICTPR, Puntos de Encuentro
communication environment analysis 135
communication for development (C4D) 4–6; addressing contradictions arising from different approaches to 144–5; definitions of 4, 7; different views on 74; importance of dialogue 5–7, 9, 11; meaning of participation in 11; role in sustainable development 4–5, 7, 12; role of 73; struggle to demonstrate importance of 5, 93; tensions between dominant and alternative approaches to evaluation of **148**, **149**; tensions between dominant and participatory approaches to **6**, 145; in the UN 6–7; UN Inter-Agency Round Tables on 6, 32; *see also* change; development communication; dialogue; evaluating C4D; participation; sustainable social change

communication for social change (CFSC) 7, 24, **39**, 40, 83, 119, 138, 152; approaches to measuring 40, 41, 119, 140
Communication Initiative Network **106**
communication systems 109–10, 155–6
communicative ecology: in AC4SC project 48, 51, 56, **80**; in Finding a Voice 48–9, 51; holistic approach in framework for evaluating C4D and 27–8, 48–9; in KCRIP (Kothmale Community Radio and Internet Project) 13; overview of concept **50**, 56
communicative ecology mapping 49, 51, 85, 135, 155; examples of **30–1, 52–5, 80**
community feedback forums **89**, 90
community multimedia centres 13, **33**
community researchers (CRs) 15, **32, 80**, 90, 102, 104, 111, 127–8, 129
community/village mapping 135, 136
complementary approaches to evaluation 69, 86, 114, 149, 159
complex adaptive systems (CAS) 47, 57–8, 64, **66**; example from LEARNERS project **59**
complex component of framework for evaluating C4D 23, 28–9, **143**; guiding principles 28
complex situations and problems 46–7, 60, 61
complexity of evaluating C4D 81, 88, 101, 147–8, 149
complexity of social change 23, 88; need to better understand context of C4D 146–7; value of complexity-based approaches for understanding 28–9, 35, 45; *see also* change; complex adaptive systems; social change; sustainable social change
complexity theory 34, 35, 45, 50; application in evaluation of Puntos de Encuentro 45, 46–7, 62; benefits and challenges 56–7; and case study approaches 133; emergence of complexity approaches 57; interdisciplinary nature of 57; interest in, for understanding development 56; key concepts 57–9; similarities with participatory approaches 45, 50; value to development and social change initiatives 28–9, 62–3; *see also* complexity-based approaches to development and social change; complexity-based approaches to evaluation; developmental evaluation; systems and complexity-based approaches to evaluation; systems thinking
complexity-based approaches to development and social change 57, 68; challenges of 56, **66**, 68–9, 147; in Puntos de Encuentro 45; value of 28–9, 56, 62; *see also* complexity of social change; complexity theory; social change

complexity-based approaches to evaluation 60, 71, 120–2, 138; challenges and contradictions 44–6, 57, 64, 68–9, 71, 147; critiques of 122; range of skills needed 146; use of simple, complicated, complex typology in 60; value of 28–9, 45–7, 57, 62–3; *see also* complexity theory; developmental evaluation; outcome mapping; systems and complexity-based approaches to evaluation; systems thinking
complicated situations and problems 46–7, 60, 61
conditions of oppression 151
context 151; assessment of 152–3; importance of understanding 9, 17, 27, 49, 72, 146–7; key methods for understanding 135; in relation to C4D 72; use of case study approach in understanding 133–4; use of EAR in understanding 13–14, 71, 113, 135; use of participatory techniques in understanding 136; use of scoping studies in understanding 79, **80**
contextual factors 71–3, 100
contradictions 68–9, 144–5; in C4D **6**; in development practices 63, 69; in ECD 100; in evaluation of C4D 44, 68–9, 144, 147; in participatory processes 125, 140; in social change process 1, 28, 44, 64
contradictory effects of development interventions 9
contribution analysis 82
contribution of C4D, as more realistic measure of effectiveness 4, 88, **149**
Cornwall, A. 9, 10, 11, 12, 65–6, 126, 131–3
cost-effectiveness of participatory and alternative approaches 12, 26, 77, 79, 83, 99, 144, 158
country-level challenges 73–4
creative, visual and technology-based methods **84**, 92, 136; use with less literate groups 136, 138
creative capacity development 92–3, **99**
Creative Capacity Development (Pearson) 92–3, **99**
creativity 92, **99**, 117, 125; definition of 92; role of participatory methods in fostering 24
critical approaches 23; to ECD 96, 108, 111, 128; to feminist research and evaluation 131, **132**; importance of taking differences in gender, power and knowledge into account 32, 65–9, 122, 126, 147; to learning 37–8, 95, 96; to research and evaluation 9, 12, 16, 41, 45, 66, **67**, 90–1, 116, 126, 140; to understanding and evaluating social change 63–5, 69
critical assessment of evaluation approaches, strategies for 156–7

critical component of framework for evaluating C4D 23, 29, 32–3, 142, **143**; guiding principles 29
Critical Listening and Feedback Sessions technique 127
critical reflection 23, 38, 49, 82, **84**, **97**, 126
CRs *see* community researchers
cultural diversity, tensions in C4D 68
culture 48, 67–8, 92, 99, 107; importance of 9, 12, 61, 92; *see also* evaluation culture; learning culture; organizational culture; research culture

data: improving quality of 110–11, 129; need for disaggregated forms 29, 34, 138
DE *see* developmental evaluation
dependency on specialists 100
design flexibility and robustness 157
design of ECD strategies 111
development: challenges and issues 91; contemporary ideas about 9; dominant approaches to 9; importance of communication to 3, 5–6, 7, 110, 150; language of 10; participatory forms of 9–11, **145**
development communication: multiple meanings of 5; need to build capacity for 6; research 42; *see also* C4D
development monitoring and evaluation, dichotomies in 2, **3**, 42, 48, **49**
development theories: contributions of feminists 151; critiques of 63–4, 69
developmental evaluation (DE): background and development 40, 70–1, 77; comparison with framework for evaluating C4D **39**; critiques of 122; as key methodology 122; role in developing innovations 40; use of evaluative processes to support development of innovations 88–9, 121, 142
Developmental Evaluation (Patton) 70
dialogue: as central to C4D 5–7, 9, 11; as central to participatory development and evaluation 1, 10, 22, 24, 36, 40, 73, **110**; in participatory research and evaluation 26, **80**, **84**, 84–5, 117, 126, 128; role of, in developing indicators 36–7, 137; role of, in promoting learning 87; role of MSC technique in encouraging 123
dichotomies: in development M&E 2, **3**, 42, 48, **49**; need to move beyond 69, **148**; role of framework for evaluating C4D in moving beyond 1, 2, 21, 42, 159; top-down versus bottom-up 42
differences: in meanings and perspectives 56, 61, 91, 116; need to acknowledge 126, 156;

need to focus on, in participatory research and evaluation 4, 13, 15, 17, 23, 29, 49, 66
digital divide 13
digital storytelling 4, 36, 85, 151
diversity 4, 19, 22, 24, 26, 41, 45, 107, 145, **149**, 156; of culture and language 72, 107; importance in social change process 58; of media 74; of perspectives 26, 63, **84**, 150; role of complexity science in reflecting 56; role of participatory methods in expressing and understanding 24, 48–9; *see also* inclusion
dominant approaches: to development 9, 48; to social change communication theories 19, 63–4; tensions between alternative approaches to ECD and **146**; tensions between participatory approaches to C4D and **6**, **145**
dominant approaches to evaluation 2, 4, 21, 45, 48, 69, 82, 115, 140, **148**, **149**; challenges to 57; inappropriateness for evaluating C4D 4, 7, 48, 69, 137; quantitative approaches 73; tensions between alternative approaches and **148**, **149**; *see also* logical framework (logframe) approach; results-based management approach; SMART indicators; upward accountability-based evaluation approaches
donors: acceptance of value of complexity theory 62; approaches to social change 44; clarifying expectations 154; conventional evaluation frameworks 45–6; *see also* attitudes and policies of funders and managers; UN (United Nations)
double-loop learning 95
downward accountability: in evaluation 3, 89, 111, 155; examples 89–90; shift towards 89
dynamics: of change 34, 56, 148; of culture 56; of power 11, 56; of systems 17, 26, 57–8; *see also* complex adaptive systems; complexity theory
dynamic social contexts 43

EAN *see* Equal Access Nepal
EAR *see* ethnographic action research
Earl, S. 8, 20, 88, 120, 121, 153
early adopters 34
ECD *see* evaluation capacity development
edge of chaos 58, 64
educational level 4, 32, **33**, **80**
efficiency: fixation on 3; focus in logframe approach 115
emergent approaches: concept of emergence 34, 65; emergence and self-organizing systems 58, 61; lack of support for 147

emergent component of framework for evaluating C4D 23, 33–4, 72, **143**; guiding principles 33–4
emergent nature of development and social change 4, 8–9, 17, 23, 28, 50, 117
empowering effects of participatory approaches 12, 25, **59**, **67**, 69, **84**, 99, 124, 137; in LEARNERS project **67**, 101
empowering forms of leadership 16
empowerment 87; of all actors in system 42; of local staff and communities **67**, 108, 111–12; of low caste women 85; need for critical approach to 12, 66, 69, 151
Enhancing Rural Women's Access to ICTs project 131
Equal Access 14–15, **97**
Equal Access Nepal (EAN) 14–15, 26, **32**, 45–6, 73, **97**, 128
Equal Access participatory monitoring and evaluation toolkit 15, **97**, 127
equitable participation 4, 12; *see also* inclusion
Estrella, M. 107, 123, 140
ethical issues 19, 25, 85, 110; in feminist participatory research **84**; in using EAR 129
ethnicity 23, **32**, **33**, 49, **80**, 130
ethnographic action research (EAR) background to 14–15; benefits and challenges of incorporating **75**; communicative ecology concept and mapping in 48, 49, **50**, 51, 126; critiques of 129; developmental nature of 71; in Finding a Voice **33**, 48–9, 51; focus on power and control in 71, **75**; as key methodology 126–7; mixed methods research and evaluation 86; problems with using data 102; ratings for 127, **114**; training in 14
ethnography 13–14
evaluability assessment 153
EvaluateIT kit **67**
evaluating C4D: challenges and issues in 70–1, 81, 144–50; challenges in assessing impacts and outcomes 79–83; challenges in conceptualizing, outsourcing and managing research and evaluation 77–9; challenges in moving beyond dominant approaches 45–6; complexity of 81–3, 88, 101, 147–8, 149; contextual and structural factors 71–3; focus on power relations, gender and social norms 65–8; good communication and feedback systems in 104, 110, 155; innovative and creative approaches to 20, 46, 62, **84**, 84–5, 128, 136; institutional and country-level challenges 73–4; key trends in 83–7; pressure to conform to externally imposed approaches **76**; simple, complicated, complex problem typology 46–7, 60–1; tensions between dominant and alternative approaches **148**, **149**; value of mixed methods approach 1, 29, 46, 85–7, 90, 150; value of systems and complexity approaches 46–7; *see also* alternative approaches to evaluation; complexity theory; framework for evaluating C4D; PM&E; systems thinking
evaluation: for achieving positive change 8, 37, 91, 144; attitudes to 26, 74–5, **76**, **78**, 79, 90, 101–2, **146**, 147, **148**; clarifying boundaries and scope of 154–5; definitions of 7–8; demystifying 99, 151; formative and summative 70; developing an evaluation culture 40, 43, 93, 94, 95; **97**, 102, 109, 111; lack of support for alternative forms of 74–76, 147, **149**; language issues in 107, 119, 120, 151; need for moving baseline in 79; need for simple, practical approach 18, 35, 36, **67**, 111, 142; new conceptualizations of 87–8, 142; as ongoing learning and organizational improvement process 8, 36, 87–8, **97**, 142; role in creating learning organizations 12, 18, 87, 95, 98, 128, 142; shift from external to internal and community accountability 89–90, 142; shift from proving impacts to developing and improving initiatives 88, 120, 142; *see also* alternative approaches to evaluation; developmental evaluation; dominant approaches to evaluation; ECD; M&E; PM&E
evaluation associations, role in ECD 105
evaluation capacity development (ECD): in AC4SC 15, 96–7, **97**, 102, 104, 108, 110–11; challenges and issues in **97**, 100–4; contextual and cultural factors in 100–1; design of 111; developing evaluative thinking 70, 98, 111, 151; evaluation and meta-evaluation of 108, 111, 152, 158–9; holistic approach to 12, 27, 28, 96, **97**, 145, **146**; importance of good communication and feedback systems 109; language issues in 107, 109; in LEARNERS project 16, **59**, **67**; maintaining and sustaining capacity 102–3, 111–12; need for alternative approach to 94–5; need for, at all levels 12, 37, 145; need for effective planning 103; need for holistic approach 145–6; need for long-term approach 37, 105; power relations in 100–1; principles related to 18, 27; as response to challenges in C4D evaluation 83; role in developing learning organizations 98, 111; strategies for effective and sustainable forms of 104–11; tensions between dominant and participatory approaches **146**; understanding and defining 93–4; value of participatory methodologies for 99–100; *see also* holistic component of framework for evaluating C4D; learning-based component of

framework for evaluating C4D; learning organizations
evaluation culture 37, 40, 42, 43, 94, 95, **97**, 102, 109, 111
evaluation field building 95
evaluation processes 110–11
evaluative thinking 12, 19, 37, 40, 98, 111, 151
exclusion 11, 12, 49, 63, 90, 152; from gender work 132; of women from evaluation 132
expert knowledge 17, 43, 90
experts, deference to 101
Eyben, R. 2, 3, 9, 47, 48, 119

farming participatory research (FPR) 123
farming systems research (FSR) 123
feedback systems 109–10, 155–6; importance of 109; lack of attention to, in evaluation 109
feminism: contribution to development theory and practice 151; issues with, in development 131; role in developing innovative solutions to development challenges 151
feminist approach to C4D, in Puntos de Encuentro 44–5
feminist approaches to research and evaluation **67**, **84**, 130–3; value of 150–1
feminist consciousness 131
feminist PAR (participatory action research) 125
field notes 135
Finding a Voice 14; barriers to participation in **33**; benefits and challenges of EAR **75**; capacity development processes **109**; communicative ecology mapping 48–9, 51; use of digital storytelling 85
flexibility, need for in evaluating C4D 18, 35, 36, 43, 84, 104, 148–9
flexible thinking-action logic 82, 116, 119, 141
focus group discussions 135, 136
FPR *see* farming participatory research
framework for evaluating C4D: comparison with other frameworks 38–42; **39**, contextual and structural factors 72–3; developmental evaluation in 71; EAR in 71; ECD and 96; general principles of 17–18; implementing 152–9; key concepts in **143**; key features and benefits of 42, 142–4; need for 2–4; origins of 13–17; overview of 21–4; practical nature of 3, 21, 23, 142; rigour of approach 21, 23, 36; seven inter-related components **22**, 22–4, **143**; as part of solution to challenges and issues in evaluating C4D 150; *see also* complex component of framework for evaluating C4D; critical component of framework for evaluating C4D; emergent component of framework for evaluating C4D; holistic component of framework for evaluating C4D; learning-based component of framework for evaluating C4D; participatory component of framework for evaluating C4D; realistic component of framework for evaluating C4D
freedom, need for in evaluation of C4D 18, 35, 36, 43, 84, 104, 148–9
FSR *see* farming systems research
funders and managers *see* attitudes and policies of funders and managers; donors

gender: complexity of 133–4; danger of slipping from development agenda 32, **132**; differences 32, 51, 66, 67, 132; discrimination 69, 85 **89**, 100, 151; in evaluating C4D 34–5, 65–8, **84**; evaluation and 32, 147; importance of taking differences into account 32, 51, 66, 67, 147; neglect of, in PRCA 130; new evaluation solutions proposed by Newton **132**; politics of research and **132**, 133; *see also* feminism; feminist approaches to research and evaluation; women
gender disaggregated data, need for 138
gender division of labour charts 136
gender-sensitive approaches to research and evaluation **84**, 130–3, **132**, 150–1
group learning 124
Gumucio Dagron, A. 5, 7, 12, 73

Hearn, G. 13, 17, 26, 27–8, 29, 37, 38, 41, 47, 48, **50**, 56, 57, 65, 66, 67, 68, 86, 104, 113, 125, 126, 129
hierarchical organizational and social structures **75**, 100, 129; challenges to PM&E approaches and 129; PAR and 100
hierarchical organizational culture 38
HIV/AIDS communication interventions 63–4, **65**
HIV/AIDS prevention programmes 61, 63–4, 134
holism, as principle of ethnography 13
holistic approach: to capacity development 43, 96, 103, 142, **146**; to ECD 12, 27, 28, 96, **97**, **145**, 146; example of, to ECD **97**; importance of 27; importance to sustainability 43; need for, to ECD 96, 145–6; to organizational capacity development 96; *see also* communicative ecology; systems and complexity-based approaches to evaluation
holistic component of framework for evaluating C4D 22, 26–8, 48, **143**; guiding principles 26–7
Horton, D. 28, 37, 87, 95, 96, 103
household interviews 135
human rights 7, 61, 89; evaluation approach 122, 130

ICD *see* information and communications for development
ICT *see* information and communication technology
ICT4D *see* information and communication technology for development
ICTPR (ICT for Poverty Reduction project) 14, 79
ILS *see* Internal Learning System
images 84–5
Imam, I. 26, 37, 38, 47, 50, 51, 62, 63
immersion, as principle of ethnography 13
impact assessment 8, 15, 19, 37, 45, 50, 60, 72, 77; AC4SC methodology 40, 127–8; attribution problem 81–2; challenges and issues in C4D 7, 32, 44, 79–83, **149**; lack of data and reports on, in C4D 6, 80; shift from proving impacts to developing and improving initiatives 88, 120, 142; timeframe issues 36, 82–3; value of alternative approaches 83; value of framework of empowerment and disempowerment in LEARNERS project 66–8
impact evaluation 68–9, 77, 80–1, 94
Impact Evaluations and Development 80
implementing framework for evaluating C4D 152–9
improvement: as focus of evaluation 77, 88, **97**, 127, 140, **147**, 150; as focus of outcome mapping 120; of organizations through evaluation 87, 98, 111; problems in demonstrating in C4D 82; role of critical reflection in 126; of women's status 32
inclusion 11, 12, 63, **145**, 147; challenges in achieving 26, 41; of poor and marginalized groups **33**, 103, **109**, 129, 156; role of complexity and systems approaches in focusing on 63; role of participatory approaches in enabling 8, 125, 143, 150
in-depth interviews 135, 139
indicators 137–40; alternatives to 37, 138–9; for assessing sustainability of C4D 138; in C4D 83, 127, 134, 137–8, 140; definition of 137; in logframe approach 115; need to be context-relevant/dependent 62, 139; participatory development of 8, 36–7, 129, 137, 139–40, **149**; pre-determined 7, 46, **66**, 75, 82, 139, 147, 148; problems and limitations with 36, 69, **78**, 82, 137–9, 141, **149**; problems in developing, in C4D 101, 129; qualitative/quantitative 19, 137, 139, 140, 147, **149**; redefinition of purpose 139, 141; setting 137–40, 149; SMART 75, 140; SPICED 140; and substantialist mode of thinking 69; tensions between dominant and alternative approaches to setting **149**; use of MSC stories in developing 139; use of ToC approach in developing **76**, **118**

indigenous knowledge *see* local and indigenous knowledge
informants, key 136
information and communication technology (ICT) 4, 13, 14, 72
information and communication technology for development (ICT4D) 13–14
information and communications for development (ICD) 77
information dissemination and use 73, **110**
INGOs *see* international non-governmental organizations
innovation: in development 62, **99**, 107; local and indigenous 95, 107, 146; use of evaluation in supporting 40, 88
innovative and creative approaches: to C4D 1, 44, 85; to capacity development/ECD 92, 107; lack of reward for 108; to research and evaluation 3, 36, **84**, 90, 107, 136
innovative C4D initiatives 18, 22, 25, 35, 44; promotion of, in framework for evaluating C4D 150; value of systems and complexity approaches in evaluating 120
innovative evaluation solutions to 'problem' of gender and development **132**
innovative research and evaluation methodologies and methods 25, 46, 62, 74, **76**, 84–5, **110**, 128, 136; challenges and issues 90; lack of support for 74, 75, 147; need for, in C4D 85, 140
Institute to Serve Facilitators of Development (VBNK) 92–3
institutional challenges 73–4
Internal Learning System (ILS) 85
international non-governmental organizations (INGOs), insights from **110**
inter-relationships, as focus of systems and complexity approaches 22, 27, 47–8, 50, 56, 155
interviews 135–6
invitational participation 11

Jallov, B. 12, 104, 123, 144

KABP surveys *see* knowledge, attitudes, behaviours and practices surveys
KCRIP *see* Kothmale Community Radio and Internet Project
key evaluation concepts, importance in defining 109
key informants 136
knowledge: in ECD 107; expert 17, 43, 90; knowledge sharing 109–10; local and indigenous 8, 43, 90, 107, 126; political nature of 90; power–knowledge nexus 68
knowledge, attitudes, behaviours and practices (KABP) surveys: as key methodology 128–9,

136; limitations of 134; in PRCA methodology 128–9; ratings for **114**, 135; strengths of 134

Kothmale Community Radio and Internet Project (KCRIP) 13–14, 129

La Boletina magazine, as example of self-organization 47, **66**

Lacayo, V. 9, 27, 28, 34, 35, 44, 45, 46–7, 57, 62, 63, 64, **66**, 69, 119, 133, 138, 151, 152

language 72, 107; of evaluation 107, 120; used in ECD 107, 109

leaders: loss of, in organizations 103; role in community development **59**; role in fostering learning cultures 87, 98, 108, 152; women **59**, **84**

leadership **59**, 108; empowering forms of 16; programme in Minnesota 70, 77; women's 15

LEARNERS process 15–16

LEARNERS project 15–16; empowering and disempowering impacts of **67**, 101; role of leaders in **59**, 108; value of meta-evaluation in 101

learning: barriers and issues with 92–3, **97**, 98, **99**, 101–4, 108; double-loop 95; from failure/mistakes 33, 37–8, 98, 108, 150; as key aspect of C4D **6**, **7**, **145**; as key aspect of evaluation process 38, 87, **149**, 154, 156; from local knowledge and innovation 90, 107, 146; role of complexity approaches in encouraging 29, 62–3; role of creative and participatory methods in encouraging 24, 85, **89**, 92–3, 99, **110**; role of images in enhancing 84; role of meta-evaluation in enhancing 152, 154; role of ToC approach in enhancing 116, 154; single-loop 95; to think evaluatively 12, 19, 37, 40, 98, 111, 151

learning culture: development of 37, 87–8, 98, 108, 152; importance for development effectiveness 37; problems with fostering 87–8, 108, **146**

learning organizations 12, 37, 87, 93, 146, 152; creative capacity development within **99**; key features of **98**

learning organization development 98, **146**; as key principle 18, 37; as part of AC4SC project and methodology 40, **97**, 103, 128; role of action learning cycle in 93; role of double-loop learning in 95; role of ECD in 98, 111

learning-based approaches 41, 92–3; of AC4SC methodology 40–1; to capacity development/ECD 92–6, **97**, **99**, 103, 107, **146**; compared with dominant evaluation approaches 21, 87–8, 101–2, 119, 146, 148–9; developing a learning culture 37, 87–8; of developmental evaluation 40, 71; of EAR 126–7; of LEARNERS process 15; to meta-evaluation 38, 152; of MSC technique 123–5; need for openness, freedom and flexibility in using different evaluation approaches, to enable 148–50; of outcome mapping 121; in PM&E 40, 122–3; of SPICED indicator approach 140

learning-based component of framework for evaluating C4D 23–4, 37–8, 96, 142–3, **143**; guiding principles 37

Lennie, J. 15, 17, 18, 19, 25, 26, 28, 36, 37, 38, 57, **59**, 63, 64, 65, 66, **67**, 68, 87, 100, 101, 102, 103, 104, 107, 108, 111, 126, 127, 128, 129, 130, 131, 137, 151, 152, 156, 159

LFA *see* logical framework (logframe) approach

listener groups **53**, **80**

listening 73, **75**; across difference 11; active/powerful 11, 23, 35, **97**, 111, 150; impact of organizational culture on **98**; as key aspect of C4D 5, 6, 7, 11, 72, 73

literacy 56, 100, 107

local and indigenous knowledge 8, 43, 90, 107, 126

local context, methods for understanding 135

logical framework (logframe) approach (LFA): challenges and issues in evaluating C4D and **76**, 101; compared with ToC approach 116, 119, 140–1, 154; critiques of 26, 44, 48, 117–19; incompatibilities with participatory approaches 12, 26, 117, 119; nature of 26, 48; overview of 115; ratings for **114**; strengths of 115, 141

longitudinal studies: issues with **149**; need for, in evaluation of C4D 35, 83, 148, 149; reluctance of donors to fund 35, 83, **149**

long-term approach: to change **3**, 4, 17, 23, 45, 74, 88, 94; to developing communication processes 119; to ECD 27, 28, 37, 74, 94, 96, 111; to researching and evaluating C4D 12, 14, 17, 23, 24, 35, 36, 83, 143

long-term view/perspective: need for 36, 43, 88, 90, 159; to using participatory evaluation approaches 12, 24, 26

M&E *see* monitoring and evaluation

mapping: communicative ecologies 49, 51, 65, **80**, 85, 155; community village 135, 136; networks and relationships 65; value of various techniques 151–2

maps, diagrams and charts, use of: in EAR 127–8; in evaluating C4D 136; for providing quantitative data 127; for representing relationships 136

maximalist participation 10–11

MDGs *see* Millennium Development Goals
measuring change/impacts: focus of dominant evaluation approaches 44, 46, 48, **49**, 70, 88, 137, **148**; issues in C4D 45, 81, 101, 134, 139–40, 147; role of indicators in 137; shift away from 7, 45, 88, 138, 141
Media Development Monitoring and Evaluation-Wiki (MediaME) 105
media development programme design 74
media usage analysis methods 135
meta-evaluation 87–8, 152, 158–9; in developing toolkits 111; methods in AC4SC project 159; need for, in developing action research theories and practices 126; as solution to challenges in evaluation of C4D 152; value of 152
methodological pluralism 23, 41, 43, 57, 85–6
methodologies, participatory: value of, for ECD 99–100; value of, for M&E 25–6, 108; *see also* AC4SC methodology; action research; EAR; MSC; outcome mapping; PAR; PRCA
methodologies and approaches for evaluating C4D: action research approaches 125–6; case study approaches 133–4; feminist and gender-sensitive approaches 130–3; participatory communication and C4D-focused methodologies 126–30; participatory evaluation approaches 122–5; quantitative survey-based methodologies 134; ratings for **114**; selecting most appropriate 156–8; systems and complexity-based approaches 120–2; understanding programme theory and process of change 115–20; using creative and innovative approaches 151–2
methodology, definition of term 113
methods: definition of term 113; key C4D evaluation methods 135–7; ratings for **135**; selecting most appropriate 156–8; strengths and limitations of 137
Millennium Development Goals (MDGs) 32, **132**
minimum critical specification 58
mixed methods research and evaluation 41, 46, 85–7, 104, 113; in AC4SC project **32**, 40; challenges and issues with 87, 104, **148**; as creative form of research 86; definition of 86; in EAR 86, 127; in evaluation of Puntos de Encuentro 46; examples of 85; as key element of framework for evaluating C4D 35, 36, 150; as moving past dichotomies/paradigm wars 86, 148; use of triangulation in **32**, 128; value of 85–7, 90; value of, in evaluating C4D 1, 29, 86, 90, 150
mode-2 programmes, role of indicators in 139
monitoring, overview of 8

monitoring and evaluation (M&E) 46, 113, 122–3; dichotomies in **3**; *see also* PM&E
most significant change (MSC) technique: in AC4SC project **32**, 124–5; as alternative to indicators 138–9; challenges and issues with 125; implementing 104; as key methodology 123–5; ratings for **114**
MSC story example **124**
MSC technique *see* most significant change technique
multiple perspectives 26, 63, **84**, 133, 150; role of complexity theory in including 57, 62–3; role of mixed methods in including 90, 150
My M&E **106**

Naya Nepal (radio programme) 15, **52–3**, 102, **118**
Nepal: communicative ecologies in **30–1, 52–3, 54–5**, 56; community feedback forums **89**, 90; community ICT centres in 14; community radio programmes 15, **80**, 102; community researchers in 15, **80**, 104, 127–8, 129; contextual and structural factors 72–3; EAR researchers in 51; ECD in 15, 96–7, 102, 104, 108, 110–11; ICT for Poverty Reduction project 79; Palpa television initiative 86; scoping studies in **80**; *see also* AC4SC project; Equal Access Nepal (EAN)
Network of Networks for Impact Evaluation 80
new ideas and ways of thinking: role of feminist research in developing 131, 151; role of outcome mapping in developing 121; role of ToC approach in developing 116–17; strategies for developing 92–3
Newton, K. 4, 32, 131, **132**, 132, 151

OM *see* outcome mapping
online communities: ECD and 105; network development and 152
online ECD initiatives, examples of **106**
open communication/dialogue 21, 26, 43, 150
openness: to alternative evaluation approaches 74, 148–9; to change 111, 112, 157; to feedback 87; as key aspect of complexity approach 57; as key element of approach to evaluating C4D 18, 22, 23, 36, **75**, 84, 144, 151, 156; to learning from evaluation 107; to learning from failure 18, 23, 33, 150; to new ideas and ways of doing things 87
optimum participation 12
organizational and social structures: effect of 100; hierarchical **75**, 100, 129; and implementation of EAR **75**
organizational capacity development 96
organizational change 57, 121, 142, **146**

organizational culture 12, 37, 107–8; hierarchical 38
outcome assessment *see* assessing outcomes
outcome mapping (OM) 8, 64, 88, 114; critiques of 122; identifying boundary partners 153; as key methodology 120–1; ratings for **114**, 121; stages of 120–1

PAR *see* participatory action research
paradigms: of C4D 5; of complexity 57, 134; of development 1, 42, **49**
paradigms, in evaluation 2, 24, 25, 88; differences between 2, 42; methodological 1, 21, 25, 42, 86; mixing, in PRCA 130; need for new 2, 42, 69, 88, 159; problems in mixing 161
paradoxes: of case study approach 133–4; of change process 28, 29, 64; in complex systems 58, **66**; in development and C4D 63, 66, 68–9, 147; in participatory processes 125
Paris Declaration on Aid Effectiveness 3, 132
Parks, W. 17, 24, 25, 26, 37, 38, 40, 41, 83, 113, 122, 123, 137, 138, 139, 140, 153
participant observation 135
participation 9–11; barriers to **33**, 38, 72, 100, 103; challenges in achieving equitable forms of 4, **145**; definitions of 10; facilitating 103; invitational 11; optimum 12; power and 10, 11; sustainability and 12; of women 64; *see also* empowering effects of participatory approaches; equitable participation
participatory action research (PAR) 8, 15, 123; in AC4SC project 26; concern with power and powerlessness in 126; effect of hierarchical social structures on 100; importance of communication and dialogue in 126; as key methodology 125–6; key principles of 26; in LEARNERS project 67; as learning-based 23–4
participatory approaches to C4D **6**, 9, **145**; tensions between dominant approaches to C4D and **6**, **145**
participatory component of framework for evaluating C4D 1, 8, 11, 22, 24–6, **143**; guiding principles 24
participatory development 9–11, **145**
participatory monitoring and evaluation (PM&E): in AC4SC project **32**, 127; approach to measuring CFSC 40; benefits and rigour of 8, 25–6, 35; challenges, limitations and issues with 101, 125, 129; definition of 123; demystifying and valuing 151; essential ingredients of, for effectiveness 153; as fundamental to C4D 24–5; as key methodology 122–3; to measuring CFSC 39, 40; mixed methods approach **32**; overview of 8, 122–3; selecting indicators for 139–40; similarities with complexity theory 50; *see also* participatory research and evaluation
participatory numbers 25
participatory research and evaluation 8, 18, 25, 36, 50, 123; in AC4SC project **80**; challenges and issues with 18–19, 26; disempowering effects of 66, **67**, 69, 101; empowering effects of 12, 25, **59**, **67**, 69, **84**, 99, 123, 137; value of 25, 36, 107; value of, for ECD 99–100; wide range of skills required for 103–4, 140, 146; *see also* action research; creative, visual and technology-based methods; PAR; PM&E; PRCA
participatory rural appraisal (PRA) 123
participatory rural communication appraisal (PRCA) 114; critiques of 129–30; as key methodology 128–9
Patton, M.Q. 20, 21, 27, 34, 35, 37, 38, 40, 47–8, 49, 50, 51, 57, 60–1, 62, 63, 65, 70, 71, 81, 83, 88–9, 98, 99, 117, 120, 121, 125, 128, 144
Pearson, J. 36, 92–3, **99**, 99
Peruvian Amazon, Minga Peru project **84**
PM&E *see* participatory monitoring and evaluation
PM&E approach to measuring CFSC 40; compared with framework for evaluating C4D 39, 41
post-conflict settings 92, 100
Poverty Reduction Strategy Papers (PRSP) 10
power: differences in 11, 29, 32, 44, 56, 66–7, 100–1, 104, 119, 126; in ECD 100–1, 107; empowering and disempowering impacts of community-based C&IT evaluation projects **67**, 69, 101; empowering local staff and communities **67**, 108, 111–12; in evaluating C4D 65–8; forms of, in evaluation of LEARNERS project **67**; Foucault's conception of 68; need to consider in C4D 32, 147; neglect of, in PRCA 130; participation and 10, 11; power–knowledge 68–9, 101; *see also* empowerment; power relations
power relations 56, 64, 65, 68, 130; challenges related to 90; between different development actors 11, 100, 103, 147; in ECD 100–1, 107; focus on, in feminist research 130, 151; involvement of C4D in challenging 11, 44, 147; use of visual approaches in reversing 85; value of Action Aid workshop on 90
PRA *see* participatory rural appraisal
practical PM&E 123
pragmatic approach 36, 86, 131, **148**; in AC4SC project **76**, 127; of practical PM&E 123; versus transformational approaches **76**

PRCA *see* participatory rural communication appraisal
principles of framework for evaluating C4D: of complex component 28; of critical component 29; of emergent component 33–4; general 17–18; of holistic component 26–7; of learning-based component 37; of participatory component 24; of realistic component 35
progress towards change, as more realistic measure of effectiveness 4, 88, **149**
projectable changes 116
PRSP *see* Poverty Reduction Strategy Papers
Puntos de Encuentro 44–5, 46, 62, **66**
Putting ICTs into the Hands of the Poor *see* ICTPR

qualitative indicators 19, 137, 139, 140, **149**; for measuring social change communication 138; need for, in C4D evaluations 137–8, **149**
qualitative methodologies 20, **79**
qualitative methods 135, 158
qualitative/quantitative sequences 134
quantitative approaches to evaluation, dominance of, in development 73
quantitative indicators 19, 137, 147
quantitative survey-based methodologies 114; ratings for **114**, 134; strengths and limitations of 134
Quarry, W. 3, 4, 6, 7, 11, 12, 72
questionnaires *see* survey questionnaires

Ramalingam. B. 9, 27, 28, 34, 35, 42, 51, 56, 57, 62
Ramirez, R. 3, 4, 6, 7, 11, 12, 72
ratings, for approaches and methodologies for evaluating C4D **114**
ratings, for methods for evaluating C4D **135**
readiness for change 107, 111
realistic approaches: to development and evaluation 35; need for, to assessing outcomes 147–8; of systems and complexity approaches 68–9
realistic component of framework for evaluating C4D 23, 35–7, **143**; guiding principles 35
relational perspective 48, **49**
relationships 26, 44, 45, **47**, 48, 61, **65**, **67**, 96, 119; gender and caste 128; hierarchical 129; importance of, in participatory and complexity approaches 2, 9, 25, 47, 51, 57, 62, **66**, 85, **97**; importance of taking time to form 19, 35, **84**, 100, 108; as key element of framework for evaluating C4D 1, 4, 28, 35, 150; of power and control 11, 65–8, 100, 117, 147; use of maps and charts in representing 136, 151

religious orientation 130
requisite variety 58
research culture **75**, **109**, 125, 127
research institutions 105
Researching, Monitoring and Evaluating Communication for Development (Lennie and Tacchi) 17
resistance: to addressing gender issues 47, 61, 132; to change 61, 92–3, 102, 129
resource constraints 157–8
results-based management approach 1, 2, 56, 73, 88, 113, 159
Retolaza, I. 82, 116, 119, 141, 154
rich pictures 85
rigour **49**, 147, **148**, **149**; in evaluation and sustainable development 18–19; of framework for evaluating C4D 21, 23, 36; of mixed methods approach 1, **32**, 36, 86–7, 90, 128, 150; of participatory approaches 25, 42, 85; role of triangulation in increasing **32**, 128
Rihani, S. 47, 51, 56, 57, 58, 62, 64
Rome Consensus 7
rural Queensland, Australia 15–16, **59**

Saathi Sanga Manka Khura (SSMK radio programme) 15, **52–3**, 102, **118**, 124–5
scoping studies 79, **80**, 155
selecting evaluation approaches, methodologies and methods 2, 23, 36, 43, 84, 86; factors to consider in 113, 156–8; principles related to 18, 35
self-organization 34, 47; in distribution of *La Boletina* 47, **66**; importance of, for social change 34, 47, 64–5, 69; participatory methodologies and 64–5, 71
sensitizing concepts 139
Servaes, J. 5, 11, 68, 138, 143, 144
Sexto Sentido (TV programme) 44, 46
sexuality 64, 130
significant change approach138; *see also* MSC
simple, complicated, complex typology 46–7, 60–1, 62, 81, 153
simple situations and problems 46–7, 60–1, 116, 117, 148
Singhal, A. 11, 44, 45, 46, 50, 61, 63, 64, **65**, **84**, 134, 151
skills: lack of, for evaluating C4D **78**; lack of, for participatory evaluation 18, 73; needed in using complexity-based approaches 122, 140; problems in maintaining 103; required for mixed methods evaluation 104; required for participatory forms of evaluation 103–4, 125, 140, **146**, **148**, 153
SMART indicators 75, 140
social change 8–9, 44, 47; beyond a focus on individual change 64; critical approaches to understanding and evaluating 63–5; critique

of dominant communication theories 63–4; importance of self-organization 64–5; related to women's lives 4, 32, 44, 85; role of framework for evaluating C4D in 41, 42, 150; sustainable forms of 7, 21, 141; value of complexity-based approaches 9, 28–9, 45; *see also* CFSC; complexity of social change; sustainable social change

social change communication: critique of dominant theories 63–4; framework for evaluating (Byrne and Vincent) 64; indicators for measuring 138

social construction of reality 32

social norms 44, 68, 151; in evaluating C4D 17, 23, 69, 134, **148**, 157; need to attend to, for sustainable interventions 68

social status 33, 56, 65, 67, 101; of women 32

socially complicated situations 61

Souter, D. 72, 77, 79, 81, 82, 83, 87, 103, 140

South Asia 47, **75**; evaluation field building in 95

South East Asia **75**

SPICED indicators, value of, in evaluation of C4D 140

Sri Lanka: community ICT centres in 14; e-Tuktuk 33; ICT for Poverty Reduction (ICTPR) project 79; KCRIP 13–14, 129

staff turnover 100, 102–3

stakeholders: accountability to 89; clarifying expectations of 154; diverse values and perspectives of 26, 29, 38, 61, 62, 104, 116, 117, 139; diversity and representativeness of 19, 111–12, 143; engaging 3, 11, 26, 79, **80**, 98, 115, 125–6, 133, 153, 157; identifying **118**, 153; participation in evaluations 7, 8, 24, 40, **76**, 83, **97**, 103, 116, 123–; relationships with and among 35, 51, 96, 147, 150; stakeholder groups 8, 94

strategies for addressing challenges of evaluating C4D 150–2

strategies for sustainable ECD 112; collaborate with other bodies 105; consider issues of power, knowledge, language and literacy 107; design and evaluation of ECD 111; develop appropriate, high quality evaluation processes 110–11; develop effective communication and feedback systems 109–10; draw on local innovation and experimentation 107; empower local staff and communities 108; engage in and support ECD networks 105; foster learning culture through leadership 108; at global and national levels 104; at organizational and community levels 105–6; take organizational culture and context into account 107–8

structural factors, effect of, on evaluation of C4D 71–3

substantialist mode of thinking 48, **49**, 119

support seeking, to implement framework for evaluating C4D 152–3

survey methods 136

survey questionnaires 25, 46, 134, 136

survey-based methodologies 114, 134

sustainability: of C&IT initiatives 15, **67**; of C4D 35, 46, 72, 93, 138, 144, 158; of capacity development **99**; challenges in achieving, related to ECD 100–4; of ECD 102–3, 112, 146; of evaluation systems and practices 36, 38, 94, 110; as focus of framework for C4D assessment (Servaes *et al.*) 138, 143–4; of learning effects 38; of organizations 37, 93; participation and **6**, 12, **145**; social norms and 68; sustainable livelihood approach 47

sustainable development 139, 144, 151; approach of framework for evaluating C4D to 3, 43, 69, 150; importance of alternative forms of evaluation in 3, 7, 12, 18, 77, 150; importance of understanding gender issues for 69, 151; indicators for 139; role of C4D in 3–6, 12, 21, 73, 150; role of empowering leadership in 16; role of learning and capacity development in 93, **99**; role of systems and complexity approaches in 19, 47, 64, 68

sustainable social change 7, 21, 41, 42, 141; challenges to 144–50

systems and complexity-based approaches to evaluation 40, 60, 120–2, 142; critiques of 122; value of 46–7, 68; *see also* complexity theory; developmental evaluation; outcome mapping; simple, complicated, complex typology

systems thinking 47; overview of systems framework 47–50; similarities with participatory approaches 45, 50; usefulness of 51, 56; value of, to development and social change initiatives 62–3; *see also* complex adaptive systems; complexity theory

Tacchi, J. 11, 12, 14, 15, 17, 20, 26, 27, 33, 40, 48, 65, 72, 73, **75**, **76**, 79, 85, 90, 100, 103, 127, 129, 137, 152

technical transfer approaches 95

technically complicated situations 61

technology-based research methods 136

theory of change (ToC): developing for C4D radio programmes **76**, **118**; of initiatives 28, 34

theory of change (ToC) approach **76**, 114; compared with logframe approach 116, 119, 140–1, 154; critiques of 119–20; key steps in creating 154; overview of, as key

methodology 116–17; ratings for **114**; strengths of 116–17, 140–1
third research movement 86
time constraints and issues 26, 35–6, **67**, **76**, 77, **78**, 102–3, 125, **146**, 157–8
timeframe issues 35–6, **78**, 82–3, 119, 148
tipping points 34
ToC *see* theory of change
top-down approaches 3, **6**, 42, 49, 57, 73, **145**
training the trainer approach 92
transformative changes 82, 116, 154
transformative PM&E 123
trends: in C4D and development 3, 42, 46, 74; in evaluation 1, 3, 5, 68, 83–90; need to consider more 46
triangulation **32**, 40, **49**, 128
trust 19, 21, 23, 40, 73, **97**, 126

UN *see* United Nations
UNAIDS: communication framework 64, **65**; evaluation framework 64
UNESCO 7; community multimedia centre 13; ICT for Poverty Reduction (ICTPR) 14, 79
United Nations (UN): approaches to evaluating C4D 73; C4D in 6–7; challenges in conceptualizing, outsourcing and managing research and evaluation 77–9; inter-agency Resource Pack for research, monitoring and evaluation of C4D 16–17; Inter-Agency Round Tables on C4D 6, 32; ratings for approaches and methodologies for evaluating C4D **114**; ratings for methods for evaluating C4D **135**; UNDP 7; UNICEF 7, 16, **106**; *see also* attitudes and policies of funders and managers; donors; UNESCO
universities, role of in ECD 105
upward accountability-based evaluation approaches 2, 4, 93, **149**; inappropriateness for evaluating C4D 4, 69, 137;
incompatibilities with learning-based approaches 21, 87, 102, 146; overview of 3
utilization of evaluation results and data 43, 62, 128; role of meta-evaluation in 152; value of complexity and systems approaches in 62

values 43, 44, **49**, 61, 66, 147, 150; focus on, in alternative evaluation approaches 21, 38, 40, 49, 62, 116, 124; role of mixed methods in capturing 29
verifying assumptions 138
visual diaries 85
visual methods **84**, 85, 92, 136, 151–2
visual participatory research methods **84**, 84–5, 136

Waisbord, S. 5, 9, 68, 74
whole systems approaches 2, 47, 71
Wilkins, K. 5, 9, 66, 130, 131, 151
women: as catalysts for change 4, **84**; and communication 51, 131; differences in access to media and information 51, 155; empowerment of 16, 85; as focus of Puntos de Encuentro initiatives 44, 47, **66**; as leaders in development process 14, **59**, **84**; need to improve conditions, status and power of 4, 32, 66, **132**; participation of, in research and evaluation 8, 129, 131, **132**, 155, 156; role and participation of, in development 4, 65, **66**, **84**; rural 15, 16, 100, 131; voice and 4, **84**, 152; *see also* gender
women and girls in development process 4, 65–6, **84**
women's rights 44
World Congress on Communication for Development (WCCD) 5–6

youth 44, **118**; rights 44
youth groups 51, **52–3**